Sale of Goods and Consumer Credit in Practice

Sale of Goods and Consumer Credit in Practice

Inns of Court School of Law
Institute of Law, City University, London

OXFORD
UNIVERSITY PRESS
Great Clarendon Street, Oxford OX2 6DP

Oxford University Press is a department of the University of Oxford.
It furthers the University's objective of excellence in research, scholarship,
and education by publishing worldwide in

Oxford New York

Auckland Bangkok Buenos Aires Cape Town Chennai
Dar es Salaam Delhi Hong Kong Istanbul Karachi Kolkata
Kuala Lumpur Madrid Melbourne Mexico City Mumbai Nairobi
São Paulo Shanghai Singapore Taipei Tokyo Toronto

and an associated company in Berlin

Oxford is a registered trade mark of Oxford University Press
in the UK and certain other countries

Published in the United States
by Oxford University Press Inc., New York

A Blackstone Press Book

British Library Cataloguing in Publication Data
Data available

Library of Congress Cataloging in Publication Data
Data available

ISBN 0-19-926602-6

1 3 5 7 9 10 8 6 4 2

Typeset by L K Murdoch, Tonbridge, Kent
Printed in Great Britain
on acid-free paper by
Ashford Colour Press, Gosport, Hampshire

FOREWORD

These Manuals are designed primarily to support training on the Bar Vocational Course, though they are also intended to provide a useful resource for legal practitioners and for anyone undertaking training in legal skills.

The Bar Vocational Course was designed by staff at the Inns of Court School of Law, where it was introduced in 1989. This course is intended to equip students with the practical skills and the procedural and evidential knowledge that they will need to start their legal professional careers. These Manuals are written by staff at the Inns of Court School of Law who have helped to develop the course, and by a range of legal practitioners and others involved in legal skills training. The authors of the Manuals are very well aware of the practical and professional approach that is central to the Bar Vocational Course.

The range and coverage of the Manuals have grown steadily. Whilst the option Manuals have been updated and revised every two years, this year the entire series has undergone a more thorough revision to ensure that they reflect the changing needs of Bar students and developments in legal skills training.

This updating and revision is a constant process and we very much value the comments of practitioners, staff and students. Legal vocational training is advancing rapidly, and it is important that all those concerned work together to achieve and maintain high standards. Please address any comments to the Bar Vocational Course Director at the Inns of Court School of Law.

With the validation of other providers for the Bar Vocational Course it is very much our intention that these Manuals will be of equal value to all students wherever they take the course, and we would very much value comments from tutors and students at other validated institutions.

The enthusiasm of the publishers and their efficiency in arranging production and publication of the Manuals is much appreciated.

The Hon. Mr Justice Elias
Chairman of the Advisory Board of the Institute of Law
City University, London
December 2003

OUTLINE CONTENTS

DETAILED CONTENTS

PREFACE

Although this Manual was originally written by two authors, I have had to take sole responsibility for this revision. My co-author, Nicholas Stanton, has been elected Leader of the Council to one of the London Boroughs and is taking a break from practice at least until the next local elections. This means that responsibility for any errors in this edition rests with me.

This Manual is aimed at providing a reasonable understanding of two important and often connected areas of civil law: sale of goods (including supply of services) and consumer credit. Few areas of law have greater impact on the daily lives of most of the population. We all make contracts for the sale of goods, almost without thinking about it. There is still confusion over the rights of the parties to such contracts. The continual growth in unsecured consumer borrowing and in the use of credit cards means that an understanding of the law relating to consumer credit is ever more important.

An understanding of the law of consumer credit is also extremely useful in other areas of practice:

(a) Practitioners undertaking road traffic work had to master the intricacies of this area of law as part of the battle between claimants and insurers which resulted in the House of Lords considering the enforceability of credit hire agreements in *Dimond v Lovell* on 11 May 2000. At one time, over 40,000 other cases were stayed pending that decision.

(b) Once the question of credit hire was resolved, the battle moved to the area of credit repair which was considered by the Court of Appeal in April 2002 in *Clark v Ardington Electrical Services*. At the time of writing the hearing of an appeal to the House of Lords by one of the unsuccessful credit repair companies in *Lagden v O'Connor* is awaited.

(c) In a case involving pawning a BMW convertible, *Wilson v First County Trust Ltd*, on 2 May 2001, the Court of Appeal made a declaration that the absolute prohibition on enforcing certain types of agreements that do not comply with the Consumer Credit Act 1974 was not compatible with the provisions of the Human Rights Act 1998. That decision was reversed by the House of Lords as recently as 10 July 2003.

(d) With the expansion of Conditional Fee Agreements, a number of credit products are available which allow claimants to pay for 'after the event insurance' on credit so as to bring a claim. Experience of the credit hire and credit repair litigation suggests that there may now be satellite litigation over the enforceability of those credit agreements.

As always, there are a number of proposals in the pipeline that may or may not result in changes in these areas of the law. The main proposals are considered in **Chapter 1** at **1.5**. Even when legislation is passed it is not always brought into force: the Easter Act 1928 was passed to fix the calendar date of this religious festival, but has yet to be brought into force. I have therefore sought to state the law as at 31 August 2003 and have mentioned possible future developments.

I would like to thank the Consumer Credit Trade Association for kindly giving us permission to reproduce some of the CCTA standard forms in this Manual. I would like to thank those who provide me with work in this interesting area and even, occasionally, provide me with funds to become a purchaser. Like many practitioners, I need little encouragement to become a debtor. Finally, I would like to thank Tony Spinak, Barrister and Principal Lecturer at the City University, Inns of Court School of Law for his extremely helpful input in updating the text and for new material.

Evan Ashfield
Temple Chambers

TABLE OF CASES

TABLE OF STATUTES

International legislation

US legislation

TABLE OF STATUTORY INSTRUMENTS

European secondary legislation

Part I

Sale of goods

1

Sources

1.1 Primary UK legislation

There are three main Acts with which you should be familiar. The most important is the Sale of Goods Act 1979 (SOGA 1979). The others are the Supply of Goods (Implied Terms) Act 1973 (SOGITA 1973) and the Supply of Goods and Services Act 1982 (SOGSA 1982).

These three Acts should be read in the light of the important amendments made by the Sale and Supply of Goods to Consumers Regulations 2002 (SI 2002 No 3045) which took effect from 31 March 2003.

1.1.1 SOGA 1979

The Sale of Goods Act 1979 is a consolidating Act which replaced the Sale of Goods Act 1893, as amended by subsequent Acts such as the Supply of Goods (Implied Terms) Act 1973. SOGA 1979 applies to the whole of the UK (although some provisions differ for Scotland and Northern Ireland). SOGA 1979 came into force on 1 January 1980 and applies to contracts for the sale of goods made after 1 January 1894, subject to certain sections being in different terms prior to the dates set out in Sch 1.

SOGA 1979 has been amended in important respects:

(a) by the Sale of Goods (Amendment) Act 1994 which came into force on 3 January 1995 and applies to contracts made after that date and abolished the market overt exception to the *nemo dat* rule (see **6.2**);

(b) by the Sale and Supply of Goods Act 1994 which came into force on 3 January 1995 and applies to contracts made after that date and which contains important changes to the implied term about quality, to acceptance of goods and to the right of partial rejection;

(c) by the Sale of Goods (Amendment) Act 1995 which came into force on 19 September 1995 and applies to contracts concluded after that date which amended the law relating to sale of unascertained goods forming part of an identified bulk, and sales of an undivided share in goods;

(d) by the Sale and Supply of Goods to Consumers Regulations 2002 which implement Directive 1999/44/EC and make important changes in relation to consumer transactions.

1.1.2 SOGITA 1973

The Supply of Goods (Implied Terms) Act 1973 contains the statutory implied terms in hire-purchase agreements as to title, description, quality and fitness, sample; modifies the statutory condition in non-consumer cases; and, contains special provisions for conditional sale agreements. SOGITA has been amended by the Sale and Supply of Goods Act 1994 which came into force on 3 January 1995 in a similar manner as SOGA 1979. Many of the provisions in SOGITA are similar to those in SOGA 1979, in particular the implied terms as to title, description, quality and fitness, so that they do not require separate consideration. Further amendments were made with effect from 31 March 2003 in relation to consumer transactions by the Sale and Supply of Goods to Consumer Regulations 2002.

1.1.3 SOGSA 1982

The Supply of Goods and Services Act 1982 is the main source of statutory implied terms for contracts dealing with the transfer of property in goods other than excepted contracts which are defined by s1(2) as:

> *(a) a contract of sale of goods;*
> *(b) a hire-purchase agreement;*
> *(c) a contract under which the property in goods is (or is to be) transferred in exchange for trading stamps on their redemption;*
> *(d) a transfer or agreement to transfer which is made by deed and for which there is no consideration other than the presumed consideration imported by the deed;*
> *(e) a contract intended to operate by way of mortgage, pledge, charge or other security.*

With effect from 31 March 2003, in relation to consumer transactions, amendments were made to SOGSA 1982 by the Sale and Supply of Goods to Consumer Regulations 2002. The changes are similar to those made to SOGA 1979.

1.1.4 Other statutes

There are a large number of other Acts which have an impact on the law of sale of goods. Although it is not necessary for you to be familiar with all of them, the main ones, in chronological order, are:

(a) Bills of Sale Acts 1878 and 1882 (as modified by the Acts of 1890 and 1891) which impose statutory formalities and registration requirements for transactions under which ownership of the goods is transferred but possession is retained;

(b) Factors Act 1889 which validates certain sales by mercantile agents, by buyers in possession and sellers in possession (see **6.2.2**);

(c) Fair Trading Act 1973 which was amended by the Competition Act 1998 and is now replaced by the Enterprise Act 2002, encouraged the provision of information to consumers and the use of Codes of Practice;

(d) Unfair Contract Terms Act 1977 (UCTA 1977) which limits the ability to avoid liability in contract or negligence or other breach of duty by contract terms or otherwise (see **4.3**);

(e) Torts (Interference with Goods) Act 1977 which contains, *inter alia*, important provisions for extinction of title on payment of damages, for allowance for improvements to goods and for sale of uncollected goods;

(f) Consumer Protection Act 1987 which contains important extensions of the privity of contract rights for consumers if goods are unsafe, so that rights also exist directly against producers and those who hold themselves out as producers;

(g) Disability Discrimination Act 1995 which contains, *inter alia*, provisions making discrimination in the supply of goods and services unlawful and which was brought into force on 2 December 1996 (see **4.7**).

(h) Late Payment of Commercial Debts (Interest) Act 1998, which creates a statutory implied term in commercial contracts that simple interest will be payable on qualifying debts, limits the power to exclude this term and makes consequential provisions (considered at **4.8** and **8.5**);

(i) Competition Act 1998, which is now substantially in force and gives very wide powers to take action against those who indulge in anti-competitive practices. Probably the highest profile inquiry has been into possible price fixing in the sale of replica sports shirts and it seems that extremely heavy fines are being imposed on a number of well-known companies;

(j) Enterprise Act 2002 the remaining provisions of which came into force on 20 June 2003. This Act includes new powers to enforce consumer laws, to promote Codes of Practice and introduces a new category of 'super-complaint' which can be made by designated consumer bodies to the Office of Fair Trading which will require the OFT to publish a response within 90 days explaining how the problem will be addressed. It repeals the Stop Now Orders (EC Directive) Regulations 2001 since those powers are replaced by those set out in Part 8 of this Act. Although the Act has only just been brought into force, there have already been three of these super-complaints. The latest is by the industry watchdog Postwatch and concerns mail consolidation.

Finally, in international sales, the Uniform Laws on International Sales Act 1967 will apply. That Act implemented two international conventions signed at the Hague on 1 July 1964 which appear as schedules to the Act. The Act came into effect on 18 August 1972. A detailed consideration of this Act is beyond the scope of this Manual as ratification of the conventions has not been as widespread as intended. The UK has not ratified the newer Vienna Convention on Contracts for the International Sale of Goods which came into force on 1 January 1980 and consideration of that convention has been omitted from this Manual.

1.2 Secondary UK legislation

The most important pieces of secondary legislation are:

(a) Consumer Protection (Cancellation of Contracts Concluded away from Business Premises) Regulations 1987 (SI 1987 No 2117) — as amended by the Consumer Protection (Cancellation of Contracts Concluded away from Business Premises) (Amendment) Regulations 1998 (SI 1998 No 3050) which create a cooling off period for contracts concluded as a result of cold-calling (see **4.4**);

(b) Unfair Terms in Consumer Contracts Regulations 1994 (SI 1994 No 3159) which create a concept of good faith in consumer contracts and apply to all contracts made on or after 1 July 1995, which were replaced with effect from 1 October 1999 by the Unfair Terms in Consumer Contracts Regulations 1999 (SI 1999 No 2083) (see **4.5**);

(c) Consumer Protection (Distance Selling) Regulations 2000 (SI 2000 No 2334) which regulate most sales of goods after 31 October 2001 which were sales via the Internet, interactive digital television, mail order, telephone or facsimile by requiring information to be provided to consumers (including written confirmation of the order) and creating a cooling-off period of seven days (see **4.9**);

(d) Stop Now Orders (EC Directive) Regulations 2001 (SI 2001 No 1422) which came into force on 1 June 2001, although they do not create individual rights they are a major new weapon in the regulation of rogue traders (see **4.10**). As from 20 June 2003, the Regulations are replaced by Part 8 of the Enterprise Act 2002;

(e) Sale and Supply of Goods to Consumers Regulations 2002 (SI 2002 No 3045) which, from 31 March 2003, amend the three main Acts (see **1.1**) in important respects where there is a contract with a consumer.

1.3 Other UK sources

SOGA 1979 expressly provides that the general common law of contract applies to contracts for the sale of goods, except where inconsistent with the provisions of the Act: s 62(2). It follows that you should have regard to the common law sources for contract and for agency. The primary legislation includes:

(a) Law Reform Frustrated Contracts Act 1943 (which is considered in **5.9.4**); and

(b) Contracts (Applicable Law) Act 1990 which ratified the Rome Convention (which appears as Sch 1 to the Act) and came into force on 1 April 1991 creating new rules governing the proper law of contracts.

The new British Standard BS8600 was launched on 12 May 1999. It is based on best practice in complaints management and on minimising hardship and inconvenience to customers. It remains to be seen whether the courts will look at this standard in cases which require an examination of complaint handling and what weight it will be given in such a dispute. It will also be interesting to see how many companies adopt this standard and whether it will reduce the current high level of consumer dissatisfaction.

1.4 EC sources

The European Community is becoming increasingly active in consumer affairs. The Consumer Protection Act 1987 has its origin in Directive 85/374. The Consumer Protection (Cancellation of Contracts Concluded away from Business Premises) Regulations 1987 have their origin in Directive 85/577. The Unfair Terms in Consumer Contracts Regulations 1994 have their origin in Directive 93/13.

The Council has made ten recommendations for consumer policy which can be summarised as follows:

(a) re-examination of the legislation in force in order to determine the areas in which legislation must be simplified or completed to allow the consumer fully to benefit from the possibilities provided by the single market, and account also to be taken of consumers' interests in all new EC legislation;

(b) improved consumer education and information;

(c) attention to be paid to the interests of consumers in financial services;

(d) consumers' interests to be safeguarded in essential public utilities;

(e) increased consumer safety for food products and increased information;

(f) preparing consumers for the information society in order to ensure easy access to new technologies;

(g) special account to be taken of vulnerable consumer groups;

(h) increased consumer representation at Community level;

(i) encouragement of the adoption of lasting consumer demand behaviour notably through better information on environmental effects;

(j) assistance to Eastern and Central Europe and developing countries in the elaboration of policies in favour of consumers.

The origin of legislation can be important for two reasons. First, courts are interpreting national legislation, so far as possible, to achieve the results intended by EC Directives. This purposive approach to national legislation has been very marked in the fields of employment and discrimination but is not limited to those fields: *Faccini Dori v Recreb Srl* (case C-91/92) [1995] All ER (EC) 1. Secondly, the question of whether national legislation complies with or fully implements an EC Directive is something which can lead to litigation. For example, the European Court of Justice has considered whether the Consumer Protection Act 1987 properly implemented Directive 85/374: *Commission v United Kingdom* [1997] All ER (EC) 481.

1.5 Proposed new legislation

As usual, there are a number of proposals for new legislation which will have an impact in this area of law. It remains to be seen how effective the new powers in the Enterprise Act 2002 will be and how often they will be invoked. It is to be hoped that the Office of Fair Trading will continue the recent higher level of active intervention in the interest of consumers. In the last 12 months over 1,500 unfair contract terms have been abandoned by traders as a result of OFT intervention, and more than 100 websites have been changed. The OFT has also produced new guidance in relation to unfair and improper practices in the sale of second-hand cars and breach may jeopardise consumer credit licences.

The OFT has continued the important work of ensuring that credit card companies accept that liability under s 75 of the Consumer Credit Act 1974 extends to overseas transactions. HSBC, Bank of Scotland and Sainsbury's bank have reached agreement with the OFT to honour valid claims for purchases made abroad rather than face action under the Stop Now Orders (EC Directive) Regulations 2001. In June 2003, proceedings were issued to resolve the issue with some other credit card suppliers.

The 1991 proposals to change the statutory provisions relating to extortionate credit bargains received more support than was expected during the consultation process. The proposed changes will mean that:

- the current 'grossly exorbitant' test is likely to be replaced by an 'excessive payments' test;
- the court will be allowed to look at matters arising after the agreement was made (perhaps including falls in interest rates);

- the court may be allowed to consider whether the transaction involved 'deceitful or oppressive or otherwise unfair or improper' conduct (the test used in determining fitness for a consumer credit licence);
- time orders will be encouraged;
- there should be power to deal with groups of similar transactions; and,
- a new restitutionary power may be granted to the OFT.

The Law Commission has produced a report which aims to replace the Unfair Contract Terms Act 1977 and the Unfair Terms in Consumer Contracts Regulations 1999 with a single Act written in plain and accessible language. The aim of a single regime for this area of control over contract terms will involve substantial changes. In addition, consideration is being given to extending some degree of control to all business to business contracts by introducing a fair and reasonable test, and extending control of exclusion or exemption notices. Finally, the scope of the existing exemptions is being reviewed.

1.6 Cases

Cases involving sale of goods disputes can be found in all the major series of law reports. Cases also appear in some specialist reports such as those dealing with company law, insolvency, consumer credit and (as so many reported cases involve motor cars) even the Road Traffic Reports. The main cases which you will need are referred to in the text of this Manual and others will be found from the major practitioner works.

As SOGA 1979 is a consolidating Act the large body of cases under the Sale of Goods Act 1893 is still a valuable source.

A table (see overleaf) showing the destination of provisions in the 1893 Act has been prepared which will assist you when looking at the old cases; the sections of SOGA 1979 which have been subsequently amended, replaced or repealed are noted in italics.

1.7 Further reading

The main text books which you should use for further reading are:

Atiyah, *The Sale of Goods*, 9th edn, Financial Times 1995

Guest, *Benjamin's Sale of Goods*, 6th edn, Sweet & Maxwell, 2002

Bowstead and Reynolds, *Law of Agency*, 17th edn, Sweet & Maxwell, 2001

Bridge, *The Sale of Goods*, 2nd edn, OUP, 1998

Beale, *Chitty on Contracts*, 28th edn, Sweet & Maxwell, 1999

Dobson, *Sale of Goods and Consumer Credit*, 6th edn, Sweet & Maxwell, 2000

Goode, R., *Commercial Law*, 3rd edn, Butterworths, 2003

Halsbury's Laws of England, Butterworths

Harvey, *The Law of Consumer Protection and Fair Trading*, 6th edn, Butterworths, 2000

McGregor, *McGregor on Damages*, 17th edn, Sweet & Maxwell, 2003

A large number of specialist works exist which you can usefully refer to for further reading on specific areas, including:

Bradgate, *Commercial Law*, 3rd edn, Butterworths, 2000

Cotter, *Defective and Unsafe Products*, Butterworths, 1996

Davies, *Equipment and Motor Vehicle Leasing and Hiring Law and Practice*, Sweet & Maxwell, 1997

Harrison, *Good Faith in Sales*, Sweet & Maxwell, 1997

Harvey and Meisel, *Auctions Law and Practice*, 2nd edn, OUP, 1995

Lawson, *Exclusion Clauses and Unfair Contract Terms*, 7th edn, Sweet & Maxwell, 2003

Lewison, *The Interpretation of Contracts*, 2nd edn, Sweet & Maxwell, 1997

McKendrick, *Force Majeure and Frustration of Contract*, Lloyd's of London Press, 1995

Murdoch, *Law of Estate Agency and Auctions*, 3rd edn, Estates Gazette, 1994

Palmer, *Bailment*, 2nd edn, Sweet & Maxwell, 1991

Palmer and McKendrick, *Interests in Goods*, 2nd edn, Informa, 1998

Pease and Chitty, *Law of Markets and Fairs*, 5th edn, Butterworths, 1998

Salinger, *Factoring: Law and Practice of Invoice Finance*, 3rd edn, Sweet & Maxwell, 1999

Treitel, *Frustration and Force Majeure*, Sweet & Maxwell, 1994.

For sample statements of case in sale of goods cases you should refer to:

Atkin's Court Forms, Volume 34(2), Butterworths

Bullen, Leake and Jacobs, *Precedents of Pleading*.

1893	SOGA 1979	1893	SOGA 1979	1893	SOGA 1979
s 1(1)	s 2(1), (2)	s 17	s 17	s 42	s 42
s 1(2)	s 2(3)	s 18	s 18	s 43	s 43
s 1(3)	s 2(4), (5)	s 19	s 19	s 44	s 44
s 1(4)	s 2(6)	s 20	s 20	s 45	s 45
s 2	s 3	s 20, proviso 1	s 20, proviso 1	s 46(1)	s 46(1), (2), (3)
s 3	s 4	s 20, proviso 2	s 20, proviso 2	s 46(2)	s 46(4)
s 4	repealed	s 21	s 21	s 47	s 47
s 5	s 5	s 22(1)	*s 22(1)*	s 48	s 48
s 6	s 6	s 22(2)	repealed	s 49	s 49
s 7	s 7	s 22(3)	*s 22(2)*	s 50	s 50
s 8(1)	s 8(1)	s 23	s 23	s 51	s 51
s 8(2)	s 8(2), (3)	s 24	repealed	s 52	s 52
s 9	s 9	s 25(1)	s 24	s 53	*s 53*
s 10(1)	s 10(1), (2)	s 25(2)	s 25(1), (2)	s 54	s 54
s 10(2)	s 10(3)	s 25(3)	s 26	s 55	Sch 1, paras 11, 12
s 11(1) Scotland	*s 11(1)*	s 27	s 27	s 55(1)	s 55(1)
s 11(1)(a)	s 11(2)	s 28	s 28	s 55(2)	s 55(2)
s 11(1)(b)	s 11(3)	s 29(1)	s 29(1), (2)	s 55A	Sch 1, para 13
s 11(1)(c)	*s 11(4)*	s 29(2)	s 29(3)	s 56	s 59
s 11(2) Scotland	s 11(1)	s 29(3)	s 29(4)	s 57	s 60
s 11(3)	s 11(6)	s 29(4)	s 29(5)	s 58	s 57
s 12	Sch 1, para 3	s 29(5)	s 29(6)	s 59 Scotland	s 58
s 12(1)(a), (b)	*s 12(1), (2)*	s 30(1)	s 30(1)	s 60	repealed
s 12(2)	s 12(3)	s 30(2)	s 30(2), (3)	s 61(1)	s 62(1)
s 12(2)(a), (b)	*s 12(4), (5)*	s 30(3)	*s 30(4)*	s 61(2)	s 62(2)
s 13(1)	*s 13(1)*, (2)	s 30(4)	s 30(5)	s 61(3)	s 62(3)
s 13(2)	s 13(3)	s 31	s 31	s 61(4)	s 62(4)
s 14	Sch 1, paras 5, 6	s 32	s 32	s 61(5)	s 62(5)
s 14(1)	*s 14(1)*	s 33	s 33	s 61(6)	s 62(6)
s 14(2)	*s 14(2)*	s 34	*s 34*	s 62(1)	*s 61(1)*
s 14(3)	*s 14(3)*	s 35	*s 35(1)*	s 62(1A)	s 14(6), s 15(3)
s 14(4)	*s 14(4)*	s 36	s 36	s 62(2)	s 61(3)
s 14(5)	s 14(5)	s 37	s 37	s 62(3)	s 61(4)
s 15	Sch 1, para 7	s 38	s 38	s 62(4)	s 61(5)
s 15(1)	s 15(1)	s 39	s 39	s 63	s 1(1)
s 15(2)	*s 15(2)*	s 40 Scotland	s 40	s 64	repealed
s 16	*s 16*	s 41	s 41		

2 Definitions and concepts

SOGA 1979 defines a number of terms which you will need to be familiar with. SOGA 1979 also creates a number of concepts which are essential to an understanding of sale of goods law.

2.1 Statutory definitions

Section 61, SOGA 1979 defines the main terms for England and Wales, unless the context or subject matter otherwise requires, as follows:

(a) Action — includes counterclaim and set-off.

(b) Bulk — means a mass or collection of goods of the same kind which (i) is contained in a defined space or area; and (ii) is such that any goods in the bulk are interchangeable with any other goods therein of the same number or quantity.

(c) Business — includes a profession and the activities of any government department or local or public authority.

(d) Buyer — means a person who buys or agrees to buy goods.

(e) Consumer contract — has the same meaning as in s 25(1), UCTA 1977; and for the purposes of SOGA 1979 the onus of proving that a contract is not to be regarded as a consumer contract shall lie on the seller; the definition in s 25(1), UCTA 1977 is that a consumer contract is a contract (not being a contract of sale by auction or competitive tender) in which (i) one party to the contract deals, and the other party to the contract ('the consumer') does not deal or hold himself or herself out as dealing, in the course of a business, and (ii) in the case of a contract such as mentioned in s 15(2)(a), UCTA 1977, the goods are of a type ordinarily supplied for private use or consumption; s 15(2)(a), UCTA 1977 concerns contracts for the transfer of ownership or possession of goods from one person to another (with or without work having been done on them).

(f) Contract of sale — includes an agreement to sell as well as a sale.

(g) Credit-broker — means a person acting in the course of a business of credit brokerage carried on by him, that is a business of effecting introductions to individuals desiring to obtain credit (i) to persons carrying on any business so far as it relates to the provision of credit, or (ii) to other persons engaged in credit brokerage.

(h) Delivery — means the voluntary transfer of possession from one person to another except that in relation to ss 20A and 20B, SOGA 1979 it includes such appropriation of goods to the contract as results in property in the goods being transferred to the buyer.

(i) Document of title to goods — has the same meaning as in the Factors Acts; the meaning in the Factors Acts is to be found in s 1(4), Factors Act 1889 and includes any bill of lading, dock, warrant, warehouse-keeper's certificate, and warrant or order for the delivery of goods, and any other document used in the ordinary course of business as proof of the possession or control of goods or authorising or purporting to authorise, either by indorsement or delivery, the possessor of the document to transfer or receive the goods thereby represented.

(j) Factors Acts — means the Factors Act 1889 and any enactment amending or substituting the same.

(k) Fault — means wrongful act or default.

(l) Future goods — means goods to be manufactured or acquired by the seller after making the contract of sale.

(m) Goods — means all personal chattels other than things in action and money; and in particular 'goods' includes emblements, industrial growing crops, and things attached to or forming part of the land which are agreed to be severed before sale or under a contract of sale and includes an undivided share in goods.

(n) Property — means the general property in goods and not merely a special property.

(o) Quality — in relation to goods, includes their state or condition.

(p) Sale — includes a bargain and sale as well as a sale and delivery.

(q) Seller — means a person who sells or agrees to sell goods.

(r) Specific goods — means goods identified and agreed on at the time a contract of sale is made and includes an undivided share, specified as a fraction or percentage, of goods identified and agreed on as aforesaid.

(t) Warranty — means an agreement with reference to goods which are the subject of a contract of sale, but collateral to the main purpose of such contract, the breach of which gives rise to a claim for damages, but not to a right to reject the goods and treat the contract as repudiated.

In addition by s 61(3), a thing is deemed to be done in good faith within the meaning of SOGA 1979 if it is done honestly, whether it is done negligently or not.

2.2 What is a contract for the sale of goods?

SOGA 1979 defines such a contract in s 2(1) as:

> *a contract by which the seller transfers or agrees to transfer the property in goods to the buyer for a money consideration called the price.*

You should note that two distinct concepts are covered. First, a sale of goods which is both a contract and a conveyance or transfer of those goods. Secondly, an agreement to sell which is only a contract. The distinction can have important effects on disputes over when risk passes (**Chapter 5**) and on remedies for breach of the contract as proprietary rights in the goods will normally only exist if there has been a sale rather than a mere agreement to sell.

2.3 Is there a contract?

There must be a consensual contract between the parties which is determined by the ordinary rules of contract. Where consent does not exist at all or does not extend to all the essential elements there is no contract.

Capacity to contract is governed by the general law (s 3(1), SOGA 1979). Contracts for necessaries sold and delivered to minors, or to persons who are incompetent by reason of mental incapacity or drunkenness are provided for by s 3(2) and (3), SOGA 1979.

There are now no formalities for a contract for the sale of goods (s 4, SOGA 1979).

There may still be a valid and binding contract for the sale of goods where no price is agreed for the goods. The price may be fixed in a manner agreed between the parties or may be determined by a course of dealing between the parties: s 8(1), SOGA 1979. Alternatively, the price may be left unstated and not capable of being determined in accordance with s 8(1), in which event a reasonable price is payable: s 8(2), SOGA 1979. Finally, s 9, SOGA 1979 provides for cases where the price for the goods is to be fixed by a third party identified in the contract.

A transfer of property pursuant to an arbitration award would not be a consensual contract, but pursuant to the award itself: *Hunter v Rice* (1812) 104 ER 782. Similarly, payment of the value of goods under a judgment under the Torts (Interference with Goods) Act 1977 extinguishes the owner's title and passes it to the person paying the value, but that is not a contract between the parties to the proceedings. An acquisition under compulsory powers would not be a contract: *Kirkness v John Hudson & Co Ltd* [1955] AC 696. A transfer pursuant to an indemnity will not be a consensual contract but by virtue of the doctrine of subrogation so that, for example, a transfer of property in a stolen car to an insurance company in return for payment pursuant to the policy would not be a sale of goods contract between the insured and the insurer. If goods are supplied under a public or statutory duty (even at a price) SOGA 1979 will not apply: *Pfizer Corporation v Ministry of Health* [1965] AC 512.

Auctions can also give rise to contracts for the sale of goods. Section 57, SOGA 1979 sets out the basic rules for the formation of the contract at auction. There is statutory regulation of undesirable practices. Mock auctions are prohibited and criminal penalties exist under the Mock Auctions Act 1961. Auction rings in which bidders agree not to bid against each other are prohibited by the Auctions (Bidding Agreements) Acts 1927 and 1969. Further discussion of auction sales can be found in the specialist books mentioned at **1.7**.

2.4 What are goods?

The definition of 'goods' to be found in s 61(1), SOGA 1979 appears above: see **2.1(m)**. Note that 'things in action and money' are expressly excluded from the definition of goods.

Problems can arise in applying the definition. It seems odd that a rare coin which is not legal tender could be goods but a rare coin which is still legal tender will not be goods as it is money. It seems that a computer disk is within the statutory definition of goods but the program itself is not: *St Albans City & District Council v International Computers Ltd* [1996] 4 All ER 481 in which Sir Iain Glidewell held, at p. 493, that the computer program itself was not 'goods' within the statutory definition in SOGA 1979 and differed on that point from the judge's finding that software probably was goods: [1995] FSR 686 at p 699.

A common problem is distinguishing between (i) contracts for the sale of goods, and (ii) contracts for work and materials which are supplies of services. The distinction is no longer relevant to formalities as neither type of contract has to be in writing. The distinction will determine whether the statutory implied terms are those found in SOGA 1979 or in SOGSA 1982, and may be important on questions of title and frustration. It is said that the intention of the parties is crucial, but it is difficult to extract clear principles from the many decided cases. In the early cases the distinction was crucial as sales of goods with a value of £10 or more had to be evidenced in writing by a note or memorandum signed by the party to be charged until s 4 of the 1893 Act was repealed in 1954.

The test can be summarised as:

(a) if there is a sale of goods which are later to be fixed to chattels or land as a subsidiary obligation, the contract will be for the sale of goods;

(b) if there is an agreement to fix goods to land or to another chattel to which the sale of the goods is a subsidiary obligation, the contract will be for supply of services;

(c) if the principal obligation is the supply of goods with any work to them being incidental, then the contract will be for sale of goods; and,

(d) if the principal materials are supplied by the customer to be worked on (with or without other materials) the contract will be for supply of services.

It can be extremely difficult to apply these principles in practice. If clothes are made or altered for a customer is there a contract of sale of the finished garment or a contract for work and materials? Similarly is a contract with the printer who prints a book one of sale of goods or work and material? In *Lee v Griffen* (1861) 121 ER 716, a case involving dentures, it was said that the test was not to be the value of the skill and labour compared to that of the material but rather the subject matter of the contract and if a sale of a chattel was involved it was for sale of goods. In *Robinson v Graves* [1935] 1 KB 579, a case involving painting a portrait, it was held that the materials sold (the canvas and paint) were only incidental to the skill of producing the portrait so that there was no sale of goods.

By s 5(1), SOGA 1979 the goods may be 'existing goods' or 'future goods'. Existing goods are goods already owned or possessed by the seller. Future goods are goods to be manufactured or acquired by the seller after the making of the contract.

A further division can be made into 'specific goods' and 'unascertained goods'. Specific goods has already been defined (see **2.1(r)**). Unascertained goods is not defined in SOGA 1979 but means all goods other than specific goods. New rules dealing with unascertained goods which form part of a bulk were introduced by the amendments to SOGA 1979 in the Sales of Goods (Amendment) Act 1995 (**5.5.2**).

2.5 Transfer of property

Transactions which do not transfer property are not sales of goods. Thus bailments are not sales of goods, nor are leases of goods. Bailments with an option to purchase (such as hire purchase agreements) are not within the definition: *Helby v Matthews* [1895] AC 471.

If the contract for sale is intended to operate by way of mortgage, charge, pledge or other security it is not a sale of goods (s 62(4), SOGA 1979).

A mortgage or charge of goods will usually fall within the Bills of Sale Acts 1878 and 1882 and the necessary statutory formalities will have to be complied with. A now common form of transaction is a 'sale and lease back' where the owner sells the goods to a finance company and then leases those same goods back. A genuine transaction will be upheld as a sale of the goods rather than a charge over them, the test being the true intention of the parties rather than the legal form: *North Central Wagon Finance Co Ltd v Brailsford* [1962] 1 WLR 1288. The result can be of considerable importance, particularly if the owner has become insolvent, as the true nature of the transaction may require legal formalities which have not been complied with such as registration of a company charge: *Re Curtain Dream plc* [1990] BCLC 925.

A pledge can exist at common law and under the Consumer Credit Act 1974 and is an actual or constructive delivery and bailment of the goods by the debtor to the creditor to be kept until the debt has been discharged. Property in the goods does not pass but the pledgee has a right to sell the goods. A pledge will not be a sale of goods transaction.

2.6 Money consideration

A gift is not provided for money consideration. Promotional gifts are unlikely to give rise to a sale of goods as the consideration is usually the purchase of other goods: *Esso Petroleum Co Ltd v Customs and Excise Commissioners* [1976] 1 WLR 1. Gifts are therefore outside the scope of SOGA 1979 and also fall outside SOGSA 1982.

A simple exchange of goods or barter is not a sale of goods. However, the statutory implied terms as to title description, quality and fitness in Part I of SOGSA 1982 will apply.

A common difficulty exists when goods are part exchanged, a practice which is, of course, extremely common with motor vehicles. Is there an exchange of goods (with some payment) or are there two separate, back-to-back, sale of goods transactions with, at most, only any credit balance being paid? The test is: what is the contractual intention?

In *G J Dawson (Clapham) Ltd v H & G Dutfield* [1936] 2 All ER 232 the purchaser failed to deliver up the part exchange vehicles and was found liable for the balance of the purchase price rather than for damages for detinue of the part exchange vehicles (which would now be wrongful interference). In practice most motor vehicle trade-in transactions are now likely to be two separate sale of goods transactions, each being separately documented. This distinction is of practical importance when considering the exception to the nemo dat principle under Part III of the Hire Purchase Act 1964; which applies only where the purchaser buys or agrees to buy or takes the vehicle on hire-purchase and not merely to an exchange of vehicles (see **6.2.7** and **16.3.5.1**).

More recently, in *Forthright Finance Ltd v Ingate (Carlyle Finance Ltd, third party)* [1997] 4 All ER 99, the Court of Appeal had to determine whether there were two separate transactions or one transaction where there had been a part exchange involving a motor car. The defendant agreed to buy a Metro under a conditional sale agreement. Before paying all the instalments the defendant decided to change her car to a Fiat Panda. The dealer agreed to buy the Metro and pay off the finance company. The sum due under the conditional sale agreement and the value of the Metro were almost identical. The defendant then agreed to buy the Fiat Panda under a new conditional sale agreement. Not unusually, the dealer failed to discharge the finance due on the Metro. The defendant had no defence to the claim under that agreement but sought an indemnity from the new finance company on the grounds that the entire transaction was a single transaction and the finance company was liable for the promises of the dealer. The Court of Appeal concluded that there was a single transaction and not two separate transactions so that the defendant was entitled to her indemnity.

3

The terms of the contract

3.1 Classification of terms

Traditionally contract terms have been divided into conditions or warranties. Conditions are terms which, if broken, enable the innocent party to treat himself as discharged from further performance of the contract and to claim damages caused by the breach. Warranties are terms which, if broken, give the innocent party only a right to claim damages, the measure of damages being defined in s 53, SOGA 1979.

It now seems plain that there is an intermediate category of contract terms which, if broken, give the innocent party one or other remedy depending upon the nature and seriousness of the breach: *Hong Kong Fir Shipping Co Ltd v Kawasaki Kisen Kaisha Ltd* [1962] 2 QB 26. Section 11(3), SOGA 1979 and s 8(3), SOGITA 1973 expressly define certain obligations as conditions or warranties. The argument that, as a result, in contracts for sales of goods and supplies of services there was no intermediate category of contract terms was rejected in *Cehave NV v Bremer Handelsgesellschaft GmbH (The Hansa Nord)* [1976] QB 44.

Section 11, SOGA 1979 provides:

> (2) *Where a contract of sale is subject to a condition to be fulfilled by the seller, the buyer may waive the condition, or may elect to treat the breach of the condition as a breach of warranty and not as a ground for treating the contract as repudiated.*
>
> (3) *Whether a stipulation in a contract of sale is a condition, the breach of which may give rise to a right to treat the contract as repudiated, or a warranty, the breach of which may give rise to a claim for damages but not to a right to reject the goods and treat the contract as repudiated, depends in each case on the construction of the contract; and a stipulation may be a condition, though called a warranty in the contract.*
>
> (4) *Subject to section 35A below where a contract of sale is not severable and the buyer has accepted the goods or part of them, the breach of a condition to be fulfilled by the seller can only be treated as a breach of warranty, and not as a ground for rejecting the goods and treating the contract as repudiated, unless there is an express or implied term of the contract to that effect.*

SOGA 1979 creates two situations in which breach of a condition will not entitle the innocent party to treat the contract as discharged but can only claim damages (as would have been the position if the condition had been a warranty). First, where the innocent party elects to treat the breach of condition as a breach of warranty (s 11(2)). Secondly, where there is a non-severable contract and the buyer has accepted the goods (s 11(4)): but note that this is now qualified by the new s 35A.

Section 15A, SOGA 1979 (which applies to contracts made after 3 January 1995) provides that:

> (1) *Where in the case of a contract of sale—*
>
> (a) *the buyer would, apart from this subsection, have the right to reject goods by reason of a breach on the part of the seller of a term implied by section 13, 14 or 15 above, but*
>
> (b) *the breach is so slight that it would be unreasonable for him to reject them,*

then, if the buyer does not deal as consumer, the breach is not to be treated as a breach of condition but may be treated as a breach of warranty.

(2) This section applies unless a contrary intention appears in, or is to be implied from, the contract.

(3) It is for the seller to show that a breach fell within subsection (1)(b) above.

The effect is that, unless a contrary intention appears or is to be implied into the contract, terms which are conditions for consumers will not be conditions for non-consumers only where it would be unreasonable for the non-consumer buyer to reject.

Section 30(2A), SOGA 1979 limits the right to reject for delivery of the wrong quantity in non-consumer cases where the difference is so slight that it would be unreasonable for the buyer to do so. Again the burden of proof is on the seller (s 30(2B)).

Under ss 15A and 30(2A) which apply only to non-consumer cases, whether the term is a condition or a warranty will depend upon the seriousness of the breach. Thus a statutory category of intermediate terms has been created for these non-consumer sales.

3.2 How do you decide what terms are conditions?

It seems plain that a term is a condition if it is expressly made such by statute. What is less clear is the effect of the label given to the obligation in the contract itself. It seems that a term need not be a condition merely because it is so described in the contract: *Wickman Machine Tool Sales Ltd v L. Schuler AG* [1974] AC 235, although contrast *Lombard North Central plc v Butterworth* [1987] QB 527. Similarly the general view that a warranty need not be only a warranty because it is so described in the contract is given statutory effect for sale of goods contracts by s 11(3), SOGA 1979.

An obligation which often has to be classified is the obligation of time for performance by one or both parties. The first question is often what is the actual time allowed by the contract? Words such as 'from' may include the day the contract is made or may start the next day. Once the obligation is established: will it be a condition or a warranty?

Section 10(1), SOGA 1979 provides that unless a different intention appears from the terms of the contract stipulations as to time of payment are not of the essence of the contract (ie, are not conditions), in effect creating a statutory presumption for the timing of payment.

Section 10(2) provides that whether any other stipulation as to time is or is not of the essence of the contract depends on the terms of the contract, the different wording making it plain that the statute is not creating a presumption either way.

3.3 Written contracts

If the contract is in writing and has been signed by a party, that party will be bound by those written terms even if he or she has not read them (*L'Estrange v F. Graucob Ltd* [1934] 2 KB 394) or was unable to understand them (*The Luna* [1920] P 22 and, more recently, *Barclays Bank plc v Schwartz* The Times, 3 August 1995). This clear rule is qualified by three important requirements. First, that the party signing must be aware that the document he or she has signed contains or refers to some written terms. Secondly, the terms referred to must actually be present or available so that, for example, where documents sent by facsimile refer to terms stated on the back which are not stated or otherwise communicated that gives rise to a cogent inference that the terms were not intended to apply: *Poseidon Freight Forwarding Co Ltd v Davies Turner Southern Ltd* [1996] CLC 1264. Finally, that the party signing has had reasonably sufficient notice of the exact term — a concept which the courts apply particularly to unusual or onerous terms (see **3.5** below). The five main exceptions to this rule are:

(a) where a complete contract already existed rather than mere negotiations between the parties so that signing a document including new terms will not bind a party unless there is a variation (for which consideration will be required) or a novation;
(b) where the contract is (i) void for mistake at common law or (ii) may not be enforced or can be rectified in equity as a result of a mistake;
(c) under the doctrine of non *est factum*, which is a rare and special category of mistake which applies only where a party to the contract has been misled into signing a contract without being negligent; see, for example, the review of this exception in *Saunders v Anglia Building Society* [1971] AC 1004;
(d) where there has been a misrepresentation of the terms or effect of a clause (*Curtis v Chemical Cleaning & Dyeing Co Ltd* [1951] 1 KB 805);
(e) where the contract is voidable as a result of duress.

When considering whether a contract is voidable for duress, it is important to note that not every form of pressure amounts to duress. Three recent cases demonstrate the problems in this area of the law.

(a) In *Atlas Express Ltd v Kafco (Importers and Distributors) Ltd* [1989] QB 833, the claimant agreed to make a series of deliveries of basketware for the defendant. After the contract had been made the claimant sought to increase the price and refused to perform the balance of the contract if that increase was not agreed. No alternative carrier was likely to be able to meet the delivery dates. If delivery dates were missed, the defendant would be sued by the buyer who would have ceased trading with them. The defendant then agreed to the increased price on the basis that no alternative course of action existed. The defendant then agreed to the increased price on the basis that no alternative course of action existed. The claimant sued for the new higher price. The claim failed as the new contract was voidable for economic duress and because there was no consideration for the new agreement.
(b) In contrast, in *CTN Cash & Carry Ltd v Gallaher Ltd* [1994] 4 All ER 714, the Court of Appeal had to consider whether a sum of money paid by the buyer to the seller could be recovered on the grounds of economic duress when it was found not to be owed. The problem arose because a delivery of cigarettes from the defendant was stolen when the cigarettes were in the claimant's warehouse. Although property in the cigarettes had not passed, the defendant demanded payment in default of which they would not in future grant credit to the claimant (the defendant believed that property had passed and the money was actually due). The claimant paid the £17,000 demanded and later sought to recover the money as a sum paid under economic duress (no claim was made for restitution on the basis of unjust enrichment, or for repayment as a payment made under a mistake). The claim for return of the money because of economic duress failed and the appeal was dismissed.
(c) The most recent case in this area is *Alf Vaughan & Co Ltd (in administrative receivership) v Royscot Trust plc* [1999] 1 All ER 856. This case involved various hire purchase agreements and lease agreements for vehicles. When administrative

receivers were appointed they wished to sell the business as a going concern with clear title to the hire purchase and leased goods. They asked the defendant for a settlement figure (ie, the sum which was required to transfer title in all the goods). The defendant then exercised a contractual right to terminate because of the appointment of the administrative receivers and offered to sell the vehicles for £82,000. The administrative receivers had a right to apply for relief from forfeiture but did not do so. The following day the defendant sought to repossess the vehicles and only withdrew on being promised payment of £82,000. The settlement figure under the various agreements was £34,386.05. The defendant was therefore making a windfall of profit of £47,613.95. When the administrative receivers sought to recover that sum as being paid under duress of goods, the claim was dismissed as the threat to the goods was not tortious, immoral or unconscionable so as to be an illegitimate threat amounting to duress.

In *PB Leasing Ltd v Patel & Patel (trading as Plankhouse Stores)* [1995] CCLR 82, the court had to consider a number of issues arising from an agreement being signed in blank. It was held that the customers could not rely on the doctrine of non est factum as they had acted without proper care in signing the agreement without reading it. The customers were not liable to the finance company in negligence for signing the agreement in blank. Fortunately for the customers, the agreement was a regulated consumer credit agreement which was unenforceable without a court order, and the court, exercising its discretion, declined to allow enforcement.

The fact that a signed written contract exists will not normally prevent there being other express terms of that contract which have not been put into the signed document, provided they are not in conflict with the written terms. However, many written contracts contain an 'entire agreement' clause which seeks to exclude the existence of other terms. Such clauses are not always wholly effective. In *Thomas Witter Ltd v TBP Industries Ltd* [1996] 2 All ER 573 (at pp. 595—98), and *Deepak Fertilisers & Petrochemicals Ltd v Davy McKee (London) Ltd* [1999] 1 All ER 69 (at p 79), there are detailed examinations of the construction and effect of entire agreement clauses. There could be a collateral contract between the same parties. If the entire agreement excludes misrepresentations or implied terms then it will be subject to the statutory qualifications considered in **Chapter 4**.

In commercial transactions there is often a dispute as to which set of standard terms applies to the contract. This is usually resolved by examining the events chronologically looking for the offer or counter offer which has actually been accepted, often by performing the contract, which means that the party firing the last shot in the negotiations will usually succeed in showing that the last terms are the basis for the contract.

3.4 Construing written contracts

The function of the court is to decide the objective intention of the parties. The question is not what the parties understood the words or document to mean, but the meaning which the document would convey to a reasonable person having all the background knowledge which would reasonably have been available to the parties in the situation in which they were at the time of the contract (*Investors Compensation Scheme Ltd v West Bromwich Building Society* [1988] 1 WLR 896). There are no special rules for mercantile contracts or business documents. The main 'rules' of construction are:

(a) the ordinary meaning of words should be used unless:
  (i) there is some well known trade custom or trade practice which means that a special meaning is to be given to words (probably the best known example being a 'baker's dozcn' meaning 13), or
  (ii) there is some local custom which means words have a particular meaning in that locality, or
  (iii) the words are technical words, in which case the normal accepted technical meaning should be used;

(b) words should be construed so as to avoid absurd or inconsistent provisions as the parties cannot have intended that the contract should be absurd or inconsistent;

(c) the entire contract will be considered so that individual words or phrases are considered in their context and any recitals may be used as a guide to the interpretation of the operative parts of a contract;

(d) in written contracts, as in statutes, general words which follow several specific words are to be construed in a similar manner — the ejusdem generis rule;

(e) finally that the term is construed more strongly against its grantor or maker — the contra proferentem rule — but this only arises where there remains an ambiguity which has not been resolved by the application of the earlier rules.

A common problem is the poorly drafted written contract. There are no special rules of construction, but in applying the rules set out above in *Antaios Compania Naviera SA v Salen Rederierna AB (The Antaios)* [1984] AC 676, Lord Diplock said:

> if a detailed semantic syntactical analysis of words in a commercial contract is going to lead to a conclusion that flouts business common sense, it must yield to business common sense.

This is an important reflection of the purpose of all rules of construction, namely to ascertain the intention of the parties.

When construing a written contract it is important to remember the effect of the parole evidence rule under which oral evidence cannot be admitted to contradict, vary, add to or subtract from the terms of a written contract. Parole evidence will not be admitted even to establish a mutual but unexpressed intention of both parties to the contract: *New Hampshire Insurance Co v MGN Ltd* The Times, 25 July 1995. The parole evidence rule will not apply if the contract is partly oral and partly in writing, or only evidenced in writing. Evidence of earlier drafts of the contract or negotiations cannot be admitted (save where the court is being asked to rectify the text of the agreement). This will not prevent evidence being admitted of the customary meaning of words in a particular trade or of a special technical meaning of words.

Another common problem in practice is construing a written contract which refers to other documents (eg, trade association standard terms) or other factors (eg, the base interest rate of a major bank). If the notice given of the incorporation of the document or factor is adequate and the term or factor is not onerous or unusual (see **3.5**), then the court will try to give effect to what the parties agreed should be incorporated. Any inconsistencies between the written contract and any terms or factors which are incorporated from elsewhere will then have to be resolved.

3.5 Onerous or unusual terms

If a contract contains some particularly onerous or unusual terms the court will look with great care to see whether the onerous term has been incorporated into the contract. This approach is at variance with the general approach that a party is bound by the terms which he or she is aware are in a written agreement even if he or she has not read them. This exception is limited to unusual or onerous terms.

The most striking description of this rule is to be found in the judgment of Denning LJ in *J. Spurling v Bradshaw* [1956] 1 WLR 461 at 466 where he said:

> Some clauses I have seen would need to be printed in red ink on the face of the document with a red hand pointing to it before the notice could be held to be sufficient.

The importance of this rule has been slightly reduced by the statutory control of exemption clauses. Nevertheless it remains an important way of challenging onerous or unusual express terms of a written contract. It is still being applied today with important consequences for the parties: see, for example, the striking decisions of the Court of Appeal in *Interfoto Picture Library Ltd v Stiletto Visual Programmes Ltd* [1989] QB 433 and *AEG (UK) Ltd v Logic Resource Ltd* [1996] CLC 265. When considering whether a term is unusual it is helpful to discover whether there are any standard terms in the industry or trade such as those appearing in any Code of Practice (see **4.2**).

3.6 Exemption and indemnity clauses

The ordinary rules of construction apply to exemption clauses which exempt one party from the consequences of some breach of contract and to indemnity clauses which require the innocent party to indemnify the party in breach against claims from third parties. When ascertaining the intention of the parties:

(a) an exemption clause must be clear so that a clause which effectively absolves one party from any performance at all may be held to be meaningless as it could not have been the intention of the parties that there were no mutual obligations (*Tor Line AB v Alltrans Group of Canada Ltd* [1984] 1 WLR 48); and,

(b) when considering exemption clauses excluding liability for negligence the three tests in *Canada Steamships Lines Ltd v The King* [1952] AC 192 are applied and it seems that:

  (i) if the clause plainly excludes such liability then (subject to statutory control) effect will be given to it,

  (ii) if the clause is unclear it will be construed contra proferentem, and

  (iii) if the clause covers liabilities other than negligence (eg, an Act of God such as damage by lightning) then it will be held not to cover negligence.

The basic rule of privity of contract applies, so that the burden and benefit of an exemption clause cannot normally be conferred on those who are not parties to the contract, save in the cases of agency, assignment and 'Himalaya' clauses.

The 'Himalaya' clause is named after the ship involved in the case of *Adler v Dickson* [1955] 1 QB 158. A 'Himalaya' clause is an exclusion of liability clause which protects not only the contracting party but that party's servants, agents and sub-contractors by conferring upon them the benefit of the clause: *New Zealand Shipping Co Ltd v A.M. Saterwaite*

& Co Ltd (The Eurymedon) [1975] AC 154, and *Port Jackson Stevedoring Pty Ltd v Salmond and Spraggon (Aust.) Pty Ltd (The New York Star)* [1981] 1 WLR 138. 'Himalaya' clauses are extremely common in carriage of goods contracts and now appear in the main Conventions: see, for example, the United Nations Convention for International Multimodal Transport of Goods, the Hamburg Rules, the Hague-Visby Rules, and the Warsaw Convention (as amended). A similar result is sometimes achieved by an express contract clause which prohibits actions against others such as sub-contractors, servants or agents and such a clause would not be subject to the test of reasonableness in UCTA 1977: *Neptune Orient Lines Ltd v JVC (UK) Ltd* [1983] 2 Lloyd's Rep 438. An agreement to indemnify and hold harmless can contain within it, by necessary implication, an implied obligation not to sue: *Deepak Fertilisers & Petrochemicals Ltd v Davy McKee (London) Ltd* [1999] 1 All ER 69.

The burden of proof is upon the party claiming that some liability is excluded to show that the particular liability falls within the ambit of the clause.

3.7 *Force majeure* clauses

There is no general concept of *force majeure* in English law and the courts have often seemed reluctant to accept the concept at all. Sale of goods contracts often contain express *force majeure* clauses which limit the seller's liability in circumstances anticipated by the clause with or without provision for notice to be given to the buyer. The true effect of a *force majeure* clause is to limit the seller's obligation to perform and it is not therefore an exemption clause which excludes liability for breach of contract as no breach will have occurred. An important consequence is that such terms may not be required to satisfy the test of reasonableness under UCTA 1977. The burden of proving that the clause applies is upon the party seeking to rely upon it, usually the seller.

3.8 Liquidated damages clauses and penalties

There are no special rules of construction for liquidated damages or penalty clauses in contracts. The onerous clauses rule and the *contra proferentem* rule are often of practical importance. If the sum stipulated in the contract is a penalty, the clause will not be enforced. If the sum is a genuine pre-estimate of damage, looked at when the contract was made, it will be a liquidated damages clause and enforceable. The label given by the parties to the clause will not determine whether it is a penalty or a liquidated damages clause: *Dunlop Pneumatic Tyre Co Ltd v New Garage and Motor Co Ltd* [1915] AC 79.

A clause will be either a liquidated damages clause or a penalty if it provides for the payment of a sum of money by a party who is in default of his or her contractual obligations in some stated way or ways. Incentives for early performance or payment will not be classified as a liquidated damages clause or as a penalty. Thus a clause, properly incorporated into the contract, which provides for a 10% discount on the agreed price if it is paid within 28 days will be upheld; but a clause which provides for a 10% increase in the contract price if the payment is received after 28 days will be unenforceable as a penalty as it is not a genuine pre-estimate of the loss suffered by payment being late. A clause which provides for the payment of a sum of money on the happening of a certain event, which is not itself a breach of contract by either party, will not be a liquidated damages or penalty clause: *Export Credits Guarantee Department v Universal Oil Products Co* [1983] 1 WLR 399.

It is unfortunate that there remains considerable uncertainty in the law of penalty clauses. The decision in *Financings Ltd v Baldock* [1963] 2 QB 104 that the clause was a penalty is to be contrasted with the decision in *Lombard North Central plc v Butterworth* [1987] 1 QB 527 in which a similar clause was upheld. In addition, if the decision of the Court of Appeal in *Lombard North Central plc v Butterworth* is followed the law of penalties can be wholly avoided by drafting the contract so that all obligations are conditions.

Confusion exists over the effect of forfeiture clauses where a sum, usually the deposit, is forfeited on breach of contract by the buyer. In *Workers Trust & Merchant Bank Ltd v Dojap Investments Ltd* [1993] AC 573, the Privy Council decided that whilst forfeiture clauses were outside the normal rules on penalty clauses the amount of the deposit had to be reasonable and, if the amount could not be shown to be reasonable, the clause was an unenforceable penalty clause. A quite different approach has been adopted in some cases concerning the creation or transfer of proprietary rights where the court has merely granted equitable relief from the forfeiture: *BICC plc v Burndy Corporation* [1985] Ch 232, a case which it is not easy to reconcile in commercial terms with the decision in *Sport International Bussum BV v Inter-Footwear Ltd* [1984] 1 WLR 776. The power to grant equitable relief has been exercised under a finance agreement: *Goker v NWS Bank* The Times, 23 May 1990 and *Transag Haulage Ltd v Leyland Daf Finance plc* [1994] BCC 356. The High Court has equitable jurisdiction to grant relief and the County Court will have a similar power: s 38, County Courts Act 1984.

3.9 Contracts wholly or partly oral

If the contract is simply an oral contract, proof of any disputed express terms of the contract will require oral evidence from those making the contract and any witnesses. Evidence of ancillary matters (eg, actions thereafter of one or more parties) may be admissible to establish the accuracy of the oral evidence, but will not prove the actual contract.

If the contract is partly oral and partly in writing proof of any disputed express terms may require oral evidence. It is commonly alleged that a contract is only evidenced in writing in an attempt to circumvent the parole evidence rule.

3.10 Implied terms

After the express terms of a contract have been ascertained it is necessary to consider what terms will be implied into the contract. Terms may be implied into a contract in three main ways:

- to reflect the actual intention of the parties — the unexpressed terms;
- to give business efficacy to the agreement — the terms which the court presumes the parties would have expressed if they had considered the position; and
- by law — not as a result of the actual or presumed intention of the parties but as a result of general considerations of policy.

The implication of a term as being the actual intention of the parties can be based on custom within the trade or locality if the custom is notorious, certain, legal and reasonable; or can be based on a previous course of dealing between the parties; or can be based on the circumstances and express obligations of the contract. There is often an overlap between the first and second category. Terms are implied to give business efficacy when they are required in order to enable the contract to work satisfactorily. No term will be implied under the first two tests if the term is unreasonable, but the mere fact that the term is reasonable will not mean that it is implied.

Most terms which are implied by law are now based upon statutory provisions, although many of the statutory provisions are a codification of the common law. The terms implied by law can be divided into two distinct categories. First, there are terms which are always implied into a contract of the particular type and which cannot be excluded by agreement between the parties. Secondly, there are those which are implied into the particular type of contract only where the parties have not reached some other arrangement. The implied terms introduced by SOGA 1979 fall into both categories.

The implied terms imposed by SOGA 1979 have to be considered in detail. Those implied terms can be varied or excluded by express agreement between the parties, by course of dealings between the parties or by such usage as binds both parties to the contract (s 55(1), SOGA 1979). The implied terms are:

- implied terms about title (s 12);
- implied terms where there has been a sale by description (s 13);
- implied terms about quality or fitness (s 14);
- implied terms where there is a sale by sample (s 15).

3.10.1 The implied terms as to title

Section 12, SOGA 1979 designates the various implied terms as conditions or warranties as to title (s 12(5)). It is vital to note that the conditions and warranties as to title apply to all contracts and not merely to those concluded by a seller in the course of a business.

The implied term which is a condition is in s 12(1):

> *... there is an implied term on the part of the seller that in the case of a sale he has the right to sell the goods, and in the case of an agreement to sell he will have the right at the time when the property is to pass.*

By s 6(1)(a), UCTA 1977 this condition cannot be excluded or restricted by reference to any contract term in consumer and non-consumer sales. The anti-avoidance provisions of s 27, UCTA 1977 apply. However, the prohibition on excluding or restricting liability does not apply to international supply contracts (s 26, UCTA 1977).

Questions of title and the exceptions to the *nemo dat* rule are considered in **Chapter 6**. A breach of this condition gives rise to a right to reject the goods even after long use and the buyer will be able to reclaim the purchase price together with interest upon the total failure of consideration despite having the benefit of the use of the goods. This right is of particular importance with depreciating goods such as motor vehicles: *Rowland v Divall* [1923] 2 KB 500 and *Butterworth v Kingsway Motors Ltd* [1954] 1 WLR 1286. Section 11(4) concerning acceptance was said not to apply to such cases.

The position where the buyer acquires good title under one of the exceptions to the *nemo dat* rule is much less clear. Although the buyer gets good title the seller did not actually have the right to sell and so seems in clear breach of s 12(1). The buyer may have real difficulty in reselling the goods. The position was considered in *Barber v NWS Bank plc* [1996] 1 WLR 641 where the Court of Appeal was concerned with the position of a hirer under a conditional sale agreement of a car to which the finance company did not have title. It seems from the judgment that had title passed under an exception to the *nemo dat* rule the outcome of the case would have been different.

Section 12(1) also applies where the seller's right to sell is restricted by some breach of civil or criminal law. 'If a vendor can be stopped by process of law from selling he has not the right to sell' and there will be a breach of s 12(1): *Niblett Ltd v Confectioners' Materials Co Ltd* [1921] 3 KB 387, per Scrutton LJ at p 398, in a case involving goods which could not properly be sold as they infringed a trade mark.

The implied term which is a warranty is in two parts to be found in s 12(2):

> *... there is ... an implied term that—*
> *(a) the goods are free, and will remain free until the time when property is to pass, from any charge or encumbrance not disclosed or known to the buyer before the contract is made, and*
> *(b) the buyer will enjoy quiet possession of the goods except in so far as it may be disturbed by the owner or other person entitled to the benefit of any charge or encumbrance so disclosed or known.*

By s 6(1)(a), UCTA 1977 this warranty cannot be excluded or restricted by reference to any contract term in consumer and non-consumer sales. The anti-avoidance provisions of s 27, UCTA 1977 apply. However, the prohibition on excluding or restricting liability does not apply to international supply contracts (s 26, UCTA 1977).

These two warranties create continuing obligations. The decision in *Niblett Ltd v Confectioners' Materials Co Ltd* was also based on breach of this warranty. In *Microbeads AG v Vinhurst Road Markings Ltd* [1975] 1 WLR 218 a breach of s 12(2) but not of s 12(1) occurred when a subsequent patent affected the goods sold. Where the buyer has to deliver up the goods to their true owner there will be a breach of s 12(2): *Mason v Burningham* [1949] 2 KB 545. Similarly, where quiet possession is interfered with by a third party with the connivance of the seller there will be a breach of s 12(2): *Empresa Exportadora de Acucar v Industria Azucarera Nacional SA (The Playa Larga and The Marble Islands)* [1983] 2 Lloyd's Rep 171. The measure of damages for breach of the warranty is governed by s 53, SOGA 1979.

Section 12(3) creates a special situation where there appears from the contract or is to be inferred from the intention of the parties that the title to be transferred is only the title which the seller or some third party may have. Section 12(4) and (5) create modified obligations as to title which apply only to this special situation and are similar to s 12(1) and (2). Sales of goods to which s 12(3) apply are rare.

For hire-purchase agreements, the implied conditions and warranties as to title are to be found in s 8, SOGITA 1973. The implied conditions and warranties are very similar to those contained in SOGA 1979. The implied conditions and warranties in hire-purchase agreements cannot be excluded by agreement: s 6(1)(b), UCTA 1977.

In contracts for work and materials, the implied conditions and warranties as to title are to be found in s 2, SOGSA 1982. Again, they are very similar to those found in SOGA 1979. The implied conditions and warranties in contracts for work and materials cannot be excluded by agreement: s 7(3A), UCTA 1977.

3.10.2 Implied terms in sales by description

Where there is a contract for sale by description the implied term is a condition, s 13(1A) and is that '... *the goods will correspond to the description*' (s 13(1)). It is vital to note that the conditions and warranties as to description apply to all contracts and not merely to those concluded by a seller in the course of a business.

Note that if the sale is by sample and description the goods must correspond to the description as well as to the sample (s 13(2)). A sale is not prevented from being by description merely because being exposed for sale or hire the goods are selected by the buyer (s 13(3)).

In consumer sales the obligations imposed by s 13, SOGA 1979 cannot be excluded or restricted by reference to any contract term (s 6(2)(a), UCTA 1977). In non-consumer sales, liability can be restricted or excluded only in so far as the exclusion satisfies the test of reasonableness (s 6(3), UCTA 1977). The anti-avoidance provisions of s 27, UCTA 1977 apply. However, the prohibition on excluding or restricting liability does not apply to international supply contracts (s 26, UCTA 1977).

Sales by description are by far the most common type of contract for the sale of goods. All sales of unascertained goods will be by description. All sales of goods which the buyer has not seen at all will be sales by description. Many sales by sample will also be sales by description. Many words used to describe the goods being sold will be a 'description' for the purposes of this section. However, words which are merely useful information will not be a description.

The courts are now moving away from excessive technicalities where every word used about the goods is a description. Two leading cases need to be considered. In a contract for the sale of mink food the manufacturer acquired from a third party Norwegian herring meal which was referred to as fair average quality of the season; by a majority the House of Lords held that this was not a description within s 13, SOGA 1979: *Christopher Hill Ltd v Ashington Piggeries Ltd* [1972] AC 441. A contract for sale of a ship said to be going to be built in a particular yard with a particular hull number when it was then built in another yard under another number was not a sale by description as the words were merely for identification and had no significance: *Reardon Smith Line Ltd v Hansen Tangen* [1976] 1 WLR 989.

The sale must be 'by' description so that where the buyer does not rely upon any words used by the seller there can be no sale by description: *Harlington and Leinster Enterprises Ltd v Christopher Hull Fine Art Ltd* [1991] 1 QB 564.

A common problem in practice is whether the sale of a second-hand motor car is a sale by description. If the seller sells in the course of his business it may not matter whether the complaint is made under s 13 or 14, SOGA 1979. If the seller is a non-business seller, the buyer may have to rely on s 13 to bring a complaint as s 14 does not apply to non-business sales. Reliance on s 13 may be the only way in which a buyer can complain about the very common problem of 'clocking' (ie, altering the odometer so that it shows that a motor vehicle has a lower mileage) in a non-business sale. 'Clocking' is a Trade Descriptions Act 1968 offence which is so prevalent that it often attracts a custodial sentence, but that is of little comfort to the buyer who has to find a civil remedy. In *Beale v Taylor* [1967] 1 WLR 1193 the claim was brought under s 13 as it was a non-business sale. The court found the seller to be quite innocent. However, the court held that a description of the motor car as a 'Herald convertible, white, 1961, twin carbs., £190', was not satisfied when the vehicle was actually the rear portion of a Triumph Herald and the front portion of an earlier model, welded together in an unsafe and unsatisfactory manner.

3.10.3 Implied terms as to quality and fitness

These are the implied terms which give rise to most claims. They are quite separate. The terms are conditions (s 14(6), SOGA 1979). The old standard of merchantable quality has been replaced by a new concept of satisfactory quality and, as decisions under the new provision are being made, it is no longer necessary to cite the older cases.

Apart from the provisions of s 14(2C), in consumer sales the obligations imposed by s 14, SOGA 1979 cannot be excluded or restricted by reference to any contract term (s 6(2)(a), UCTA 1977). In non-consumer sales, liability can be restricted or excluded only in so far as the term satisfies the test of reasonableness (s 6(3), UCTA 1977). The anti-avoidance provisions of s 27, UCTA 1977 apply. However, the prohibition on excluding or restricting liability does not apply to international supply contracts (s 26, UCTA 1977).

The implied term arises where the seller sells in the course of a business (s 14(2)). The words 'in the course of a business' appear in a number of statutes. The courts seemed to be moving towards a single interpretation of those words, but the Court of Appeal recently decided that the words do not have the same meaning in all statutes: *Stevenson v Rogers* [1999] 1 All ER 613. This problem is considered in more detail later (see **4.3.1**).

Satisfactory quality means '*the standard that a reasonable person would regard as satisfactory, taking account of any description of the goods, the price (if relevant) and all other relevant circumstances*' (s 14(2A)). Quality of goods '*includes their state and condition and the following (among others) are in appropriate cases aspects of the quality of goods (a) fitness for the purpose for which goods of the kind in question are commonly supplied; (b) appearance and finish; (c) freedom from minor defects; (d) safety; and (e) durability*' (s 14(2B)).

The implied term of satisfactory quality '*does not extend to any matter making the goods unsatisfactory (a) which is specifically drawn to the buyer's attention before the contract is made, (b) where the buyer examines the goods before the contract is made, which that examination ought to reveal, or (c) in the case of a contract for sale by sample, which would have been apparent on a reasonable examination of the sample*' (s 14(2C)).

A term of fitness for a particular purpose is implied where the seller sells in the course of a business and the buyer makes known any particular purpose for which the goods are being bought, except where the circumstances show that the buyer does not rely or that it is unreasonable for him or her to rely on the skill or judgment of the seller s 14(3)). The particular purpose will not merely be the general purpose of the goods: *Slater and others v Finning Ltd* [1996] 3 All ER 398.

The circumstances which can amount to a breach of these implied terms are considered in **Chapter 10**.

The Sale and Supply of Goods to Consumers Regulations 2002 amended s 14 in an important respect, by introducing a new s 14(2D)–(2F). If the buyer deals as a consumer, then the relevant circumstances for the purposes of s 14(2A) include public statements on the specific characteristics of the goods made by the seller, the producer or his or her representative, particularly in advertising or on labelling. The seller can avoid this liability in limited circumstances under the new s 14(2E) if the buyer was not aware of the public statement, it had been withdrawn or corrected, or the decision to buy had not been influenced by the public statement. One example of the decision not being influenced by the statement is, presumably, where the consumer buyer had not heard or read the public statement prior to the decision to purchase.

3.10.4 Sale by sample

The implied conditions in a contract of sale by sample are: (a) that the bulk will correspond to the sample in quality, s 15(2)(a); and (b) that the goods will be free from any defect making their quality unsatisfactory which would not be apparent on reasonable examination of the sample (s 15(2)(c)).

In consumer sales the obligations imposed by s 15, SOGA 1979 cannot be excluded or restricted by reference to any contract term (s 6(2)(a), UCTA 1977). In non-consumer sales liability can be restricted or excluded only in so far as the exclusion satisfies the test of reasonableness (s 6(3), UCTA 1977). The anti-avoidance provisions of s 27, UCTA 1977 apply. However, the prohibition on excluding or restricting liability does not apply to international supply contracts (s 26, UCTA 1977).

4 Statutory protection

The common law protection afforded by the rules of incorporation of onerous terms and construction of contract clauses have already been considered in **Chapter 3**. The statutory implied terms in sale of goods contracts have been considered in **Chapter 3**. Further civil statutory protection is to be found in the Misrepresentation Act 1967, Fair Trading Act 1973, Unfair Contract Terms Act 1977, the Consumer Protection (Cancellation of Contracts Concluded away from Business Premises) Regulations 1987, the Unfair Terms in Consumer Contracts Regulations 1999, the Consumer Protection Act 1987 and the Disability Discrimination Act 1995. There are numerous statutes and regulations which give rise to criminal sanctions and various powers to prohibit particular undesirable trade practices, but those are beyond the scope of this Manual.

4.1 Misrepresentation Act 1967

Section 3 of the Misrepresentation Act 1967 (as inserted by UCTA 1977) prohibits any contract term which would exclude or restrict (a) liability for a misrepresentation made before the contract was made or (b) any remedy by reason of such misrepresentation, unless the term satisfies the requirement of reasonableness in s 11(1), UCTA 1977. The burden of showing that the term satisfies the test of reasonableness is on the party relying upon it: *Thomas Witter Ltd v TBP Industries Ltd* [1996] 2 All ER 573.

4.2 Fair Trading Act 1973

Section 124(1) of the Fair Trading Act 1973 gives the Director of Fair Trading the power to arrange for the publication of information and advice to consumers. Section 124(3) creates a duty of the Director to encourage relevant trade associations to prepare and disseminate to their members Codes of Practice for guidance in safeguarding and promoting the interests of consumers. Relevant trade associations are widely defined by s 124(4). A large number of Codes of Practice have been prepared and disseminated by trade associations. The Director will now endorse Codes which comply with his best practice guidelines, one of which is that the Code must give the consumer genuine benefits which are beyond legal requirements. Various Codes have been prepared covering, inter alia, businesses in the following areas: antiques, the motor industry, the motor repair industry, credit companies, direct sales and mail order, electrical goods and services, footwear, glass and glazing, holidays and holiday caravans, introduction agencies, laundry and vehicle rental. In some cases such as the credit industry, there are numerous Codes produced by different trade associations.

The Codes of Practice can be important for the individual customer for a number of reasons. In particular, the Codes create rights which go beyond the ordinary rights of the consumer (eg, a guarantee for the product) and may be incorporated into the individual contract, or may constitute a collateral contract with the supplier or manufacturer, or an actionable misrepresentation so that the consumer can enforce these rights; and the Codes will give guidance as to trade practice and common standard terms of trading which can be useful if a clause in an individual contract is being challenged as being onerous (see **3.5**). Rights such as those in a guarantee will not reduce the ordinary rights enjoyed by the buyer; they are merely additional rights: *Rogers v Parish* [1987] QB 933.

Another important area of the work of the Director General is his use of Part III of the Fair Trading Act 1973 which obliges him to seek assurances from traders who persistently fail to fulfil their obligations to customers. Examples of the assurances sought and given appear in the Annual Report. In 1995 one undertaking given by a second-hand car dealer was 'not to threaten violence against customers who complain'. Breach of an undertaking is punishable as a contempt of court. However, breach of an undertaking creates no private law right: *Mid-Kent Holdings plc v General Utilities plc* [1997] 1 WLR 14.

The Unfair Contract Terms Unit of the Office of Fair Trading is becoming increasingly active in requiring business to stop using contract terms which are unfair. Most companies agree to abandon terms rather than face OFT claims for an injunction to prevent the use of such terms. In 1999, after complaints from the Air Transport Users' Council, airlines were told to expect legal action if they did not stop using contract terms which are unfair to passengers involving issues such as non-transferable ticketing arrangements, re-scheduling or flights without compensate and limits on liability for damaged goods. The International Air Transport Association (IATA) was told to review the standard terms, which have now been amended. Changes have also been required from several mobile telephone companies. Regular bulletins are issued which give details of the action taken. About 5,000 standard term contracts are now investigated each year.

The OFT is continuing the campaign to require the deletion of all 'full payment in advance' clauses from home improvement contracts.

The Competition Act 1998 has made changes to UK competition law and has amended the Fair Trading Act 1973. Those changes and the new power to obtain Stop Orders (injunctions against rogue traders) are designed to give much greater protection to consumers. The Enterprise Act 2002 replaces the powers under the Fair Trading Act 1973 with wider powers and introduces new powers that are, again, designed to enhance the protection given to consumers. Investigations and action taken under the 1973 Act continue, so the provisions of this Act will continue to be important for several years.

4.3 Unfair Contract Terms Act 1977

Innovative controls of exclusion of contractual and tortious liability were introduced by UCTA 1977. The general provisions in ss 2–5 can apply to sale of goods contracts or guarantees. Sections 6 and 7 are of particular importance to contracts for the sale and supply of goods. Section 10 prohibits the use of separate contracts to limit or exclude liability. Section 26 excludes international supply contracts. Section 27 restricts the use of choice of law clauses. The Law Commission has proposed a new single Act to replace UCTA 1977 and the Unfair Terms in Consumer Contracts Regulations 1999 with a clearer and considerably wider regime of control. Unless and until those proposals are brought into force, UCTA 1977 remains an important control.

The OFT is becoming increasingly active in the area of standard terms which are unfair. Regular Unfair Contract Terms Bulletins are now issued outlining the action taken and the terms which are unacceptable. Many companies or groups of companies (eg, mobile telephone companies) have agreed to change their business practices by introducing new contracts and by agreeing not to enforce the offending terms in current contracts.

The prohibitions which particularly affect sale of goods are as follows:

(a) the absolute prohibition on excluding or restricting the implied undertakings as to title (s 6(1)(a), UCTA 1977);

(b) the absolute prohibition in consumer cases on excluding or restricting the implied terms in SOGA 1979, ss 13–15 as to sale by description, quality or fitness, and sale by sample; and,

(c) the qualified prohibition in non-consumer cases on excluding or restricting the implied terms in SOGA 1979, ss 13–15 as to sale by description, quality or fitness, and sale by sample, so that to be effective an exclusion or restriction must satisfy the test of reasonableness in s 11 and Sch 2, UCTA 1977.

4.3.1 Dealing as consumer

Dealing as a consumer is defined in s 12(1), UCTA 1977 as being where a party neither makes the contract in the course of a business nor holds himself out as doing so, and the other party makes the contract in the course of a business, and in the case of sales of goods, the goods passing under or in pursuance of the contract are of a type ordinarily supplied for private use or consumption. With effect from 31 March 2003, the definition in UCTA 1977 has been amended by the Sale and Supply of Goods to Consumers Regulations 2002 by inserting a new s 12(1A) and by a replacement wording for s 12(2).

A business may deal as a consumer if the transaction is not entered into as an integral part of the business carried on and is not a transaction carried on with some regularity: *R & B Customs Brokers Co Ltd v United Dominion Trust Ltd* [1988] 1 WLR 321. In the R & B Customs Brokers case the court was concerned with a claim by a company in business as freight forwarders and shipping agents that a Colt Shogun was defective. The Shogun was being bought under a conditional sale agreement from the defendant finance company. Saunders & Abbott (1980) Limited, the suppliers, were joined as a third party (Part 20 defendant). The Shogun had numerous defects including a leaking roof and was found to be unfit for the purpose of being used in English weather. The judge found that the company was dealing as a consumer. As a result, the defendant's clause excluding any warranty or condition as to the condition, description, quality or fitness of the Shogun did not operate. The claimant succeeded against the defendant and the defendant succeeded against the third party (Part 20 defendant). The Court of Appeal dismissed the appeal by the third party (Part 20 defendant). The Shogun was only the second or third vehicle acquired by the claimant company on finance in a five year period and the requisite degree of regularity was not established so that this became an integral part of the business, rather than something merely incidental to it.

The Court of Appeal revisited the question of transactions in the course of a business in *Stevenson v Rogers* [1999] 1 All ER 613. The dispute concerned the sale by a fisherman of his fishing vessel. If the sale was in the course of his business there would be an implied term of merchantability (now satisfactory quality): s 14(2) SOGA. The court held that the sale was in the course of a business. It now seems that the concept of a sale in the course of a business under SOGA is different from the test under the Trade Descriptions Act 1968 and UCTA 1977.

The European Court had to consider whether a guarantee was given in the course of a business for the purposes of Directive 85/577/EC (see **4.4**) in *Bayerische Hypotheken und Wechselbank AG v Dietzinger* [1998] 1 WLR 1035. The guarantee was connected to a contract which was plainly a business contract and was therefore not covered by the Directive. The Court ruled that the contract of guarantee was ancillary to the business contract and was therefore not a consumer contract which attracted the cooling-off period.

4.3.2 Reasonableness

Section 11, UCTA 1977 provides:

> (1) *In relation to a contract term, the requirement of reasonableness for the purposes of this Part of this Act ... is that the term shall have been fair and reasonable one to be included having regard to the circumstances which were, or ought reasonably to have been, known to or in the contemplation of the parties when the contract was made.*
>
> (2) *In determining for the purposes of section 6 or 7 above whether a contract term satisfies the requirement of reasonableness, regard shall be had in particular to the matters specified in Schedule 2 to this Act; but this subsection does not prevent the court or arbitrator from holding, in accordance with any rule of law, that a term which purports to exclude or restrict any relevant liability is not a term of the contract.*

Schedule 2, UCTA 1977 provides as follows:

> *The matters to which regard is to be had in particular for the purposes of section 6(3), 7(3) and (4), 20 and 21 are any of the following which appear to be relevant —*
>
> (a) *the strength of the bargaining positions of the parties relative to each other, taking into account (among other things) alternative means by which the customer's requirements could have been met;*
>
> (b) *whether the customer received an inducement to agree to the term, or in accepting it had an opportunity of entering into a similar contract with other persons, but without having to accept a similar term;*
>
> (c) *whether the customer knew or ought reasonably to have known of the existence and extent of the term (having regard, among other things, to any custom of the trade and any previous course of dealing between the parties);*
>
> (d) *where the term excludes or restricts any relevant liability if some condition is not complied with, whether it was reasonable at the time of the contract to expect that compliance with that condition would be practicable;*
>
> (e) *whether the goods were manufactured, processed or adapted to the special order of the customer.*

There are an ever increasing number of decisions applying the test of reasonableness to particular contracts. One of the leading cases is still *George Mitchell (Chesterhall) Ltd v Finney Lock Seeds Ltd* [1983] 2 AC 803 in which unmerchantable seed was planted over 60 acres of land and, although it germinated, the crop was commercially useless. The loss to the claimant was £61,000. The liability of the defendant supplier was limited to replacement or the value of the seed which was £192. The Court of Appeal dismissed the appeal upholding the decision that the clause was not reasonable within the meaning of the then provisions of s 55(4), Sale of Goods Act 1893 (as substituted by s 4, SOGITA 1973).

In *Watford Electronics Ltd v Sanderson CFL Ltd* [2001] 1 All ER (Comm) 696, the Court was considering standard terms of trading and Chadwick LJ said:

> Where experienced businessmen representing substantial companies of equal bargaining power negotiate an agreement, they may be taken to have had regard to the matters known to them. They should, in my view be taken to be the best judge of the commercial fairness of the agreement which they have made; including the fairness of each of the terms in that agreement. They should be taken to be the best judge on the question whether the terms of the agreement are

reasonable. The court should not assume that either is likely to commit his company to an agreement which he thinks is unfair, or which he thinks includes unreasonable terms. Unless satisfied that one party has, in effect, taken unfair advantage of the other — or that a term is so unreasonable that it cannot properly have been understood or considered — the court should not interfere. (para 55)

4.3.3 Statements of case and the burden of proof

In *Sheffield v Pickfords Ltd & Another* [1997] CLC 648, the Court of Appeal held that where a party (in that case the defendant) in his statement of case relied on standard conditions, it is implicit in that statement of case that, if UCTA 1977 applies to those standard conditions, the party relying upon them is asserting that they satisfy the test of reasonableness and that it is for the party relying on the terms and not the party seeking to avoid them to allege reasonableness. The court accepted that this has not been pleading practice hitherto. It was suggested that at least a general averment of reasonableness should be made by the party relying on the terms, of which particulars of the specific facts and matters relied upon can then be ordered or given. In reaching this extraordinary conclusion, the Court of Appeal seemed to be influenced by the burden of proof under UCTA 1977.

The burden of proof under UCTA 1977 is important not only because of the new approach to statements of case outlined above, but because of the need to adduce evidence to deal with some or all of the factors which the court has to consider under the test of reasonableness. The burden of proof is as follows:

- the burden is on the party claiming that the other party does not deal as a consumer to establish that fact (s 12(3), UCTA 1977); and
- the burden of showing that a contract term or notice satisfies the requirement of reasonablenes is upon the party making the claim (s 11(5), UCTA 1977).

4.4 Consumer Protection (Cancellation of Contracts Concluded away from Business Premises) Regulations 1987

These Regulations apply to contracts made on or after 1 July 1988 and create a statutory cooling-off period which gives the consumer a right to cancel contracts which are within the scope of the Regulations. The Regulations implement Council Directive EEC 85/577 and should be interpreted, so far as possible, to achieve the result intended by the Directive: *Faccini Dori v Recreb Srl* [1995] All ER (EC) 1.

The Regulations were amended by the Consumer Protection (Cancellation of Contracts Concluded away from Business Premises) (Amendment) Regulations 1998. The definition of an unsolicited visit has been amended to give greater protection to the consumer. An offence has been created where a trader does not give notice of the right to cancel the contract which is to be enforced by Trading Standards Officers.

The Regulations apply to contracts (other than excepted contracts) for the supply of goods or services to a consumer which are made during unsolicited visits by a trader to the consumer's home or to the home of another person, or to the consumer's place of work; and to contracts made during a visit at the request of the consumer where the goods or services to which the contract relates are other than those concerning which the consumer requested the visit (provided that when the visit was requested the consumer did not know, or could not reasonably have known, that the supply of goods or services formed part of the trader's business activities); and to contracts made on an excursion organised by the trader away from business premises on which he is carrying any business.

'Unsolicited visit' is widely defined in reg 3(3) as a visit by a trader, whether or not he is the trader who supplies the goods or services, which does not take place at the express request of the consumer and includes a visit which takes place after a trader telephones the consumer (otherwise than at his express request) indicating expressly or by implication that he is willing to visit the consumer.

Excepted contracts are defined in reg 3(2) and include transactions relating to land; contracts for sale of goods by regular roundsmen; insurance contracts; investment agreements within the Financial Services Act 1986 or the Banking Act 1987 (which have their own statutory cancellation system); any contract under which the total payments to be made by the consumer do not exceed £35; and any contract under which credit within the Consumer Credit Act 1974 is provided not exceeding £35 (other than a hire-purchase or conditional sale agreement). A further important exempt category exists for contracts which fulfil all of these three conditions, namely:

(a) the terms of the contract are contained in a trader's catalogue which is readily available to the consumer to read in the absence of the trader or his representative before the conclusion of the contract;

(b) the parties intend that there shall be maintained continuity of contact between the trader or his representative and the consumer in relation to the transaction in question or any subsequent transaction; and

(c) both the catalogue and the contract contain or are accompanied by a prominent notice indicating that the consumer has a right to return to the trader or his representative goods supplied to him within the period of not less than seven days from the date on which the goods are received and otherwise to cancel the contract within that period without incurring any liability (other than a liability which may arise from the failure of the consumer to take reasonable care of the goods while they are in his possession).

If the Regulations apply, no contract shall be enforceable against the consumer unless the trader has delivered to the consumer notice in writing indicating the right to cancel the contract within the period of seven days, the notice containing both the information set out in Part I of the Regulations and a Cancellation Notice (reg 4(1)). If the consumer does cancel then the contract is treated as if it had never been entered into by the consumer (reg 4(6)). The Regulations then make provision for return of money paid (reg 5); repayment of credit (reg 6); return of the goods (reg 7); and return or payment for goods part-exchanged (reg 8). Hardly surprisingly there is a prohibition on contracting out (reg 10).

These important Regulations are widely ignored by firms and companies engaged in cold-calling. The failure to comply renders the contract unenforceable against the consumer and not merely unenforceable without, say, leave of the court. It is unfortunate that consumers are not better informed of their rights under these Regulations.

The cancellation provisions in these Regulations can usefully be compared with the cancellation rights which exist under the Consumer Credit Act 1974 which are considered in detail at **Chapter 15**.

4.5 Unfair Terms in Consumer Contracts Regulations 1999

The Unfair Terms in Consumer Contracts Regulations 1994 apply to contracts made on or after 1 July 1995. The 1999 Regulations came into force on 1 October 1999 when the 1994 Regulations were revoked.

The main changes introduced by the 1999 Regulations are the right for a qualifying body listed in Sch 1 to consider complaints about unfair terms and to seek an injunction on behalf of consumers to prevent the continued use of an unfair term provided that prior notice has been given to the Director General of Fair Trading. Qualifying bodies may also require traders to produce copies of their standard terms of trading.

The regulations differ from UCTA 1977 as they only apply to consumer contracts. Surprisingly, in the regulations a consumer is defined as a natural person who in making the contract is acting for purposes which can be regarded as outside his business — a definition which is narrower than UCTA where consumer can include a company or partnership. Regulation 3(1) defines both seller and supplier as someone acting for purposes relating to his business and would not apply to non-business transactions. The Regulations then apply to any term which is not individually negotiated and which is unfair. Regulation 7(2) introduces a *contra proferentem* rule of construction for written terms.

4.5.1 Core terms

The Regulations do not permit terms to be challenged as unfair to the extent that under reg 6(2) they define the subject matter of the contract or concern the adequacy of the price or remuneration as against the goods or services sold. What amounted to core terms was one of the matters considered by the House of Lords in *Director General of Fair Trading v First National Bank* [2002] 1 All ER 97.

4.5.2 Individually negotiated?

The burden of showing that the term was individually negotiated is upon the seller or supplier — reg 5(4). A term shall always be regarded as not having been individually negotiated if it is drafted in advance and the consumer has not been able to influence the substance of the term — reg 5(2). If certain terms or certain aspects of the contract have been individually negotiated the regulations apply to the rest of the contract if an overall assessment of the contract indicates that it is a pre-formulated contract — reg 5(3).

4.5.3 Unfair?

An unfair term is one which, contrary to the requirement of good faith, causes a significant imbalance in the parties' rights and obligations under the contract to the detriment of the consumer — reg 5(1). The assessment of the unfair nature of a term shall be made taking into account the nature of the goods or services for which the contract was concluded and referring, as at the time of the conclusion of the contract, to all circumstances attending the conclusion of the contract or of another contract upon which it is dependent — reg 6(1).

Schedule 2 contains a non-exhaustive list of terms which may be regarded as unfair:

1. *Terms which have the object or effect of—*
   (a) *excluding or limiting the legal liability of a seller or supplier in the event of the death of a consumer or personal injury to the latter resulting from an act or omission of that seller or supplier;*
   (b) *inappropriately excluding or limiting the legal rights of the consumer vis-à-vis the seller or supplier or another party in the event of total or partial non-performance or inadequate performance by the seller or supplier of any of the contractual obligations, including the option of offsetting a debt owed to the seller or supplier against any claim which the consumer may have against him;*
   (c) *making an agreement binding on the consumer whereas provision of services by the seller or supplier is subject to a condition whose realisation depends on his own will alone;*
   (d) *permitting the seller or supplier to retain sums paid by the consumer where the latter decides not to conclude or perform the contract, without providing for the consumer to receive compensation of an equivalent amount from the seller or supplier where the latter is the party cancelling the contract;*
   (e) *requiring any consumer who fails to fulfil his obligation to pay a disproportionately high sum in compensation;*
   (f) *authorising the seller or supplier to dissolve the contract on a discretionary basis where the same facility is not granted to the consumer, or permitting the seller or supplier to retain the sums paid for services not yet supplied by him where it is the seller or supplier himself who dissolves the contract;*
   (g) *enabling the seller or supplier to terminate a contract of indeterminate duration without reasonable notice except where there are serious grounds for doing so;*
   (h) *automatically extending a contract of fixed duration where the consumer does not indicate otherwise, when the deadline fixed for the consumer to express this desire not to extend the contract is unreasonably early;*
   (i) *irrevocably binding the consumer to terms with which he had no real opportunity of becoming acquainted before the conclusion of the contract;*
   (j) *enabling the seller or supplier to alter the terms of the contract unilaterally without a valid reason which is specified in the contract;*
   (k) *enabling the seller or supplier to alter unilaterally without a valid reason any characteristics of the product or service to be provided;*
   (l) *providing for the price of goods to be determined at the time of delivery or allowing a seller of goods or supplier of services to increase their price without in both cases giving the consumer the corresponding right to cancel the contract if the final price is too high in relation to the price agreed when the contract was concluded;*
   (m) *giving the seller or supplier the right to determine whether the goods or services supplied are in conformity with the contract, or giving him the exclusive right to interpret any term of the contract;*
   (n) *limiting the seller's or supplier's obligation to respect commitments undertaken by his agents or making his commitments subject to compliance with a particular formality;*
   (o) *obliging the consumer to fulfil all his obligations where the seller or supplier does not perform his;*
   (p) *giving the seller or supplier the possibility of transferring his rights and obligations under the contract, where this may serve to reduce the guarantees for the consumer, without the latter's agreement;*
   (q) *excluding or hindering the consumer's right to take legal action or exercise any other legal remedy, particularly by requiring the consumer to take disputes exclusively to arbitration not covered by legal provisions, unduly restricting the evidence available to him or imposing on him a burden of proof which, according to the applicable law, should lie with another party to the contract.*
2. *Scope of subparagraphs 1(g), (j) and (l)*
   (a) *Subparagraph 1(g) is without hindrance to terms by which a supplier of financial services reserves the right to terminate unilaterally a contract of indeterminate duration without notice where there is a valid reason, provided that the supplier is required to inform the other contracting party or parties thereof immediately.*
   (b) *Subparagraph 1(j) is without hindrance to terms under which a supplier of financial services reserves the right to alter the rate of interest payable by the consumer or due to the latter, or the amount of other charges for financial services without notice where there is a valid reason,*

provided that the supplier is required to inform the other contracting party or parties thereof at the earliest opportunity and that the latter are free to dissolve the contract immediately.

Subparagraph 1(j) is also without hindrance to terms under which a seller or supplier reserves the right to alter unilaterally the conditions of a contract of indeterminate duration, provided that he is required to inform the consumer with reasonable notice and that the consumer is free to dissolve the contract.

(c) *Subparagraphs 1(g), (j) and (l) do not apply to:*
- *transactions in transferable securities, financial instruments and other products or services where the price is linked to fluctuations in a stock exchange quotation or index or a financial market rate that the seller or supplier does not control;*
- *contracts for the purchase or sale of foreign currency, traveller's cheques or international money orders denominated in foreign currency;*

(d) *Subparagraph 1(l) is without hindrance to price indexation clauses, where lawful, provided that the method by which prices vary is explicitly described.*

4.5.4 The effect of an unfair term

By reg 8 if a term is found to be unfair within the meaning of the regulations then it is not binding on the parties to the contract; and the contract will continue to bind the consumer if it is capable of continuing in existence without the unfair term.

By regs 10–15, complaints can be considered by the Director General of Fair Trading or a qualifying body, injunctions can be sought to prevent the use of unfair terms, documents and information can be sought and published. These powers are much wider than the powers under the 1994 Regulations under which the Director General was to consider complaints and, if he considered terms unfair, he could require undertakings or seek injunctions.

The Unfair Contract Terms Bulletins issued periodically by the Director contain details of the action taken, specifying the contract term challenged, the exact regulations which might be infringed and the changes made by the trader.

4.6 Consumer Protection Act 1987

The Consumer Protection Act 1987 introduced important new statutory rights and remedies for consumers so that the producer becomes directly liable to the consumer for the damage caused by unsafe products (liability exists towards anyone injured, not just the buyer). 'Producer' and 'product' are defined in s 1(2), Consumer Protection Act 1987. Defect is defined as being where the safety is not such as persons generally are entitled to expect (s 3(1)). The damage for which liability can be claimed is any damage, including personal injury and loss exceeding £275, other than damage to the goods themselves.

4.7 Disability Discrimination Act 1995

Part III of the Disability Discrimination Act 1995 relates to the provision of goods and services. The Act came into force on 2 December 1996. Section 19 renders it unlawful for a provider of services to discriminate against a disabled person. Note that s 19(2)(b) extends the meaning of services to include goods and services. The definition of disability and disabled person are to be found in s 1 of the Act. The discrimination in respect of goods and services is:

(a) refusing to provide or deliberately not providing to the disabled any service which he provides or is prepared to provide to the public;

(b) failing to comply with the duty imposed by s 21 in circumstances in which the effect of that failure is to make it impossible or unreasonably difficult for the disabled person to make use of any such service — s 21 creates a duty to make adjustments so as to enable the disabled to have access to goods and services;

(c) in the standard of service which he provides to the disabled person or the manner in which he provides it; or

(d) in the terms on which he provides a service to the disabled.

The remedy for discrimination contrary to the Act is enforcement in the county court. The damages will be based on the tortious measure of damages (s 25(1)). Damages for injury to feelings may be awarded (s 25(2)). The right is therefore very similar to that in non-employment cases under the Sex Discrimination Act 1975 and the Race Relations Act 1976. It may be that guidance on the level of awards can be obtained from the reported decisions under these two Acts.

The predicted rush of cases under the Disability Discrimination Act 1995 has not yet materialised. Nevertheless, there have been some interesting claims. Many are settled without any admission of liability and cannot be regarded as creating a precedent. In one recent claim a person with visual impairment objected to a requirement that she should have a detailed contract read over to her by her solicitor (who, needless to say, charged for that difficult work) before she signed it: the claim was settled when her costs were reimbursed by the supplier of the services.

The Disability Rights Commission Act 1999 was brought into force on 6 August 1999. The Commission has been set up and can now investigate complaints and support claims by individuals.

4.8 Late Payment of Commercial Debts (Interest) Act 1998

The Late Payment of Commercial Debts (Interest) Act 1998 is intended to give additional protection to sellers, particularly small businesses by introducing a right to interest on late payments: see **8.5**. The Act was brought into force in stages. From 1 November 1998 the Act applied to contracts between any small business and a large business. From 1 July 1999 it was extended to contracts between any small business and certain public authorities. In September 2000 three further public bodies were added to the list. In November 2000 the Act was extended to contracts between a small business and a small business purchaser. Unfortunately, it is not proposed that the Act be extended to late payment of barristers' fees.

4.9 Consumer Protection (Distance Selling) Regulations 2000

The Consumer Protection (Distance Selling) Regulations 2000 implement the EC Distance Contracts Directive (97/7/EC) and are designed to protect consumers where goods or services are to be supplied by means of distance communications. The Regulations came into force on 31 October 2000.

Distance communication is any means which, without the simultaneous physical presence of the supplier and the consumer, may be used for the conclusion of a contract between those parties; and an indicative list of such means is contained in Sch 1 to the Regulations. The indicative list is as follows: unaddressed printed matter; addressed printed matter; letter; press advertising with order form; catalogue; telephone with human intervention; telephone without human intervention (automatic calling machine, audiotext); radio; videophone (telephone with screen); videotext (microcomputer and television screen) with keyboard or touch screen; electronic mail; facsimile machine (fax) and television (teleshopping).

A 'distance contract' means any contract concerning goods or services concluded between a supplier and a consumer under an organised distance sales or service provision scheme run by the supplier who, for the purpose of the contract, makes exclusive use of one or more means of distance communication up to and including the moment at which the contract is concluded.

4.9.1 Excluded contracts

Regulation 5 lists excluded contracts which are in six main categories: certain contracts concerning land, building contracts, financial service contracts (examples of which appear in Sch 2), automated vending machines, telephone contracts using public payphone, and auctions.

Regulation 6 lists the partially excluded contracts. Only certain regulations apply to timeshare contracts (which are, in any event, governed by the Timeshare Act 1992). Similarly, only certain regulations apply to any 'package' within the meaning of the Package Travel, Package Holidays and Package Tours Regulations 1992. The more common partial exemptions are:

(a) contracts for the supply of food, beverages or other goods intended for everyday consumption supplied to the consumer's residence or to his workplace by regular roundsmen; and

(b) contracts for the provision of accommodation, transport, catering or leisure services, where the supplier undertakes, when the contract is concluded, to provide these services on a specific date or within a specific period.

4.9.2 Effect of the regulations

If the Regulations apply:

(a) the consumer is entitled to have specified (detailed) information about the contract 'in good time' prior to the conclusion of the contract (reg 7) to be followed up in writing (reg 8);

(b) the consumer has a cooling-off period in which the contract can be cancelled (regs 10–12);

(c) the effect of exercise of the right to cancel is specified (including the timing of refunds and automatic cancellation of any related credit agreement) (regs 14–17) and provision is made for goods which were part-exchanged (reg 18);

(d) there is a requirement for the contract to be performed by the supplier within 30 days unless the parties agree otherwise (reg 19).

Detailed provisions amend the law relating to unsolicited goods (described in the Regulations as inertia selling).

4.10 Stop Now Orders (EC Directive) Regulations 2001

The Stop Now Orders (EC Directive) Regulations 2001 implement the EC Directive 98/27/EC and the Injunctions Directive. The Regulations came into force on 1 June 2001. Certain public bodies (including every weights and measures authority in Great Britain) can bring proceedings under the Fair Trading Act 1973 (as amended by the Regulations) to apply to the court to stop a trader carrying on business in the objectionable manner. A stop order can be obtained if there is a breach of consumer protection directives (described as 'community infringements'). The main legislation on sale of goods is that set out at **4.5** and **4.9** above.

Except in urgent cases, the trader will be notified before action is taken and given two weeks to stop the infringement. Successful court action against a trader leads to a stop order being made and the court may order publication of the order and/or publication of a corrective statement with a view to eliminating the effect of any infringement.

These Regulations do not permit individual action. However, most cases will start with a complaint by an individual (or his or her solicitor) to one of the bodies which can seek a stop order.

Although these Regulations were repealed and replaced by Part 8 of the Enterprise Act 2002, action taken under the Regulations can continue. The terms of the Regulations and the action taken will remain relevant for many years. In June 2003 an individual involved with a number of kitchen suppliers was jailed for nine months for contempt for breach of an order made under the Regulations. The court allowed his release after only five weeks after he apologised and gave suitable undertakings about future compliance with the order.

5

Passing of property, risk and frustration

As already noted at 2.2, a sale of goods contract as defined by s 2(1), SOGA 1979 includes both a sale of goods which is a contract and conveyance, and an agreement to sell which is only a contract. The agreement to sell will usually be converted into a sale when property actually passes. The difference between a sale and an agreement to sell is important for deciding when title to property actually passes and for deciding the remedy for breach of contract: *Re Goldcorp Exchange (in receivership)* [1994] 2 All ER 806. This chapter is concerned with the passing of title or property, the passing of risk and frustration.

5.1 The concepts

Three basic concepts have to be considered: property, possession, and risk.

5.1.1 Property

Property in the sense of title or ownership or a proprietary right in the goods may be transferred to the buyer before delivery, at the time of delivery or after delivery, and will be important on insolvency and in deciding when the seller can sue for the price. The actual point in time at which property has to be considered will depend upon the circumstance of the sale. For example, on insolvency, if the seller is an individual the important date is the date on which the bankruptcy order is made: ss 278(a) and 283(1), Insolvency Act 1986. In relation to the insolvency of a company there are two important dates (a) if there is a voluntary liquidation, the date on which the resolution for winding up is passed (s 86, Insolvency Act 1986) and (b) if there is a compulsory winding up the date when the petition was presented (s 129, Insolvency Act 1986).

The implied conditions and warranties of title by a seller have already been considered (**Chapter 3**). The ability of certain non-owners to transfer good title under the exceptions to the *nemo dat* rule will be considered later (**Chapter 6**). The remedies for breach of the condition and warranties of title are considered later (**Chapter 10**).

5.1.2 Possession

Possession is not to be confused with property or ownership and is not defined in SOGA 1979. However, s 1(2), Factors Act 1889 provides that a person shall be deemed to be in possession of goods or of the documents of title to goods where the goods or documents are in his actual custody or are held by any other person subject to his control or for him or on his behalf. Further guidance on the meaning of possession can be gained from the cases involving the exceptions to the *nemo dat* rule which involve possession of goods (see **Chapter 6**); for the unpaid seller's lien on the goods (see **9.3**); and from the cases deciding whether it is the seller or the buyer who has rights against third parties who have possession of the goods.

5.1.3 Risk

Risk is a concept which is important where the goods are damaged or destroyed: *Leigh & Sillivan Ltd v Aliakmon Shipping Co Ltd (The Aliakmon)* [1986] AC 785; where the contract is frustrated; and in deciding whether an insurable interest in the goods exists for the buyer or the seller or, very rarely, for both.

5.2 The passing of property

The basic principles are:

(a) No property in unascertained goods can pass until the goods are ascertained (s 16, SOGA 1979); but this must now be read subject to s 20A, SOGA 1979.

(b) Property in specific goods passes when it is intended to pass having regard to the intention of the parties (s 17(1), SOGA 1979).

(c) The intention of the parties is to be ascertained from the terms of the contract, the conduct of the parties and the circumstances of the case (s 17(2), SOGA 1979); but, unless a different intention appears, the rules in s 18, SOGA 1979 must be applied.

(d) Risk is transferred when title to or property in the goods passes — *res perit domino* (s 20(1), SOGA 1979); but this principle may be excluded by agreement or by usage.

5.3 Specific or unascertained goods?

Specific goods are defined by s 61(1) as being goods identified and agreed on at the time a contract of sale is made and this includes an undivided share, specified as a fraction or percentage, of goods identified and agreed on as aforesaid. All other goods are unascertained at the time the contract is made. The goods become ascertained when they are identified: *Re Wait* [1927] 1 Ch 606. Goods do not become specific goods when they are ascertained.

5.4 Passing of property in specific goods

There are two situations which have to be considered. First, where the intention of the parties is clear. Secondly, where the intention of the parties is not clear.

5.4.1 Clear intention

If the intention of the parties is clear from the terms of the contract, the conduct of the parties and the circumstances of the case, then property passes in accordance with that intention (s 17(2), SOGA 1979).

5.4.2 Unclear intention

Unless a different intention appears the provisions of s 18, SOGA 1979 must be used to ascertain the intention of the parties as to the time at which property in the goods is to pass to the buyer. Section 18, SOGA 1979 contains five rules which must be considered in turn.

5.4.2.1 Rule 1

Where there is an unconditional contract for the sale of specific goods in a deliverable state the property in the goods passes to the buyer when the contract is made, and it is immaterial whether the time of payment or the time of delivery or both be postponed.

The important features are that the contract must be unconditional and the goods must be in a deliverable state. 'Unconditional' is not defined in SOGA 1979 but the early attempts by the courts to construe this as meaning a contract without any essential undertakings or promises should not now be followed in the light of the prohibitions on excluding the statutory implied conditions and warranties: the better interpretation is simply that there are no later conditions which must be fulfilled such as payment of the price before property passes. 'Deliverable state' means that the goods are in such a condition that the buyer would under the contract be bound to take delivery of them (s 61(5), SOGA 1979). Contracts falling within Rule 1 are not common as the courts are very ready to infer that property only passes upon payment: *Ward RV Ltd v Bignall* [1967] 1 QB 534.

5.4.2.2 Rule 2

Where there is a contract for the sale of specific goods and the seller is bound to do something to the goods for the purpose of putting them into a deliverable state, the property does not pass until the thing is done and the buyer has had notice that it has been done.

The important features are that it is the seller's obligation to do something to put the goods in the deliverable state (which will have the same meaning as above), that the seller has done that thing, and the buyer has notice that it has been done. It may be difficult in each case to distinguish between things which the seller must do so as to put the goods into a deliverable state (ie, the state in which the buyer is bound to accept delivery) and mere ancillary obligations. However, if the seller and buyer agree that something will be done to the goods at the seller's expense after delivery, it is difficult to see how this rule can apply.

5.4.2.3 Rule 3

Where there is a contract for the sale of specific goods in a deliverable state but the seller is bound to weigh, measure, test, or do some other act or thing with reference to the goods for the purpose of ascertaining the price, the property does not pass until the act or thing is done and the buyer has had notice that it has been done.

The obligation to weigh, measure, test or do some other act must be on the seller, and the act must be for the purpose of ascertaining the price of goods already in the deliverable state. As with Rule 2 notice to the buyer that the step has been taken is also required. This rule is of limited practical significance.

5.4.2.4 Rule 4

When goods are delivered to the buyer on approval or on sale or return or other similar terms the property in the goods passes to the buyer—

(a) when he signifies his approval or acceptance to the seller or does any other act adopting the transaction;

(b) if he does not signify his approval or acceptance to the seller but retains the goods without giving notice of rejection, then, if a time has been fixed for the return of the goods, on the expiration of that time, and, if no time has been fixed, on the expiration of a reasonable time.

Sales on approval and transactions involving sale or return are common, and this rule will govern the passing of title if the parties have not reached some other agreement. The words 'any other act adopting the transaction' can cause difficulties although some acts such as pledging the goods to a pawnbroker will certainly be such an act: *Kirkham v Attenborough* [1897] 1 QB 291. The words 'on the expiration of a reasonable time' are also likely to cause difficulty: what is a reasonable time will be a question of fact (s 59, SOGA 1979).

In *Atari Corp (UK) Ltd v Electronics Boutique Stores (UK) Ltd* [1998] 1 All ER 1010, the Court of Appeal had to consider whether a letter was a sufficient notice of rejection of some goods and an exercise of the right of return of goods under rule 4 of s 18. The Court adopted a 'common sense' approach to the letter and held that the absence of a clear identification of the goods to be returned beyond those then unsold did not prevent the notice being valid. The Court also decided that it was not essential for the notice to be valid that the goods were available for return at the date of the notice. The House of Lords dismissed the petition for permission to appeal so these points must now be regarded as settled law.

5.5 Passing of property in unascertained goods

The facts in *Re Stapylton Fletcher Ltd* [1995] 1 All ER 192, a case involving rights to wine stored by wine merchants on the insolvency of the merchants (decided prior to the amendments to SOGA 1979), neatly illustrate the practical problems in deciding whether the parties have reached agreement on ascertainment. In the absence of agreement the position is governed by s 18(1), SOGA 1979, Rule 5 which provides:

(1) Where there is a contract for the sale of unascertained or future goods by description, and goods of that description and in a deliverable state are unconditionally appropriated to the contract, either by the seller with the assent of the buyer or by the buyer with the assent of the seller, the property in the goods passes to the buyer; and the assent may be express or implied, and may be given either before or after the appropriation is made.

(2) Where, in pursuance of the contract, the seller delivers the goods to the buyer or to a carrier or other bailee or custodier (whether named by the buyer or not) for the purpose of transmission to the buyer, and does not reserve the right of disposal, he is to be taken to have unconditionally appropriated the goods to the contract.

(3) Where there is a contract for the sale of a specified quantity of unascertained goods in a deliverable state forming part of a bulk which is identified either in the contract or by subsequent agreement between the parties and the bulk is reduced to (or less than) the quantity, then, if the buyer under that contract is the only buyer to whom the goods are then due out of the bulk—

(a) the remaining goods are to be taken as appropriated to that contract at the time when the bulk is so reduced; and

(b) the property in those goods passes to the buyer.

> *(4) Paragraph (3) above applies also (with the necessary modification) where the bulk is reduced to (or to less than) the aggregate of the quantities due to a single buyer under separate contracts relating to that bulk and he is the only buyer to whom goods are then due out of that bulk.*

5.5.1 Rules 5(1) and 5(2)

These Rules deal with the unconditional appropriation of deliverable goods to the contract by agreement express or implied. 'Appropriation' is not defined in SOGA 1979 but means an intention to attach the contract irrevocably to those goods so that those goods and no others are the subject of the sale and become the property of the buyer: *Carlos Federspiel & Co SA v Charles Twigg & Co Ltd* [1957] 1 Lloyd's Rep 240. The appropriation must be unconditional and so could not, for example, be linked to payment of the purchase price.

Rule 5(2) lays down that delivery of the goods to the buyer or to a carrier for transmission to the buyer will be an unconditional appropriation. There will be no appropriation until the goods are identifiable: *Healy v Howlett & Sons* [1917] 1 KB 337. At common law this unconditional appropriation can take place by ascertainment by exhaustion or by ascertainment by consolidation: *Karlshamns Olje Fabrike v Eastport Navigation Corp* [1982] 1 All ER 208.

Where goods are stored in bulk after sale, segregation of the bulk from the seller's stock will suffice to create ascertainment for the purpose of s 16, SOGA 1979. Each purchaser of a part of the bulk will become a tenant in common of the entire stock in the proportion that his goods bear to the total in store for the time being: *Re Stapylton Fletcher Ltd* [1995] 1 All ER 192.

5.5.2 Rules 5(3) ans 5(4)

These rules were introduced by the Sale of Goods (Amendment) Act 1995 and apply to contracts made on or after 19 September 1995. They give statutory effect to the common law concept of the appropriation or ascertainment by the process of exhaustion of the bulk or by consolidation of contracts between the same parties.

5.6 Shares in bulk goods

Bulk is defined in s 61(1), SOGA 1979, as amended, as a mass or collection of goods of the same kind which (a) is contained in a defined space or area; and (b) is such that any goods in the bulk are interchangeable with any other goods therein of the same number or quantity.

For contracts made on or after 18 September 1995 the passing of property in goods forming part of a bulk is governed by s 20A, SOGA 1979 which states:

> *(1) This section applies to a contract for the sale of a specified quantity of unascertained goods if the following conditions are met—*
> *(a) the goods or some of them form part of a bulk which is identified either in the contract or by subsequent agreement between the parties; and,*
> *(b) the buyer has paid the price for some or all of the goods which are the subject of the contract and which form part of the bulk.*
>
> *(2) Where this section applies, then (unless the parties agree otherwise), as soon as the conditions specified in paragraphs (a) and (b) of subsection (1) above are met or at such later time as the parties may agree—*
> *(a) property in an undivided share in the bulk is transferred to the buyer; and*

(b) the buyer becomes an owner in common of the bulk.

(3) Subject to sub-section (4) below, for the purposes of this section, the undivided share of the buyer in a bulk at any time shall be such share as the quantity of goods paid for and due to the buyer out of the bulk bears to the quantity of goods in the bulk at that time.

(4) Where the aggregate of the undivided shares of the buyers in a bulk determined under subsection (3) above would at any time exceed the whole of the bulk at that time, the undivided share in the bulk of each buyer shall be reduced proportionately so that the aggregate of the undivided shares is equal to the whole of the bulk.

(5) Where the buyer has paid the price for only some of the goods due to him out of the bulk, any delivery to the buyer out of the bulk shall, for the purposes of this section, be ascribed in the first place to the goods in respect of which payment has been made.

(6) For the purposes of this section payment of part of the price for any goods shall be treated as payment for a corresponding part of the goods.

The practical workings of the co-ownership created by s 20A are set out in s 20B. Section 20A applies where the goods (or some of them) form part of a bulk which is identified either in the contract or by subsequent agreement between the parties and the buyer has paid the price for some or all of the goods which are the subject of the contract and which form part of that bulk. Unless the parties otherwise agree, as soon as this has happened, property in an undivided share in the bulk is transferred to the buyer, and the buyer becomes an owner in common of the bulk. The undivided share of the buyer is his pro rata share and, if the bulk is too small for the total quantity bought, each buyer's share is reduced pro rata. Section 20B provides that once the buyer has become the owner in common, he is deemed to consent to specified dealings with goods in the bulk.

5.7 Mixture, accession and new goods

Three further concepts have to be considered for their effect upon transfer of property under English law. First, there is the mixture of goods belonging to different owners — *confusio* or *commixtio*. Secondly, there is the accession of one thing to the property of another — *accessio* or *adjunctio*. Finally, there is the creation of a new thing made wholly or partly from materials belonging to another — *specificatio*.

5.7.1 Mixture

Where the goods of several owners are mixed without their consent they become owners in common according to their contribution to the resulting mass: *Sandeman & Sons v Tyzack and Branfoot* [1913] AC 680 and *Indian Oil Corporation Ltd v Greenstone Shipping SA (The Ypatianna)* [1988] 1 QB 345. Section 188, Law of Property Act 1925 applies, but only where the application is made by a person interested in a moiety or more of the mixture. Section 10, Torts (Interference with Goods) Act 1977 provides that co-ownership is no defence to an action where the defendant without authority destroys the goods or disposes of goods in a way giving good title to the entire property in the goods or otherwise does anything which is equivalent to the destruction of the goods or disposes of the goods in a way which gives good title.

5.7.2 Accession

Where goods are attached to the property of another and cannot readily be removed or separated therefrom, ownership of those goods will pass to the owner of the goods to which they become attached. If separation is easy that will not be the result: *Hendy Lennox (Industrial Engines) Ltd v Grahame Puttick Ltd* [1984] 1 WLR 111. The House of Lords considered a difficult question of annexation to land in the recent case of *Elitestone Ltd v Morris & another* [1997] 2 All ER 513. In that case it was suggested that the traditional twofold distinction between chattels and fixtures should be replaced by a threefold classification of an object brought onto land as (a) a chattel, (b) a fixture, or (c) part and parcel of the land itself. Objects placed into categories (b) or (c) would then become part of the land.

Difficult questions of fact can arise as to what is the main object and what is the attachment, or is there merely an entirely new product created. For example, if a crane is fitted to a flat-bed lorry is the resulting mobile crane an accession (a) of the lorry to the crane, or (b) of the crane to the lorry, or (c) is it an entirely new product? Some of the practical difficulties are resolved by the statutory allowance for improvement to goods made by someone honestly in the mistaken belief of having good title which is to be found in s 6, Torts (Interference with Goods) Act 1977, but those provisions will not assist when there has been a deliberate attachment of goods belonging to different owners.

5.7.3 New goods

Where goods have lost their separate identity and have been incorporated into a wholly new product the owner of the original goods will have lost title: *Borden (UK) Ltd v Scottish Timber Products Ltd* [1981] Ch 25.

5.8 Seller reserving a right of disposal

Section 19(1), SOGA 1979 states the general position where the seller has reserved a right of disposal of goods. Sub-sections (2) and (3) give examples of the application of the general rule. Section 19 reads:

> (1) *Where there is a contract for the sale of specific goods or where goods are subsequently appropriated to the contract, the seller may, by the terms of the contract or appropriation, reserve the right of disposal of the goods until certain conditions are fulfilled; and, in such a case, notwithstanding the delivery of the goods to the buyer, or to a carrier or other bailee or custodier for the purpose of transmission to the buyer, the property in the goods does not pass to the buyer until the conditions imposed by the seller are fulfilled.*
>
> (2) *Where goods are shipped, and by the bill of lading the goods are deliverable to the order of the seller or his agent, the seller is prima facie to be taken to reserve the right of disposal.*
>
> (3) *Where the seller of goods draws on the buyer for the price, and transmits the bill of exchange and bill of lading to the buyer together to secure acceptance or payment of the bill of exchange, the buyer is bound to return the bill of lading if he does not honour the bill of exchange, and if he wrongfully retains the bill of lading the property in the goods does not pass to him.*

Conditional contracts falling within s 19 are now extremely common. Since the decision in *Aluminium Industrie Vaassen BV v Romalpa Aluminium Ltd* [1976] 1 WLR 676 many companies have adopted 'Romalpa' clauses to retain title to goods until they are paid for them. Such clauses can give priority over other creditors and a right to trace and claim proceeds of sale. The drafting of effective retention of title clauses has become difficult as the drafting seeks to cover every eventuality. There are publications which deal only with this area and there is an ever growing list of reported decisions. The precise drafting of the clauses is extremely important. For example, in *Re Bond Worth Ltd* [1980] Ch 228 it was held that the particular clause created a charge on the assets of the buyer company and so was void for want of registration under s 395, Companies Act 1985. A charge on the property of an individual will usually fall within the Bills of Sale Acts 1878 and 1882, and would require registration. The Insolvency Act 1986 also had an impact on such clauses as it prohibits enforcement against an administrator without his or her consent or permission of the court.

An important qualification on the use of retention of title clauses to re-take possession of the goods, and to sell them whilst the contract is still subsisting, is that the seller can only re-take and re-sell sufficient goods to discharge the debt and must account to the buyer for any surplus: *Clough Mill Ltd v Martin* [1985] 1 WLR 111. If the contract has been terminated, the seller does not have to account for any profit made on a subsequent sale unless the seller is claiming damages from the buyer.

5.9 The importance of risk as a concept

Risk is of crucial importance in sale of goods contracts. If the goods are destroyed or damaged or have deteriorated it will determine whether the parties are bound by the terms of the contract. Similarly, risk is of importance when considering whether the contract has been discharged by frustration. Finally, risk can be of importance when considering contracts which are conditional, such as those involving growing crops: *H R & S Sainsbury Ltd v Street* [1972] 1 WLR 834.

5.9.1 Passing of risk

Risk is presumed by s 20, SOGA 1979 to pass with property. Section 20 provides that:

> (1) *Unless otherwise agreed, the goods remain at the seller's risk until the property in them is transferred to the buyer, but when property in them is transferred to the buyer the goods are at the buyer's risk whether delivery has been made or not.*
>
> (2) *But where delivery has been delayed through the fault of either the buyer or the seller, the goods are at the risk of the party at fault as regards any loss which might not have occurred but for such fault.*
>
> (3) *Nothing in this section affects the duties or liabilities of either seller or buyer as a bailee or custodier of the goods of the other party.*
>
> (4) *In a case where the buyer deals as a consumer ... subsections (1) to (3) above must be ignored and the goods remain at the seller's risk until they are delivered to the consumer.*

Subsection (4) was added, with effect from 31 March 2003, by the Sale and Supply of Goods to Consumers Regulations 2002.

Section 20(1) creates the statutory presumption which applies if the parties have not made other arrangements. Section 20(2) distinguishes between delivery and the passing of property and is therefore concerned with risk and possession. Similarly, s 20(3) means that the party in possession of the goods will be liable as bailee, whatever the position over property.

The presumed link between risk and property in s 20(1), SOGA 1979 may be contrasted with modern systems such as the Uniform Law on International Sales, the Vienna Convention on International Sales, and the United States Uniform Commercial Code where risk is linked to possession on the assumption that the person in possession of the goods is in the best position to care for them. If the statutory presumption applies, the position of the buyer can be weak. If, for example, a buyer purchases goods for delivery at a later date so that property and risk vest in the buyer at purchase: what happens if the goods are destroyed by fire? The seller as bailee of the goods may not be liable if adequate care was taken. The seller may have insurance which would compensate for the loss, and the money should then be held on constructive trust for the buyer. However, it is certainly arguable that the seller has no insurable interest in the goods if property and risk have passed.

5.9.2 Delayed delivery

If one party to the contract is at fault in delaying delivery, that party will bear the risk of any loss which occurs as a result of the delay (s 20(2), SOGA 1979).

5.9.3 Risk in transit

Special provisions for risk in transit are to be found in ss 32 and 33, SOGA 1979. Three situations are covered:

(a) If the seller makes an unreasonable contract with the carrier having regard to the nature of the goods and the other circumstances of the case, the buyer may decline to treat the delivery to the carrier as delivery to himself or may hold the seller responsible in damages (s 32(2), SOGA 1979).

(b) Unless otherwise agreed, if the seller send the goods by sea transit to the buyer under circumstances in which it is usual to insure, the seller must give such notice to the buyer as may enable him to insure and if the seller fails to do so the goods are at his risk during such sea transit (s 32(3), SOGA 1979).

(c) Unless otherwise agreed, where the seller of goods agrees to deliver them at his own risk at a place other than that where the goods are when sold, the buyer must nevertheless take any risk of deterioration in the goods necessarily incident to the course of transit (s 33, SOGA 1979). The seller must despatch the goods in such a condition that they would endure a normal journey: *Mash & Murrel Ltd v Joseph I Emmanuel Ltd* [1961] 1 WLR 862.

Just as the Sale and Supply of Goods to Consumers Regulations 2002 amended s 20 by adding a new subsection (4), in consumer cases s 32 is amended to make the risk in transit a risk of the seller.

5.9.4 Frustration and mistake

As already discussed, the common law rules of contract are applicable to contracts for the sale of goods (s 62(2), SOGA 1979). Frustration and mistake are concepts which must be considered in the light of the particular provisions of ss 6 and 7, SOGA 1979. (It will be rare for frustration to apply to unascertained goods as the goods contracted for can usually be obtained from other sources.)

Section 6, SOGA 1979 provides:

> Where there is a contract for the sale of specific goods, and the goods without the knowledge of the seller have perished at the time when the contract is made, the contract is void.

There is no statutory meaning for 'perish'. It may include goods which have been stolen, and goods which have totally changed their character by being damaged. Much will depend upon the character of the goods and the nature or extent of the damage.

Section 7, SOGA 1979 provides:

> *Where there is an agreement to sell specific goods and subsequently the goods, without any fault on the part of the seller or buyer, perish before the risk passes to the buyer, the agreement is avoided.*

In this situation the contract is avoided and the provisions of the Law Reform (Frustrated Contracts) Act 1943 relating to apportionment of loss do not apply. If the specific goods are an undivided share of goods within s 61(1), as amended, presumably the goods which perish must be those identified and agreed upon. It is important to note that if there has been fault by either party this provision will not apply, nor will it apply where risk has already passed to the buyer.

In cases not falling within ss 6 or 7, SOGA 1979, the provisions of the Law Reform (Frustrated Contracts) Act 1943 apply. The 1943 Act makes important provision for money paid or payable, for instalment contracts to be severed, and for part delivery. However, the provisions of the Act only apply where there is nothing in the contract which provides for the particular circumstances.

Destruction of the goods and frustration of the contract are considered in more detail later (see **Chapter 10**).

6

Transfer of title by non-owners

6.1 Title

The general rule is that no-one can pass a better title than he himself possesses. This is usually referred to by the Latin maxim *nemo dat quod non habet* which is often shortened and described as the *nemo dat* rule.

6.2 Exceptions to the *nemo dat* rule

There are now seven main exceptions to the *nemo dat* rule. The exceptions are policy based and it is not always easy for the court to determine which policy considerations prevail when interpreting the exceptions. All the exceptions to the *nemo dat* rule need to be considered carefully as the exceptions tend to be narrowly construed.

An example of changing policy considerations can be seen in the abolition of the market overt exception. Section 22, SOGA 1979 contained the market overt exception to the *nemo dat* rule. It applied where a buyer bought goods in good faith and without notice of any defect or want of title on the part of the seller in a market overt. A 'market overt' meant a public market established by statute, charter or very long use and, by custom, extended to every shop in the City of London. It was proposed by the Law Reform Committee 12th Report that this exception be extended to all retail establishments, but that extension of the exception was never enacted. This exception was totally repealed (rather than extended to all retail establishments) by the Sale of Goods (Amendment) Act 1994 in respect of any contracts made after 3 January 1995.

The seven main exceptions to the *nemo dat* rule are:

- estoppel (s 21(1), SOGA 1979);
- sales under the Factors Acts (s 21(2)(a), SOGA 1979);
- sales under special powers (s 21(2)(b), SOGA 1979);
- sales under voidable title (s 23, SOGA 1979);
- sales by seller in possession (s 24, SOGA 1979);
- sales by buyer in possession (s 25, SOGA 1979);
- sales of motor vehicles within Part III of the Hire Purchase Act 1964.

Another exception could be said to exist as a result of the ordinary law of agency whereby the agent (who has no title at all) can pass title on behalf of his principal if he has actual or apparent authority to bind his principal. The common law rules of agency apply to sales of goods contracts (s 62(2), SOGA 1979).

An exception also exists under the Torts (Interference With Goods) Act 1977 in the sense that it is possible to acquire title under the provisions of that Act by payment of the value of the goods (see **6.3** below).

A further exception can be said to exist under the Limitation Act 1980 as an owner will have his own title to goods extinguished after expiry of the relevant limitation period. Finally, although not an exception to the *nemo dat* rule, it is possible to agree to transfer only such title as the seller possesses (s 12, SOGA 1979) (see **3.10.1**).

6.2.1 Estoppel

Section 21(1), SOGA 1979 applies where the owner of the goods is, by his conduct, precluded from denying the seller's authority to sell. It applies where the owner is not the actual seller. The conduct of the owner will be either a representation or negligent conduct. If this exception applies the buyer will acquire a title which is good against the world.

Estoppel by representation exists where the owner (or his agent) makes a clear and unambiguous representation to the actual buyer, who relies upon it, which misleads the buyer into believing that the seller was entitled to sell the goods: *Eastern Distributors Ltd v Goldring* [1957] 2 QB 600. A mere parting with possession by the owner is not sufficient to create such a representation: *Central Newbury Car Auctions Ltd v Unity Finance Ltd* [1957] 1 QB 371. Thus, for example, if you return your goods to the shop for service or repair and the shop sells your goods to another you would not lose title under this exception.

Estoppel by negligence will exist where there is a duty of care owed by the owner to the buyer, breach of that duty, and the breach was causative of the buyer entering into the transaction: *Mercantile Credit Co Ltd v Hamblin* [1957] 2 QB 242. It is the first element which it is difficult to establish as mere carelessness in relation to the goods or carelessness such as a failure to register an interest with Hire-Purchase Information (HPI) will not suffice: *Moorgate Mercantile v Twitchings* [1977] AC 890, *Debs v Sibec* [1990] RTR 91. (For an explanation of HPI see **6.2.7** below.)

A limit to the scope of this exception was found in *Shaw v Commissioner of Police* [1987] 1 WLR 1332. In that case the court was faced with the common situation of a student parting with possession of his Porsche Turbo. Unusually he supplied a letter stating that he had sold it to a Mr London when he had not. The student's conduct was held to be sufficient to give rise to an estoppel. However, crucially, Mr London had not sold the car on to the claimant dealer; he had only entered into an agreement for sale in which property was not to pass until he was paid, which never happened. An agreement to sell does not involve the transfer of property (s 2(5), SOGA 1979) and is not covered by this exception. The result was that the fortunate student remained the owner of the Porsche Turbo.

The policy basis for this exception to the *nemo dat* rule is that the conduct of the true owner is blameworthy in the sense that the true owner has encouraged or allowed the transaction by the non-owner: *Lickbarrow v Mason* (1787) 2 TR 63. This exception can be seen as being very similar to the doctrine of reputed ownership of goods which applies to the law of distress and to execution against goods.

6.2.2 Sales under the Factors Act 1889

There have been five Factors Acts starting with that passed in 1823 and culminating in that passed in 1889 which was an Act amending and consolidating the earlier legislation. A careful explanation of the history and purpose of those Acts is to be found in the judgment of Lord Goff of Chievely in *National Employers' Mutual General Insurance Association Ltd v Jones* [1990] AC 24. Nothing in SOGA 1979 affects the Factors Acts (s 21(2)(a), SOGA 1979). Nothing in the Factors Act 1889 affects the common law rules of agency (s 13, Factors Act 1889).

The crucial sections of the Factors Act 1889 are s 1(1) which defines a mercantile agent; s 2 which deals with dispositions by mercantile agents; s 8 which deals with dispositions by sellers remaining in possession; and s 9 which deals with buyers obtaining possession. The protection of the Act applies only where property has actually passed to the buyer under the agreement: *Re Highway Foods International Ltd* [1995] 1 BCLC 209.

Section 2(1) of the Factors Act 1889 validates any sale pledge or other disposition:

- if it is by a mercantile agent who is in possession of the goods or documents of title of the goods as mercantile agent;
- with the consent of the true owner — which is presumed in the absence of evidence to the contrary: s 2(4);
- the sale pledge or other disposition is in the ordinary course of business as a mercantile agent; and,
- the person taking the goods is acting in good faith and without notice of any want of authority to make the disposition.

Section 2(2) of the Factors Act 1889 validates any sale pledge or other disposition taking place after termination of the consent to possession by the true owner, provided the person taking the goods has no notice of the determination of consent.

Section 8 of the Factors Act 1889 validates a sale pledge or other disposition by a seller who remains in possession of the goods or documents of title to the goods (or by a mercantile agent acting for him) to a person acting in good faith and without notice of the previous sale. The wording of this section is very similar to s 24, SOGA 1979 which is considered below. The only difference is that s 8, Factors Act 1889 applies where the second transaction is an agreement for sale pledge or other disposition and is therefore wider than s 24, SOGA 1979. The differences in wording were noted in *Newtons of Wembley Ltd v Williams* [1965] 1 QB 560. Section 8 of the Factors Act 1889 provides:

> *Where a person having sold goods continues, or is, in possession of the goods or of the documents of title to the goods, the delivery or transfer by that person, or by a mercantile agent acting for him, of the goods or documents of title under any sale, pledge, or other disposition thereof, or under any agreement for sale, pledge, or other disposition thereof to any person receiving the same in good faith and without notice of the previous sale, has the same effect as if the person making the delivery or transfer were expressly authorised by the owner of the goods to make the same.*

Note: the underlined words appear in the s 8, Factors Act but not s 24, SOGA 1979.

Section 9 of the Factors Act 1889 validates a sale by a person who: (a) has bought or agreed to buy goods and obtains with consent of the seller possession of the goods or the documents of title to the goods; and (b) then delivers or transfers the goods or the documents of title (or his mercantile agent does so) under any sale pledge or other disposition or under any agreement for sale pledge or other disposition; (c) to any person receiving them in good faith and without notice of any lien or other right of the original seller.

The provisions of ss 2(1) and 9 of the Factors Act 1889 were considered in *Re Highway Foods International Limited* [1995] 1 BCLC 209. Large quantities of meat had been supplied under a contract with a retention of title clause. The meat was then sold and delivered to a sub-purchaser under a contract with another retention of title clause. The court had to decide whether title had passed to the sub-purchaser and held that it had not.

The wording is very similar to that in s 25, SOGA 1979 although, as with s 8 of the Factors Act 1889, s 9 of the 1889 Act applies where the second transaction is an agreement for sale pledge or other disposition and is therefore wider than s 25, SOGA 1979. Conditional sale agreements are excluded from being agreements to buy for this purpose (s 9(i), Factors Act 1889, as inserted by the Consumer Credit Act 1974).

6.2.3 Sales under special powers

This exception to the *nemo dat* rule covers three distinct situations (s 21(2)(b), SOGA 1979). First, sales under common law powers. Secondly, sales under statutory powers. Finally, sales by order of a court of competent jurisdiction.

The use of common law powers of sale is now rare. However, such powers arise from pledges, certain exceptional liens (by custom or arrangement) and where the concept of agency of necessity applies. Sale of goods distrained upon by landlords which was originally a common law power is now largely governed by statute.

An important statutory right of sale of goods is to be found in s 48, SOGA 1979 (see **9.3.4**). There are a very large number of other statutory powers of sale. The most common is that for uncollected goods (ss 12–13, Torts (Interference with Goods) Act 1977). Other statutory powers include the powers for landlords to sell goods distrained upon under the various powers starting with the Distress for Rent Act 1689 and ending with the Law of Distress Amendment Act 1908 and the Distress for Rent Rules 1988; sale of guests' belongings for unpaid hotel fees under s 1, Innkeepers Act 1878 and the Hotel Proprietors Act 1956; sales of goods by certain warehousemen under Merchant Shipping Act 1894; sales of pawned goods under the Consumer Credit Act 1974; sales by mortgagors, receivers and under bills of sale; sales under the Insolvency Act 1986 and, a sale by a local authority of an abandoned motor vehicle will pass title to the purchaser: *Bulbruin Ltd v Romanyszyn* [1994] RTR 273.

Most court orders for sale of goods will be in aid of execution under a statutory power and could be regarded as either statutory sales or sales under a court order. Apart from sales in aid of execution the court can order a sale of perishable goods or where it is desirable to sell goods forthwith: CPR, r 25.1(c)(v) (formerly RSC O 29, r 4 and CCR O 13, r 7(1)(f)).

6.2.4 Sales under voidable title

Section 23, SOGA 1979 provides that a sale by someone with voidable title which has not been avoided to a buyer in good faith without notice of the defect in title will be valid. When considering this exception to the *nemo dat* rule it is crucial to distinguish between contracts which are void and those which are merely voidable. Contracts which are voidable will include those induced by misrepresentation, undue influence, mistake and duress.

The most common practical problem is where there has been a sale to a rogue who usually pays for the goods with a worthless cheque. Is the sale void for mistake as to identity or merely voidable? *Ingram v Little* [1961] 1 QB 31 where the contract was found to be void is not now likely to be followed since the decision in *Lewis v Averay* [1972] 1 QB 198.

If the contract is voidable how is it to be avoided if the buyer is a rogue? Normally avoidance has to be communicated to the other party to the contract. However, where the other party cannot be traced, it is sufficient if steps are taken to trace and notify the other such as informing the police: *Car and Universal Finance Co Ltd v Caldwell* [1965] 1

QB 525. Avoidance of the contract will not mean that the buyer did not obtain possession of the goods with the consent of the owner.

In some cases avoidance of the contract will not be sufficient as any subsequent sale by the rogue may fall within s 25(1), SOGA 1979 or the Factors Act 1889 as a sale by a buyer in possession: *Newtons of Wembley Ltd v Williams* [1965] 1 QB 560. It is sometimes suggested that that case has destroyed the practical effect of avoiding any contract. In that case, unusually and crucially, the subsequent sale by the rogue (after avoidance of the contract) was in the then well-established Warren Street W1 second-hand car street market, so that the subsequent sale by the rogue was something which would have been done in the ordinary course of the business of a mercantile agent and title passed notwithstanding the prior avoidance of the original contract with the rogue.

Extraordinarily, under s 23, SOGA 1979 the burden of showing a lack of good faith or notice is upon the original owner: *Whitehorn Bros v Davidson* [1911] 1 KB 463. That is in stark contrast to the normal position where the burden is on the buyer to show these requirements.

6.2.5 Sale by seller in possession

Section 24, SOGA 1979 is in similar terms to s 8, Factors Act 1889 which is considered above. Section 24 is slightly narrower as it excludes second transactions which are only agreements for a sale, agreements to pledge, or agreements for some other disposition. Section 24, SOGA 1979 provides that:

> *Where a person having sold goods continues or is in possession of the goods, or of the documents of title to the goods, the delivery or transfer by that person, or a mercantile agent acting for him, of the goods or documents of title under any sale, pledge, or other disposition thereof, to any person receiving the same in good faith and without notice of the previous sale, has the same effect as if the person making the delivery or transfer were expressly authorised by the owner of the goods to make the same.*

There are five points to note if this exception to the *nemo dat* rule is to apply:

(a) 'having sold' means there must be a relationship of buyer and seller under which title has passed to the first buyer;

(b) 'continues or is in possession' means that the seller, despite the change in ownership of the goods, must retain possession of them or of the documents of title and continuous possession is the essential element: *Worcester Works Finance Ltd v Cooden Engineering Co Ltd* [1972] 1 QB 210;

(c) there is no requirement for the continuing possession to be with the consent of the buyer (the new owner);

(d) 'delivery or transfer' of the goods or documents of title to the second purchaser must take place;

(e) the second owner must receive the goods or documents of title in good faith and without notice of the previous sale.

Proof of good faith and the absence of notice seems to rest on the second buyer: *Heap v Motorists Advisory Agency Ltd* [1923] 1 KB 577.

6.2.6 Buyer in possession

Section 25(1), SOGA 1979 is in similar terms to s 9, Factors Act 1889, but s 25(1) is slightly narrower as it excludes second transactions which are only agreements for a sale, agreements to pledge, or agreements for some other disposition. Section 25(1), SOGA 1979 provides that:

> (1) *Where a person having bought or agreed to buy goods obtains, with the consent of the seller, possession of the goods or the documents of title to the goods, the delivery or transfer by that person, or a mercantile agent acting for him, of the goods or documents of title under any sale, pledge, or other disposition thereof, to any person receiving the same in good faith and without notice of any lien or other right of the original seller in respect of the goods, has the same effect as if the person making the delivery or transfer were a mercantile agent in possession of the goods or documents of title with the consent of the owner.*

There are six points to note if this exception to the *nemo dat* rule is to apply:

(a) 'bought or agreed to buy' means there must be a contract of sale rather than a bailment or contract for work and materials, a conditional sale is specifically excluded by s 25(1), and a contract which is voidable will suffice;

(b) 'with the consent of the seller' means actual consent when possession first passed to the buyer — fraud would not vitiate that original consent, nor would a subsequent withdrawal of consent to possession by the buyer by, for example, the seller avoiding the contract: *Newtons of Wembley Ltd v Williams* [1965] 1 QB 560;

(c) 'possession of the goods' can be constructive possession in the sense of possession by a sub-purchaser: *Four Point Garage Ltd v Carter* [1985] 3 All ER 12;

(d) 'delivery or transfer' of the goods or documents of title to the second purchaser must take place;

(e) the disposition has the same effect as if made by a mercantile agent in possession of the goods or documents of title with the consent of the true owner, so for title to pass the second disposition must fall within the definition of a disposition by a mercantile agent and the seller must have title to pass to the buyer for this exception to apply: *National Employers' Mutual General Insurance Association Ltd v Jones* [1990] AC 24;

(f) the second owner must receive the goods or documents of title in good faith and without notice of the previous sale.

A very detailed analysis of this provision is to be found in *Forsythe International (UK) Limited v Silver Shipping Company Ltd* [1994] 1 WLR 1334.

Proof of good faith and the absence of notice seems to rest on the second buyer: *Heap v Motorists Advisory Agency Ltd* [1923] 1 KB 577.

6.2.7 Part III, Hire Purchase Act 1964

Part III of the Hire Purchase Act 1964 contains an exception to the *nemo dat* rule which is of enormous practical effect. Part III has been amended and extended by the Consumer Credit Act 1974.

When Hire Purchase Information was set up, the majority of finance companies registered their interest in all motor vehicles so that a reasonably comprehensive check could be made by motor dealers and other finance companies before the purchase of second-hand cars to ensure that the vehicle was not owned by a finance company. The information stored has been extended to some stolen or seriously damaged vehicles (usually reported by insurance companies). Until very recently, access to HPI was restricted to traders and finance companies, so that it was difficult for anyone intending to purchase a motor vehicle to make an independent inquiry to see if it was on hire-purchase or conditional sale. Access to HPI is now available to everyone on payment of a search fee. As there is no obligation on finance companies to register an interest, a search is not a guarantee that the car is not owned by someone other than the keeper who is trying to sell it.

Section 27, Hire Purchase Act 1964, as amended, provides that where:

> (a) *a motor vehicle is bailed under a hire-purchase agreement or agreed to be sold under a conditional sale agreement;*
> (b) *the debtor disposes of the motor vehicle before property has become vested in him;*
> (c) *the disposition is to a private purchaser who is a purchaser in good faith without notice of the hire-purchase or conditional sale agreement*
>
> *the sale shall operate as if the creditor's title was vested in the debtor immediately before the disposition.*

Private purchaser is a concept which can cause difficulties as repairing second hand cars is a widespread hobby. It can be difficult to decide when a hobby becomes a business. It is now clear that if the purchaser is in business as a motor trader he will not be protected by these provisions even if the particular purchase was not connected with that business but was for his own use: *Stevenson v Beverley Bentinck Ltd* [1976] 1 WLR 483.

This provision remains of practical importance but the statute has to be construed carefully. In *Hichens v General Guarantee Corporation Ltd* [2001] EWCA Civ 359 the Court of Appeal had to consider whether the agreement came into effect when the car was handed over or, subsequently, when the paperwork was finalised. The judge, adopting a similar approach to that adopted in *Carlyle Finance Ltd v Pallas Industrial Finance* [1999] RTR 281 (which had not been cited to him), found that the contract was made when the car was handed over so that the requirements of the section applied. The Court of Appeal dismissed the appeal.

This exception to the *nemo dat* rule is further extended as follows:

(a) where the first sale by the debtor is to a trade purchaser so that the section does not apply (and the trader will not have title), a sale by the trader to a first private purchaser shall operate as if the creditor's title was vested in the debtor immediately before the disposition, so the first private purchaser gets good title (s 27(3));

(b) where the first private purchaser takes the motor vehicle on hire-purchase, the effect will be that the sale by the creditor of that agreement to the first private purchaser under that agreement shall operate as if the creditor's title was vested in the debtor immediately before the disposition, so the first private purchaser gets good title (s 27(4));

(c) there is a rebuttable presumption that the sale was by the debtor (s 28(2));

(d) if the s 28(2) presumption is rebutted, there is a rebuttable presumption that the sale was by the debtor to a private purchaser without notice of the agreement and the relevant person claiming title is claiming under the person to whom the debtor disposed of the vehicle (s 28(3));

(e) if it is proved that the presumptions in s 28(2) and (3) are rebutted, there is a rebuttable presumption that the first private purchaser was a purchaser in good faith and without notice and the person now claiming title is claiming under the original purchaser (s 28(4)); and

(f) 'notice' means actual notice of the agreement not merely constructive notice and if, for example, the purchaser is told that the agreement has been paid up he does not have actual notice of it: *Barker v Bell* [1971] 1 WLR 983;

(g) the meaning of 'sale' extends to an agreement to sell (including a conditional sale agreement) and a bailment under a hire-purchase agreement: s 29(1) and *Dodds v Yorkshire Bank Finance* [1992] CCLR 92.

This exception is still causing practical problems when the person entering into the agreement is an impostor. If, as sometimes happens, an agreement is reached with an impostor and he takes away the car, can that impostor pass title? This was the situation considered by the Court of Appeal in *Shogun Finance Ltd v Hudson* [2002] 4 All ER 572. By a majority the Court of Appeal decided that the impostor was not the debtor under an agreement for the purpose of s 27 so that title had not passed and (unusually) the finance company were able to recover the vehicle or its value (by agreement in that particular case the claim was for the value). The further appeal to the House of Lords was heard in July 2003. Judgment was reserved and is still awaited at the time of writing.

Although the title which passes is only the title which the creditor had immediately before the disposition by the hirer, that title will normally be full ownership of the vehicle in view of the statutory obligation on the creditor under s 8(1), SOGITA 1973 and the usual contract terms giving effect to that obligation: *Barber v NWS Bank Plc* [1996] 1 WLR 641.

6.3 Torts (Interference with Goods) Act 1977

The Torts (Interference with Goods) Act 1977 contains two provisions which affect title. First, there is the extinction of title on payment of damages (s 5). Secondly, there is the statutory right to sell uncollected goods (ss. 12 and 13) — an exception to the *nemo dat* rule, preserved by under s 21(2)(b), SOGA 1979, which is an example of sales under special powers (see **6.2.3**).

Although not often described as an exception to the *nemo dat* rule, it is important to note the effect of s 5 of the Torts (Interference with Goods) Act 1977. By s 5 where damages for wrongful interference are assessed on the footing that the claimant is being compensated for the whole of his interest in the goods, payment of the damages or a settlement of the claim extinguishes the claimant's title.

7 Performance by the seller

The seller's duty is to deliver the goods to the buyer in accordance with the terms of the contract (s 27(1), SOGA 1979). Delivery is to be distinguished from passing title in the goods as title can pass before delivery, at the time of delivery or after delivery. The obligation to deliver the goods may be separate from the obligation to pay for them, but in the absence of agreement they are concurrent conditions (s 28, SOGA 1979). Section 29, SOGA 1979 sets out the rules for delivery; s 30 deals with the quantity to be delivered; s 31 deals with instalments; s 32 sets out the rules for delivery to carriers; and s 33 deals with deliveries to the buyer at a distant place. This chapter is concerned with the obligations on the seller, the consequences of a breach of these obligations is considered in **Chapter 10**.

7.1 Delivery

Section 61(1), SOGA 1979 defines delivery as the voluntary transfer of possession from one person to another. The definition was extended as from 18 September 1995 by the amendments to SOGA 1979 so that delivery, in relation to ss 20A and 20B, SOGA 1979, includes such appropriation of goods to the contract as results in property in the goods being transferred to the buyer. 'Possession' is not a concept which is defined in SOGA 1979 and is notoriously difficult to define.

7.2 Timing of delivery

A common question is whether the stipulation as to time for delivery is a condition or warranty or intermediate term (see **3.2**). Section 10(2), SOGA 1979 provides that whether time is of the essence (ie, is a condition) depends upon the terms of the contract. It is open to the parties to make time of the essence.

7.3 What must be delivered

The delivery must be of the goods contracted for, and:

- in the case of specific goods — the actual goods agreed upon;
- in the case of ascertained goods — the goods ascertained;

- in the case of unascertained goods — goods corresponding to the description, since the sale will be by description (see **3.10.2**);
- in the case of a sale of goods by sample — the goods must correspond to the sample; and
- in the case of goods where property passes before delivery — the goods the buyer then owns.

7.4 The rules for delivery to the buyer

Section 29 provides:

> (1) *Whether it is for the buyer to take possession of the goods or for the seller to send them to the buyer is a question depending in each case on the contract, express or implied, between the parties.*
> (2) *Apart from any such contract, express or implied, the place of delivery is the seller's place of business if he has one, and if not, his residence; except that, if the contract is for the sale of specific goods, which to the knowledge of the parties when the contract is made are in some other place, then that place is the place of delivery.*
> (3) *Where under the contract of sale the seller is bound to send the goods to the buyer, but no time for sending them is fixed, the seller is bound to send them within a reasonable time.*
> (4) *Where the goods at the time of sale are in the possession of a third person, there is no delivery by the seller to the buyer unless and until the third person acknowledges to the buyer that he holds the goods on his behalf; but nothing in this section affects the operation of the issue or transfer of any document of title to goods.*
> (5) *Demand or tender of delivery may be treated as ineffectual unless made at a reasonable hour; and what is a reasonable hour is a question of fact.*
> (6) *Unless otherwise agreed, the expenses of and incidental to putting the goods into a deliverable state must be borne by the seller.*

In the absence of an express or implied term of the contract, the place and time of delivery are fixed by s 29, SOGA 1979. In the absence of agreement, the expenses of putting the goods into deliverable state are borne by the seller. However, no provision exists in SOGA 1979 providing for the actual expenses of delivery in default of agreement. At common law the rule is that the expenses of the delivery fall on the seller but the expenses of receiving the goods on the buyer. The common law position is often varied by express agreement and certain well known terms have been established such as c.i.f. (cost, insurance and freight); f.o.b. (free on board); f.a.s. (free alongside ship); f.o.r. (free on rail); f.o.q. (free on quay); ex-ship. Ex-works is an expression in common commercial use which confirms the obligation in s 29(2) applies and delivery is at the seller's place of business — the works.

Section 29(4) does not affect the operation or issue of documents of title so that delivery of a document of title (such as a bill of lading) will avoid the need for the acknowledgment of the third party to the buyer that he holds the goods on the buyer's behalf before delivery to the buyer takes place.

7.5 The quantity to be delivered

Section 30, SOGA 1979 provides:

> (1) *Where the seller delivers to the buyer a quantity of goods less than he contracted to sell, the buyer may reject them, but if the buyer accepts the goods so delivered he must pay for them at the contract rate.*
>
> (2) *Where the seller delivers to the buyer a quantity of goods larger than he contracted to sell, the buyer may accept the goods included in the contract and reject the rest, or he may reject the whole.*
>
> (2A) *A buyer who does not deal as consumer may not—*
>
> (a) *where the seller delivers a quantity of goods less than he contracted to sell, reject the goods under subsection (1) above, or*
>
> (b) *where the seller delivers a quantity of goods larger than he contracted to sell, reject the whole under subsection (2) above,*
>
> *if the shortfall or, as the case may be, excess is so slight that it would be unreasonable for him to do so.*
>
> (2B) *It is for the seller to show that a shortfall or excess fell within subsection (2A) above.*
>
> (3) *Where the seller delivers to the buyer a quantity of goods larger than he contracted to sell and the buyer accepts the whole of the goods so delivered he must pay for them at the contract rate.*
>
> (5) *This section is subject to any usage of trade, special agreement, or course of dealing between the parties.*

Sub sections 2A and 2B were added with effect from 3 January 1995 and should be compared to s 15A, SOGA 1979 . The repeal of sub-section 4 which dealt with delivery of mixed goods took effect on the same date. The provisions of s 30 create a comprehensive code dealing with the quantity to be delivered.

7.6 Instalment deliveries

Section 31(1), SOGA 1979 provides:

> (1) *Unless otherwise agreed, the buyer of goods is not bound to accept delivery of them by instalments.*
>
> (2) *Where there is a contract for the sale of goods to be delivered by stated instalments, which are to be separately paid for, and the seller makes defective deliveries in respect of one or more instalments, or the buyer neglects or refuses to take delivery of or pay for one or more instalments, it is a question in each case depending on the terms of the contract and the circumstances of the case whether the breach of contract is a repudiation of the whole contract or whether it is a severable breach giving rise to a claim for compensation but not to a right to treat the whole contract as repudiated.*

If there is an express agreement for instalment deliveries then the obligation on the seller is to deliver in accordance with the agreement reached. Agreement to instalment deliveries may be inferred from other terms of the contract or from the general circumstances. Agreement is often inferred from contracts where the period for delivery is fixed as being over a period of time, as that suggests more than one delivery. Similarly agreement can sometimes be inferred from standard clauses such as 'each delivery shall be paid for ...'. In some cases the seller will have some of the goods in stock and will have to obtain or manufacture others; in which case, if that fact is known to the buyer, the court could easily infer an agreement to delivery by instalments. If the court is to infer an agreement to accept instalment deliveries each delivery would have to be of a reasonable quantity of the goods and at a reasonable time. What is a reasonable time would be a question of fact (s 59, SOGA 1979).

Where a series of deliveries are made it may be difficult to determine whether there is a single contract comprising each separate delivery or a single contract comprising several deliveries. The difference could be of considerable importance when considering the terms of the contract (as a series of separate contracts could lead to incorporation of terms into the later contracts by the course of dealing) and to the rights of the parties on a default by the other: see, for example, *Maple Flock Co Ltd v Universal Furniture Products (Wembley) Ltd* [1934] 1 KB 148.

7.7 Delivery to carrier

Section 32, SOGA 1979 provides:

> (1) *Where, in pursuance of a contract of sale, the seller is authorised or required to send the goods to the buyer, delivery of the goods to a carrier (whether named by the buyer or not) for the purpose of transmission to the buyer is prima facie deemed to be a delivery of the goods to the buyer.*
> (2) *Unless otherwise authorised by the buyer, the seller must make such contract with the carrier on behalf of the buyer as may be reasonable having regard to the nature of the goods and the other circumstances of the case; and if the seller omits to do so, and the goods are lost or damaged in course of transit, the buyer may decline to treat the delivery to the carrier as a delivery to himself or may hold the seller responsible in damages.*
> (3) *Unless otherwise agreed, where goods are sent by the seller to the buyer by a route involving sea transit, under circumstances in which it is usual to insure, the seller must give such notice to the buyer as may enable him to insure them during their sea transit; and if the seller fails to do so, the goods are at his risk during such sea transit.*
> (4) *In a case where the buyer deals as consumer ... subsections (1) to (3) above must be ignored, but if in pursuance of a contract of sale the seller is authorised or required to send the goods to the buyer, delivery of the goods to the carrier is not delivery of the goods to the buyer.*

The new subsection (4) was introduced, with effect from 31 March 2003, by the Sale and Supply of Goods to Consumers Regulations 2002.

If the carrier is the servant or agent of the seller this section will not apply. There is no general duty on the seller to insure the goods in transit merely to make a contract with the carrier which is reasonable, but the absence of insurance may be a factor making the contract unreasonable: *Young (T.) & Sons v Hobson and Partner* (1949) 65 TLR 365. If the journey involves sea transit s 32(3), which concerns insurance, will apply.

7.8 Delivery to distant places

Section 33, SOGA 1979 provides:

> *Where the seller of goods agrees to deliver them at his own risk at a place other than that where they are when sold, the buyer must nevertheless (unless otherwise agreed) take any risk of deterioration in the goods necessarily incident to the course of transit.*

The effect of this rule is reasonably plain, if the seller agrees to accept the risk of delivery, in the absence of further agreement, the buyer will take the risk of deterioration necessarily incident to the transit. The risk on the seller is therefore only the risk of some extraordinary or unusual deterioration.

7.9 Common delivery terms

Most standard form contracts contain clauses permitting the seller to suspend delivery, extend the time for delivery, or cancel the whole or part of the contract if he or she is prevented from performing by something outside his control. These clauses, known as force majeure clauses, are subject to the same rules of construction and incorporation as other contract clauses (see **3.7**) but may not be subject to the statutory tests of reasonableness. The burden is on the seller to show that the clause excuses proper performance on the particular facts.

8

Performance by the buyer

The buyer's duty is to accept the goods and pay for the goods in accordance with the terms of the contract (s 27, SOGA 1979). The obligation of the seller is to deliver the goods to the buyer in accordance with the contract (s 27).

8.1 Meaning of 'acceptance' and 'accept'

The concept of acceptance is extremely important. 'Accept' or 'acceptance' are used in the following places in SOGA 1979:

- s 11(4) makes a breach of condition by the seller only a breach of warranty where the buyer has 'accepted' the goods;
- s 19(3) uses 'acceptance' in relation to a bill of exchange in the context of payment;
- s 27 sets out the obligation of the buyer to accept the goods;
- s 30(1), (2) and (3) use 'accept' in the context of an election by the buyer to sanction a delivery of an incorrect quantity of goods;
- s 31(1) uses 'accept' in the context of an election by the buyer to sanction instalment deliveries;
- s 35(1) sets out the rules for deeming a buyer to have accepted goods;
- s 35A(1) explains the right of partial rejection where some goods have been accepted;
- s 36 deals with the return of goods which have not been accepted;
- s 50 sets out the damages recoverable for non-acceptance.

8.2 The rules for acceptance

Section 35, SOGA 1979 provides:

> *(1) The buyer is deemed to have accepted the goods subject to subsection (2) below—*
> *(a) when he intimates to the seller that he has accepted them, or*
> *(b) when the goods have been delivered to him and he does any act in relation to them which is inconsistent with the ownership of the seller.*
> *(2) Where goods are delivered to the buyer, and he has not previously examined them, he is not deemed to have accepted them under subsection (1) above until he has had a reasonable opportunity of examining them for the purpose—*
> *(a) of ascertaining whether they are in conformity with the contract, and*

> (b) *in the case of a contract for sale by sample, of comparing the bulk with the sample.*
>
> (3) *Where the buyer deals as consumer or (in Scotland) the contract of sale is a consumer contract, the buyer cannot lose his right to rely on subsection (2) above by agreement, waiver or otherwise.*
>
> (4) *The buyer is also deemed to have accepted the goods when after a lapse of a reasonable time he retains the goods without intimating to the seller that he has rejected them.*
>
> (5) *The questions that are material in determining for the purposes of subsection (4) above whether a reasonable time has elapsed include whether the buyer has had a reasonable opportunity of examining the goods for the purpose mentioned in subsection (2) above.*
>
> (6) *The buyer is not by virtue of this section deemed to have accepted the goods merely because—*
>
> (a) *he asks for, or agrees to, their repair by or under an arrangement with the seller, or*
>
> (b) *the goods are delivered to another under a sub-sale or other disposition.*
>
> (7) *Where the contract is for the sale of goods making one or more commercial units, a buyer accepting any goods included in a unit is deemed to have accepted all the goods making the unit; and in this subsection 'commercial unit' means a unit division of which would materially impair the value of the goods or the character of the unit.*

8.2.1 Reasonable time

One common area of dispute is: what is a reasonable time within s 35(4)? In the notorious case of *Bernstein v Pamson Motors (Golders Green) Ltd* [1987] 2 All ER 220 the court had to consider whether retaining a new car for less than a month and travelling 140 miles before the car broke down meant that the buyer had lost his right to reject for the defects leading to the breakdown. Astonishingly the judge found that the right to reject had been lost. The buyer's appeal to the Court of Appeal was compromised without a hearing. In cases such as *Rogers v Parish* [1987] QB 993 a more appropriate approach was taken and it was not even argued (either at trial or in the Court of Appeal) that after six months and 5,500 miles the right to reject had been lost.

Crucially this question has now been considered by the Court of Appeal in *Clegg v Olle Andersson (trading as Nordic Marine)* [2003] 1 All ER (Comm) 721. In a claim involving the sale of a new yacht, the buyers accepted delivery on 12 August 2000 and did not reject until 6 March 2001. The Court of Appeal found that the goods were not of satisfactory quality and the right to reject had not been lost. The Court of Appeal did not decide whether the decision in *Bernstein* was correct when it was decided, but did hold that it did not represent the law now (after the amendment to s 35 effected by the 1994 Act).

8.3 Examination

Subject to the terms of the contract, the buyer is entitled to a reasonable opportunity to inspect the goods when they are tendered for delivery (s 34(2), SOGA 1979). The buyer is not obliged to accept goods if any contractual or the statutory right of inspection is wrongly refused by the seller. In the absence of agreement to the contrary the place of examination is the place of delivery.

8.4 Payment

The obligation upon the buyer is to make payment in accordance with the terms of the contract between the parties.

The price to be paid will be ascertained by applying s 8 or 9, SOGA 1979. The price is usually agreed between the parties and fixed in the contract. The price may be fixed in some manner agreed in the contract. The price may be determined by a course of dealing between the parties. Finally, the price may be simply a reasonable price. If the price is to be determined by some third party and the third party cannot or does not make the valuation, the agreement is avoided; but if the goods or any part of them have been delivered to and appropriated by the buyer he must pay a reasonable price for them. Where the third party is prevented from making the valuation by the seller or buyer, the party not at fault may maintain an action for damages against the party at fault.

8.4.1 Time of payment

Section 28, SOGA 1979 provides:

> *Unless otherwise agreed, delivery of the goods and payment of the price are concurrent conditions, that is to say, the seller must be ready and willing to give possession of the goods to the buyer in exchange for the price and the buyer must be ready and willing to pay the price in exchange for possession of the goods.*

Although s 28 makes the obligation to pay a condition of the contract you should note the effect of s 10(1) which provides:

> (1) *Unless a different intention appears from the terms of the contract, stipulations as to time of payment are not of the essence of a contract of sale.*

Finally you should note the effect of s 48(3) which provides:

> (3) *Where the goods are of a perishable nature, or where the unpaid seller gives notice to the buyer of his intention to re-sell, and the buyer does not within a reasonable time pay or tender the price, the unpaid seller may re-sell the goods and recover from the original buyer damages for any loss occasioned by his breach of contract.*

If the contract does not otherwise provide, the result of those three provisions is as follows:

(a) if time for delivery is of the essence then so is the time for payment as they are concurrent obligations;

(b) conversely, if time for delivery is not of the essence then neither is the time of payment;

(c) if the goods are perishable or if notice of intention to resell has been given by the seller, then time for payment becomes within a reasonable time and of the essence.

If the seller has waived or is estopped from relying upon the original date of payment, the buyer may argue that no new date for payment has been agreed and that no reasonable notice has been given: *Charles Rickards Ltd v Oppenhaim* [1950] 1 KB 616, *State Trading Corporation of India Ltd v Compagnie Française d'Importation et de Distribution* [1983] 2 Lloyd's Rep 679.

8.4.2 Place of payment

The place of payment may be specified in the contract in which case the payment must be made at that place. Where there is no express provision in the terms of the contract the intention of the parties may be determined from the surrounding circumstances, or from the method of payment provided for. If the intention of the parties cannot be ascertained then, by ss 28 and 29(2), SOGA 1979 the obligation seems to be to make payment at the seller's place of business or residence: *Malik v Narodny Bank Ceskoslovenska* [1946] 2 All ER 663. The place of payment is now rarely a practical problem.

8.4.3 Manner of payment

In default of agreement between the parties, the manner of payment is cash. The defence of tender before action which is available to the buyer in an action by the seller for the price depends upon tender having taken place in cash unless the contract otherwise provides or unless the seller has waived his right to demand cash payment.

With the full introduction of the Euro in 11 countries, problems of the currency in which payment is to be made in cross-border sales in Europe should be reduced. As the UK has not joined the Euro, it remains important that the currency of payment is expressly agreed in international contracts.

Payment by post will be at the seller's risk of loss or delay only if payment by that method is expressly or impliedly authorised by the contract. Four other methods of payment call for special mention:

(a) If payment is made by a negotiable instrument there is a presumption that it is conditional upon the instrument being honoured on the due date, and the seller's remedy of an action for the price is suspended until that due date.

(b) If payment is made by a cheque accompanied by a cheque guarantee card it seems that the presumption that the cheque must be honoured may be displaced merely by the presentation of the guarantee card which is seen as a unilateral contract between the card issuer and the seller that the payment would be made: *First Sport Ltd v Barclays Bank Plc* [1993] 1 WLR 1299, a case involving an impostor using a switch card. The Court of Appeal did not follow the view of Millett J at first instance in *Re Charge Card Services Ltd* [1987] 1 Ch 150 which was left open when that case was decided by the Court of Appeal. However, since the decision in the First Sport case the banks have changed the standard conditions for use of the cheque guarantee cards so that this decision may not now be followed and cheques accompanied by a cheque guarantee card may be treated in the same way as negotiable instruments.

(c) If payment is made by credit card, charge card or debit card there is no presumption that the contract is conditional upon the payment actually being made by the credit or charge card company. Whether the contract is conditional or whether payment by the card is a satisfaction of the buyer's obligations will depend upon the circumstances of the case: *Re Charge Card Services Ltd* [1989] 1 Ch 497. In **Chapter 24** there is a more detailed examination of the use of 'plastic' as a means of payment.

(d) There are also a range of fund transfer systems between banks including giro transfer; BACS (Bankers' Automated Clearing Services); CHAPS (Clearing House Automated Payments System) and its American relation CHIPS (Clearing House Interbank Payments System) both of which offer RTGS (realtime gross settlement system); and, SWIFT (Society for Worldwide Interbank Financial Telecommunication). If payment is by funds transfer the actual documents giving the instructions are not negotiable instruments: *Tenax Steamship Co Ltd v Brimnes (Owners of) (The Brimnes)* [1975] 1 QB 929. It seems that the payment is treated as conditional: *Awilco A/S of Oslo v Fulvia SpA Di Navigazione of Lagliari (The Chikuma)* [1981] 1 WLR 314.

8.5 Late payment

Late payment of money due under sales of goods contracts is widespread. Standard terms of trading and individually negotiated contracts often contain a provision requiring the payment of contractual interest. For purely commercial reasons, these clauses are often not enforced. Statutory interest under s 69, County Courts Act 1984 or s 35A, Supreme Court Act 1981 is only available from the court. This problem is now being addressed by the Late Payment of Commercial Debts (Interest) Act 1998. The Act creates a statutory implied term that qualifying debts carry simple interest. There are detailed provisions which restrict the right to contract out of the provisions of the Act. The UCTA test of reasonableness is imported to restrict the right to postpone the creation of a qualifying debt by contract terms. The 1998 Act has been introduced in four stages (see **4.8**). Such research as has been carried out suggests that the Act has made little practical difference for most small businesses.

9 Remedies of the seller

The obligations of the buyer are to accept the goods and to pay for them in accordance with the terms of the contract (see **Chapter 8**). It is necessary to consider the effect of a failure by the buyer to perform each of those separate obligations. This chapter assumes that there has been no breach of contract by the seller which would discharge the buyer from performance of his obligations.

9.1 Seller's rights on a failure to accept goods

Section 37, SOGA 1979 provides:

> *(1) When the seller is ready and willing to deliver the goods, and requests the buyer to take delivery, and the buyer does not within a reasonable time after such request take delivery of the goods, he is liable to the seller for any loss occasioned by his neglect or refusal to take delivery, and also for a reasonable charge for the care and custody of the goods.*
>
> *(2) Nothing in this section affects the rights of the seller where the neglect or refusal of the buyer to take delivery amounts to a repudiation of the contract.*

Although it may be possible for the seller to maintain an action for the price of the goods, the more common course is to simply seek damages (see **9.4.2** below). Seeking damages avoids the possible problem for the seller of keeping the goods, since the seller cannot receive the price and keep the goods.

9.2 Seller's rights on a failure by the buyer to pay for the goods

The unpaid seller's rights can be divided into three categories. First, there are the seller's rights in the goods. Secondly, there are the seller's financial claims. Finally, there are the miscellaneous claims which the seller may have. Before turning to those three categories it is necessary to define an unpaid seller. Section 38, SOGA 1979 provides that:

> *(1) The seller of goods is an unpaid seller within the meaning of this Act—*
>
> *(a) when the whole of the price has not been paid or tendered;*
>
> *(b) when a bill of exchange or other negotiable instrument has been received as conditional payment, and the condition on which it was received has not been fulfilled by reason of the dishonour of the instrument or otherwise.*
>
> *(2) In this Part of this Act 'seller' includes any person who is in the position of a seller, as, for instance, an agent of the seller to whom the bill of lading has been indorsed, or a consignor or agent who has himself paid (or is directly responsible for) the price.*

9.3 The unpaid seller's rights in the goods

The seller's rights in the goods will be of particular importance on the insolvency of the buyer. Section 55(1), SOGA 1979 makes it plain that the rights which arise by implication of law, which include the unpaid seller's rights in the goods, can be varied or excluded by agreement between the parties. The most common variation is some form of Romalpa clause (see **5.8**). In the absence of any other contract terms, the unpaid seller's rights are to be found in s 39, SOGA 1979 which provides:

> (1) *Subject to this and any other Act, notwithstanding that the property in the goods may have passed to the buyer, the unpaid seller of goods, as such, has by implication of law—*
> (a) *a lien on the goods or right to retain them for the price while he is in possession of them;*
> (b) *in case of the insolvency of the buyer, a right of stopping the goods in transit after he has parted with the possession of them;*
> (c) *a right of re-sale as limited by this Act.*
>
> (2) *Where the property in goods has not passed to the buyer, the unpaid seller has (in addition to his other remedies) a right of withholding delivery similar to and coextensive with his rights of lien or retention and stoppage in transit where the property has passed to the buyer.*

Insolvency is defined in SOGA 1979 by s 61(4):

> (4) *A person is deemed to be insolvent within the meaning of this Act if he has either ceased to pay his debts in the ordinary course of business or he cannot pay his debts as they become due.*

9.3.1 The unpaid seller lien

Section 41, SOGA 1979 provides:

> (1) *Subject to this Act, the unpaid seller of goods who is in possession of them is entitled to retain possession of them until payment or tender of the price in the following cases—*
> (a) *where the goods have been sold without any stipulation as to credit;*
> (b) *where the goods have been sold on credit but the term of credit has expired;*
> (c) *where the buyer becomes insolvent.*
>
> (2) *The seller may exercise his lien or right of retention notwithstanding that he is in possession of the goods as agent or bailee or custodier for the buyer.*

9.3.2 Exercise of the statutory unpaid seller's lien

The right given to the seller by s 39(1) exists where property may have passed to the buyer; and the right given by s 39(2) exists where property has not passed. If property and possession have passed s 39 will not assist the seller. The lien which arises is a form of charge over the property and normally would not arise over the seller's own property. Section 39(2) creates a statutory right equivalent to a lien over the seller's own property.

9.3.3 Lien on part delivery

Section 42, SOGA 1979 provides that:

> *Where an unpaid seller has made part delivery of the goods, he may exercise his lien or right of retention on the remainder, unless such part delivery has been made under such circumstances as to show an agreement to waive the lien or right of retention.*

9.3.4 Effect of the lien

The justified exercise by the seller of his lien does not involve a rescission or discharge of the contract (s 48(1), SOGA 1979). As the retention of the goods is for the seller's benefit no expenses can be claimed from the buyer, unless the contract otherwise provides. If the seller re-sells the goods the new buyer will acquire good title (s 48(2), SOGA 1979). The right to re-sell arises:

(a) where the goods are of a perishable nature or where the unpaid seller gives notice to the buyer of his intention to re-sell and the buyer does not within a reasonable time pay or tender the price (s 48(3), SOGA 1979); and

(b) where the contract makes express provision for re-sale the contract is rescinded without prejudice to any claim for damages (s 48(4), SOGA 1979).

9.3.5 Termination of lien

The seller's lien may be lost in a number of ways. The lien can be lost upon the buyer tendering the price. The lien will also be lost if the seller assents to a sub-sale. Section 43, SOGA 1979 provides:

> *(1) The unpaid seller of goods loses his lien or right of retention in respect of them—*
> *(a) when he delivers the goods to a carrier or other bailee or custodier for the purpose of transmission to the buyer without reserving the right of disposal of the goods;*
> *(b) when the buyer or his agent lawfully obtains possession of the goods;*
> *(c) by waiver of the lien or right of retention.*
> *(2) An unpaid seller of goods who has a lien or right of retention in respect of them does not lose his lien or right of retention by reason only that he has obtained judgment or decree for the price of the goods.*

9.3.6 Stoppage in transit

The unpaid seller also has the right to stop the goods in transit on the insolvency of the buyer (s 44, SOGA 1979). The meaning of transit for this purpose is to be found in s 45, SOGA 1979. The right is exercised by taking possession of the goods or by giving notice of the claim to the carrier or other bailee (s 46, SOGA 1979). The effect of a lawful exercise of this right is the same as for a lawful exercise of the unpaid seller's lien which has already been considered (see **9.3.1** above).

9.4 The unpaid seller's financial claims

The unpaid seller's financial claims will normally be either (a) to sue the buyer for the contract price or (b) to seek damages from the buyer. There are only two exceptions, where the buyer can recover the price and damages. First, where the second rule in *Hadley v Baxendale* (1854) 9 Ex 341 is satisfied whereupon the seller may recover any special damages incurred such as the cost of financing the money: *Wadsworth v Lydall* [1981] 1 WLR 598, approved in *President of India v La Pintada Compagnia Navigacion SA* [1985] AC 105. Secondly, where the seller has incurred expenses for care of the goods as a result of the delay (s 37(1), SOGA 1979).

In some circumstances the seller will have no choice but to claim damages. Where the seller has a choice between a claim for the price or damages, the seller will have to consider the following practical points:

(a) a claim for the price will avoid the need for the seller to prove that any loss has been suffered;

(b) a claim for the price will avoid any difficult arguments over foreseeability of loss, remoteness, and mitigation;

(c) a claim for the price can be easier than a claim for damages even if the contract contains a liquidated damages clause as a claim for the price avoids any challenge to the clause on the issue of incorporation into the contract, or as a penalty;

(d) a claim for the price will be a liquidated claim upon which an enforceable default judgment could be obtained rather than judgment for damages to be assessed;

(e) on a successful application for summary judgment an enforceable judgment could be obtained rather than judgment for damages to be assessed.

9.4.1 The seller's claim for the price

A claim for the price can be brought by the seller where:

(a) property in the goods has passed to the buyer (s 49(1), SOGA 1979);

(b) when the price is payable under the contract irrespective of delivery of the goods (s 49(2), SOGA 1979).

If the buyer has wrongfully rejected the goods a claim for the price can be made. A wrongful rejection is a rejection where the buyer had no right to reject at all or where that right has been lost (see **10.3.6**). If the goods delivered were not in accordance with the contract the seller may still bring a claim for the price where:

(a) the risk of non-conformity, such as deterioration, was with the buyer;

(b) the contract excludes the implied terms in ss 13–15, SOGA 1979 (see **Chapter 3**);

(c) there has only been a breach of warranty, or where the breach of condition has been treated by the buyer as a breach of warranty, but this will not prevent a claim for damages by the buyer;

(d) where the wrong quantity is delivered but the buyer is a non-consumer and ss 15A and 30(2A) are satisfied (see **7.5**);

(e) where the buyer is unable to return the non-conforming goods because, for example, they have deteriorated or been damaged further, but this will not prevent a claim for damages by the buyer.

9.4.1.1 Interest

Apart from any contractual claim for interest, or any claim for interest made in litigation under s 69, County Courts Act 1984 or s 35A, Supreme Court Act 1981, a claim for interest may exist under the Late Payment of Commercial Debts (Interest) Act 1998: see **8.5**.

9.4.2 The seller's action for damages

The principles for assessing the damages recoverable by the seller are the same whether the claim arises from non-acceptance of the goods by the buyer, or from a failure to pay for the goods. Damages for non-acceptance are governed by s 50 which provides:

(1) *Where the buyer wrongfully neglects or refuses to accept and pay for the goods, the seller may maintain an action against him for damages for non-acceptance.*

(2) *The measure of damages is the estimated loss directly and naturally resulting, in the ordinary course of events, from the buyer's breach of contract.*

(3) *Where there is an available market for the goods in question the measure of damages is prima facie to be ascertained by the difference between the contract price and the market or current price at the time or times when the goods ought to have been accepted or (if no time was fixed for acceptance) at the time of the refusal to accept.*

In *Bem Dis a Turk Ticaret S/A TR v International Agri Trade Co Ltd* [1999] 1 All ER (Comm) 619, the Court of Appeal had to consider the measure of damages payable to a seller where the buyer refused a delivery of tapioca sold under GAFTA form 100 terms before the ship had been loaded. The court had to consider the position under s 50, SOGA 1979 and then consider whether that position had been altered under clause 28 of the GAFTA contract. The Appeal Board of GAFTA awarded US$65,000 wasted expenditure in cancelling the charterparty. The judge upheld that award as recoverable under s 50(2), SOGA 1979 a decision which was not affected by clause 28. The Court of Appeal dismissed the appeal.

9.4.2.1 Where there is an available market for the goods

Section 50(3) applies where the buyer has not paid the price and has not accepted the goods. If there is an available market for the goods the seller should sell and his damages will be the difference between the contract price and the market price. The seller may claim any reasonable costs of securing the market price for the goods (s 54). If there is a fixed price for the goods the seller's damages will be limited to nominal damages unless the supply of goods exceeded the demand as only then will the loss of a particular customer, the defaulting buyer, result in an actual loss to the seller. It seems that the burden is on the seller to show that supply exceeded demand.

9.4.2.2 Where there is no available market for the goods

Where there is no available market the seller must take reasonable steps to mitigate his loss by selling the goods. It has been held that there is no available market for second-hand cars as, unlike new cars, each one is unique: *Lazenby Garages v Wright* [1976] 1 WLR 459. With the current trend for each new car to be made to order, with a selection of optional equipment, it may be extremely difficult to maintain the distinction which means that there is no available market within s 50(3), SOGA 1979 for new cars. In *Shearson Lehman Hutton Inc v Maclaine Watson & Co Ltd (No 2)* [1990] 1 Lloyd's Rep 441, earlier cases were reviewed and the test was stated to be:

> that if the seller actually offers the goods for sale there is no available market unless there is one actual buyer on that day at a fair price; and that if there is no actual offer for sale, but only a notional or hypothetical sale for the purposes of s 50(3), there is no available market unless on that day there are in the market sufficient traders potentially in touch with each other to evidence a market in which the actual or notional seller could if he wished sell the goods.

Where there is no available market, s 50(2) gives statutory effect to the first limb of *Hadley v Baxendale* (1854) 9 Ex 341. Again any claim for recoverable expenses incurred by the seller is preserved by s 54.

9.5 Miscellaneous claims of the seller

In most cases the action by the seller for the price has a similar effect to an action for specific performance as the buyer will pay the price and will usually then take the goods.

Specific performance will not normally be ordered in favour of the seller. Injunctions will rarely be sought in cases other than 'solus' agreements but can be sought if appropriate: *Metropolitan Electric Supply Co Ltd v Ginder* [1901] 2 Ch 799. The seller may seek a declaration setting out his legal rights: *Household Machines Ltd v Cosmos Exporters Ltd* [1947] KB 217. A declaration can also be useful where it is necessary for one party to have a clear statement of rights which can be shown to third parties: *Patten v Burke Publishing Co Limited* [1991] 1 WLR 541.

The seller may have a right to forfeit any deposit paid by the buyer (see **3.8**).

The unpaid seller may also have claims in wrongful interference against third parties who hold his goods. If title to the goods has passed to the person holding them under an exception to the *nemo dat* rule (see **6.2**), the seller will have no claim against the person in possession but only against the buyer. If title has not passed the seller will have a claim against the person with possession of the goods for delivery up and/or damages under s 3, Torts (Interference with Goods) Act 1977. The seller may be able to trace any proceeds of any sub-sale into the hands of the buyer. Allowance will be made to the person in possession for any improvement to the goods (s 3(7), Torts (Interference with Goods) Act 1977). In such a claim the court can:

- order delivery up of the goods together with any consequential damages;
- on the application of the owner, order the delivery up or the value, together with any consequential damages;
- on the application of the owner, the payment of damages.

9.6 Practical aspects of the claim by the seller

Whether the seller makes a claim against the buyer for the price, for damages, or for some other remedy, the buyer may set up a counterclaim. It is important to distinguish between simple counterclaims and those cross-claims which also operate as a set-off creating a defence to the seller's action.

The effect of the doctrine of set-off has been criticised as unsatisfactory, but is quite plain. At law a set-off only exists where the claims are debts which are liquidated. In equity debts which are unliquidated may be set-off if they are connected. There is no set-off between debts which are both unliquidated and unconnected: *Axel Petroleum AB v MG Mineral Group AG (The Obelix)* [1992] 1 WLR 270. The landmark case of *Hanak v Green* [1958] 2 QB 9 set out the degree of connection required. Where the parties deal with each other on a regular basis a claim arising out of one contract will not given rise to a defence of set-off to a claim for the price under another separate contract: *B. Hargreaves Ltd v Action 2000 Ltd* [1993] BCLC 1111. The right of set-off is preserved by s 53, SOGA 1979. If the defence of set-off is not available the court has a discretion to grant a stay of execution on any claim pending the trial of the counterclaim.

The doctrine of set-off can be excluded by custom or agreement. Set-off is generally excluded in respect of freight charges so that claims for losses or delay in delivery operate only as a counterclaim.

Care must be taken when deciding how to plead any defence in view of the costs implications in actions involving claims and counterclaims: *Medway Oil and Storage Co Ltd v Continental Contractors Ltd* [1929] AC 88 and *NV Lucifersfabrieken v H and T Trading Agencies Ltd (The Dutch Match)* [1940] 1 All ER 587.

10

Remedies of the buyer

The obligations of the seller are to deliver the goods in accordance with the terms of the contract (see **Chapter 7**). It is necessary to consider the effect of a failure by the seller to deliver (i) in accordance with the terms of the contract, and (ii) goods which are in accordance with the contract. The buyer's right of rejection and the consequences of rejection have to be considered. Thereafter the various remedies available to the buyer will be considered in detail.

The remedies of the buyer must be considered in the light of the new rights for consumers created by the Sale and Supply of Goods to Consumers Regulations 2002 which introduced an important new Part 5A into SOGA 1979. The new rights are a right to require the goods to be repaired or replaced, the right to require the purchase price to be reduced by an appropriate amount and the right to rescind the contract.

10.1 Failure to deliver in accordance with the terms of the contract

The buyer can claim damages for non-delivery under s 51, SOGA 1979 and any special damages and interest under s 54, SOGA 1979. The buyer may also be able to seek specific performance under s 52, SOGA 1979 if the goods were specific or ascertained goods.

Section 51 provides:

(1) Where the seller wrongfully neglects or refuses to deliver the goods to the buyer, the buyer may maintain an action against the seller for damages for non-delivery.

(2) The measure of damages is the estimated loss directly and naturally resulting, in the ordinary course of events, from the seller's breach of contract.

(3) Where there is an available market for the goods in question the measure of damages is prima facie to be ascertained by the difference between the contract price and the market or current price of the goods at the time or times when they ought to have been delivered or (if no time was fixed) at the time of the refusal to deliver.

Section 51 is in similar terms to s 50 which was considered in **Chapter 9**.

10.2 Reasons for seller failing to deliver

Assuming that the buyer is not himself in breach of any obligation under the contract (such as paying for the goods, or paying a deposit), the main reasons for a failure to deliver are:

- a simple refusal by the seller to perform the contract;
- the goods have been sold to another buyer;

- delay in delivery;
- the goods have been lost before delivery;
- performance is prevented in other ways;
- insolvency.

The seller's right of disposal under the statutory lien may also be a reason for refusing to deliver the goods, but the exercise of that lien is dependent upon the buyer being in breach of contract and is therefore considered under the seller's remedies (**Chapter 9**).

10.2.1 Refusal by seller to perform

An outright refusal by the seller to perform his obligations will amount to a repudiatory breach of contract unless the seller's obligations under the contract were limited, or the contract has become frustrated (see **Chapter 5**). The ordinary contract law concepts of repudiatory breach, the need for acceptance of that breach, and of anticipatory breach will apply.

A seller's obligation to perform may be a limited obligation qualified by words such as to use his best endeavours. The obligation may be conditional on acts or events not within the seller's contract, such as a crop growing to maturity.

If a repudiatory breach exists and is accepted by the buyer, the buyer will have the following remedies:

- a claim in restitution for the money paid, on a total failure of consideration;
- a claim for damages for non-delivery;
- a claim for specific performance if the goods are specific goods or are ascertained goods.

10.2.2 Goods sold to another buyer

If the buyer has a right to possession of the goods, a second sale by the seller will amount to a wrongful interference with the buyer's goods. The right to possession is not dependent upon property having passed (see **Chapter 5**). A right to possession can only exist where the goods are specific, or have become ascertained goods by the time of the second sale.

If the buyer has no right to possession of the goods, the buyer's remedies will be only against the seller and will be:

- a claim in restitution for the money paid, on a total failure of consideration;
- a claim for damages for non-delivery.

If the buyer has a right to possession and the seller has sold the goods to someone else, the buyer will have remedies against the seller and may have remedies against the subsequent buyer. The buyer's remedies against that subsequent buyer will depend upon whether that subsequent buyer obtained title to the goods under an exception to the *nemo dat* rule. The exceptions which need to be considered are sales under the Factors Acts (see **6.2.2**) and sales by seller in possession: s 24, SOGA 1979 (see **6.2.5**). The subsequent buyer could also obtain good title on damages being paid under the Torts (Interference with Goods) Act 1977 (see **9.5**). If the subsequent buyer has obtained good title no claim will exist against him. If the subsequent buyer has not obtained good title he will be liable to the buyer for wrongfully interfering with the goods. The remedies of the buyer against the seller will be:

- a claim in restitution for the money paid, on a total failure of consideration;
- a claim in restitution for the money received by the seller on the subsequent sale; or
- a claim for damages for non-delivery; or
- a claim in wrongful interference with goods.

10.2.3 Delay in delivery

If the time for delivery is of the essence, or more than a reasonable time for the delivery has passed and the seller has not delivered the goods, the seller will be in repudiatory breach of contract: *Hartley v Hymans* [1920] 3 KB 475. The buyer will then be able:

- to accept the repudiatory breach and claim damages for non-delivery; or
- rarely, to seek specific performance of the contract.

10.2.4 Goods lost before delivery

Goods may be lost before the contract is made, partially lost before the contract was made, or may be lost between contract and delivery.

10.2.4.1 Goods lost before the contract is made

If all the goods are lost before the contract was made and the contract is for unascertained generic goods then the goods cannot easily be said to be lost as another source should be available and if the seller does not deliver the buyer will have the following remedies:

- a claim in restitution for the money paid, on a total failure of consideration;
- a claim for damages for non-delivery.

If all the goods are lost before the contract is made and the contract is for goods from a specific source or there is only one source then the contract may be void for mistake: *Bell v Lever Brothers Ltd* [1932] AC 161. The buyer will then recover any money paid. Damages will only be awarded to the buyer if the seller has warranted that the goods exist. Similarly if by the contract the buyer has accepted the risk that the goods may not exist, the contract will not be void for mistake and the buyer will have to pay the contract price.

If all the goods are lost before the contract is made and the contract is for specific goods within the extended statutory meaning (see **Chapter 5**), the perishing of those goods may enable the parties to treat the contract as void (s 6, SOGA 1979). The buyer will then recover any money paid. However, it is open to the parties to make this a risk of the buyer or seller: *McRae v Commonwealth Disposals Commission* (1951) 84 CLR 377.

10.2.4.2 Partial loss before the contract is made

If there has been only a partial loss of goods before the contract was made the position is:

(a) It is a question of construction whether the parties intended that the contract be wholly discharged or not, and if it is not to be wholly discharged the seller must deliver and the buyer must pay for the goods which have not been lost: *H R & S Sainsbury Ltd v Street* [1972] 1 WLR 834.

(b) If the seller has warranted the existence of the goods he must make delivery of the quantity which is not lost and the ordinary rules applying to delivery of a wrong quantity will apply (see **7.5**).

(c) If the risk of loss is on the buyer, the seller must deliver the goods which have not been lost and the buyer must pay for them.

10.2.4.3 Loss after the contract is made

A distinction must be drawn between specific and unascertained goods.

Where specific goods perish and (a) property and risk have not vested in the purchaser and (b) there is no fault by either party, the contract will be avoided (s 7, SOGA 1979). Where s 7 applies, the Law Reform (Frustrated Contracts) Act 1943 does not apply and the common law rules must be used: if there has been a total failure of consideration the money paid can be recovered and no allowance is made for the seller's expenses. Where s 7 applies, but only part of the specific goods perish, it seems that the seller is not obliged to tender what remains: *Barrow, Lane & Ballard Ltd v Phillip Phillips & Co Ltd* [1929] 1 KB 574, but contrast *H.R. & S Sainsbury Ltd v Street* [1972] 1 WLR 834. Where there is a partial failure of consideration on a non-severable contract the common law rules apply: the seller cannot compel payment but the buyer cannot compel the return of money already paid. If the seller has undertaken absolutely to deliver the goods s 7 will not apply and on a failure to deliver the buyer will have the following remedies:

- a claim in restitution for the money paid, on a total failure of consideration;
- a claim for damages for non-delivery.

Where the goods are unascertained goods the seller will only be able to argue that the contract has been frustrated if all sources of supply have been destroyed. In most situations the seller will have to obtain the goods from another source and failure to do so will give the buyer the following remedies:

- a claim in restitution for the money paid, on a total failure of consideration;
- a claim for damages for non-delivery.

In the absence of an absolute warranty by the seller or buyer, destruction of quasi-specific goods without fault before property or risk has passed may enable the seller to argue frustration at common law. If there is only a partial destruction it seems that the buyer may be able to argue frustration even where the remaining goods have been allocated to another contract, if that is reasonable: *Continental Grain Export Corp v STM Grain Ltd* [1979] 2 Lloyd's Rep 460, *Intertradex SA v Lesieur-Tourteaux* [1978] 2 Lloyd's Rep 509, *Pancommerce SA v Veecheema BV* [1982] 1 Lloyd's Rep 645.

10.2.5 Performance prevented in other ways

The general rules of frustration will apply so that events such as import or export controls or the outbreak of war can frustrate a contract. In the absence of specific contract terms, the provisions of the Law Reform (Frustrated Contracts) Act 1943 will apply.

10.2.6 Insolvency

A very common problem is what happens to goods when the seller becomes insolvent. If property has already vested in the buyer he can claim the goods. The question of vesting of property has already been considered (**Chapter 5**). If the seller is an individual the important date is the date on which the bankruptcy order is made (ss 278(a) and 283(1),

Insolvency Act 1986). In relation to the insolvency of a company there are two important dates. First, if there is a voluntary liquidation, the date on which the resolution for winding up is passed (s 86, Insolvency Act 1986). Secondly, if there is a compulsory winding up the date when the petition was presented: s 129, Insolvency Act 1986.

10.3 Goods not in accordance with the contract

The buyer may have the following rights if the goods delivered are not in accordance with the contract: a right of rejection, a right to claim return of the price, a right to damages, a proprietary right in goods, and a right to seek specific performance of the contract. The rights available will depend upon the circumstances of the case and it is convenient to consider breaches of the implied terms which are conditions, then breaches of other terms.

Where the buyer is a consumer, from 31 March 2003, he may also have the rights set out in the new Part 5A, SOGA 1979 which was introduced by the Sale and Supply of Goods to Consumers Regulations 2002. The new rights are a right to require the goods to be repaired or replaced, the right to require the purchase price to be reduced by an appropriate amount and the right to rescind the contract.

Part 5A provides as follows:

48A Introductory

(1) This section applies if—

(a) the buyer deals as consumer or, in Scotland, there is a consumer contract in which the buyer is a consumer, and

(b) the goods do not conform to the contract of sale at the time of delivery.

(2) If this section applies, the buyer has the right—

(a) under and in accordance with section 48B below, to require the seller to repair or replace the goods, or

(b) under and in accordance with section 48C below—

(i) to require the seller to reduce the purchase price of the goods to the buyer by an appropriate amount, or

(ii) to rescind the contract with regard to the goods in question.

(3) For the purposes of subsection (1)(b) above goods which do not conform to the contract of sale at any time within the period of six months starting with the date on which the goods were delivered to the buyer must be taken not to have so conformed at that date.

(4) Subsection (3) above does not apply if—

(a) it is established that the goods did so conform at that date;

(b) its application is incompatible with the nature of the goods or the nature of the lack of conformity.

48B Repair or replacement of the goods

(1) If section 48A above applies, the buyer may require the seller —

(a) to repair the goods, or

(b) to replace the goods.

(2) If the buyer requires the seller to repair or replace the goods, the seller must—

(a) repair or, as the case may be, replace the goods within a reasonable time but without causing significant inconvenience to the buyer;

(b) bear any necessary costs incurred in doing so (including in particular the cost of any labour, materials or postage).

(3) The buyer must not require the seller to repair or, as the case may be, replace the goods if that remedy is—

(a) impossible, or

(b) disproportionate in comparison to the other of those remedies, or

(c) disproportionate in comparison to an appropriate reduction in the purchase price under paragraph (a), or rescission under paragraph (b), of section 48C(1) below.

(4) One remedy is disproportionate in comparison to the other if the one imposes costs on the seller which, in comparison to those imposed on him by the other, are unreasonable, taking into account—

(a) the value which the goods would have if they conformed to the contract of sale,

(b) the significance of the lack of conformity, and

(c) whether the other remedy could be effected without significant inconvenience to the buyer.

(5) Any question as to what is a reasonable time or significant inconvenience is to be determined by reference to—

(a) the nature of the goods, and

(b) the purpose for which the goods were acquired.

48C Reduction of purchase price or rescission of contract

(1) If section 48A above applies, the buyer may—

(a) require the seller to reduce the purchase price of the goods in question to the buyer by an appropriate amount, or

(b) rescind the contract with regard to those goods,

if the condition in subsection (2) below is satisfied.

(2) The condition is that—

(a) by virtue of section 48B(3) above the buyer may require neither repair nor replacement of the goods; or

(b) the buyer has required the seller to repair or replace the goods, but the seller is in breach of the requirement of section 48B(2)(a) above to do so within a reasonable time and without significant inconvenience to the buyer.

(3) For the purposes of this Part, if the buyer rescinds the contract, any reimbursement to the buyer may be reduced to take account of the use he has had of the goods since they were delivered to him.

48D Relation to other remedies etc.

(1) If the buyer requires the seller to repair or replace the goods the buyer must not act under subsection (2) until he has given the seller a reasonable time in which to repair or replace (as the case may be) the goods.

(2) The buyer acts under this subsection if—

(a) in England and Wales or Northern Ireland he rejects the goods and terminates the contract for breach of condition;

(b) in Scotland he rejects any goods delivered under the contract and treats it as repudiated;

(c) he requires the goods to be replaced or repaired (as the case may be).

48E Powers of the court

(1) In any proceedings in which a remedy is sought by virtue of this Part the court, in addition to any other power it has, may act under this section.

(2) On the application of the buyer the court may make an order requiring specific performance or, in Scotland, specific implement by the seller of any obligation imposed on him by virtue of section 48B above.

(3) Subsection (4) applies if—

(a) the buyer requires the seller to give effect to a remedy under section 48B or 48C above or has claims to rescind under section 48C, but

(b) the court decides that another remedy under section 48B or 48C is appropriate.

(4) The court may proceed—

(a) as if the buyer had required the seller to give effect to the other remedy, or if the other remedy is rescission under section 48C

(b) as if the buyer had claimed to rescind the contract under that section.

(5) If the buyer has claimed to rescind the contract the court may order that any reimbursement to the buyer is reduced to take account of the use he has had of the goods since they were delivered to him.

(6) The court may make an order under this section unconditionally or on such terms and conditions as to damages, payment of the price and otherwise as it thinks just.

48F Conformity with the contract
For the purposes of this Part, goods do not conform to a contract of sale if there is, in relation to the goods, a breach of an express term of the contract or a term implied by section 13, 14 or 15 above.

10.3.1 Breach of implied condition of title

As seen at **3.10.1**, except in cases of sale of a limited title, there is in a contract for the sale of goods an implied statutory condition and two implied statutory warranties as to title.

The implied condition in s 12(1), SOGA 1979 is that the seller will have a right to sell the goods at the time property is to pass. The remedy for breach of the implied condition is that the buyer has three choices:

(a) The buyer can treat the contract as repudiated and sue for return of the contract price on a total failure of consideration: *Rowland v Divall* [1923] 2 KB 500 and *Butterworth v Kingsway Motors Ltd* [1954] 1 WLR 1286. The statutory concept of acceptance in s 11(4), SOGA 1979 will not preclude such a claim even if the buyer has used the goods for a considerable period of time, provided that the buyer has not acquired good title. This right is of considerable importance when dealing with depreciating goods such as most motor cars.

(b) The buyer can treat the contract as repudiated and sue for damages, but will be required to prove the damage suffered. This remedy would be used where the goods were appreciating as the buyer could recover the higher cost of replacement goods.

(c) The buyer can affirm the contract and claim damages in which case the damages will be based on normal contractual principles (ss 53 and 54, SOGA 1979).

Where the implied condition has been broken by the seller but the buyer acquired title under one of the exceptions to the nemo dat rule it seems that this condition will be treated as not being broken at all: *Barber v NWS Bank Plc* [1996] 1 WLR 641.

The implied warranties in s 12(2) are that the goods are free of undisclosed charges or encumbrances and that the buyer will enjoy quiet possession of the goods. As a warranty the buyer will only be able to claim damages for a breach and the damages will be based on normal contractual principles (ss 53 and 54, SOGA 1979). Such a breach will exist:

(a) where the buyer cannot use or sell the goods, for example, because of a patent infringement — *Niblett Ltd v Confectioners' Materials Co Ltd* [1921] 3 KB 387, *Microbeads AG v Vinhurst Road Markings Ltd* [1975] 1 WLR 218;

(b) where the buyer has to deliver up the goods to their true owner — *Mason v Burningham* [1949] 2 KB 545; and

(c) where quiet possession is interference by a third party with the connivance of the seller — *Empresa Exportadora de Acucar v Industria Azucarera Nacional SA (The Playa Larga and The Marble Islands)* [1983] 2 Lloyd's Rep 171.

10.3.2 Breach of implied condition in sales by description

As seen at **3.10.2**, there is in a contract for the sale of goods an implied statutory condition that the goods correspond to the description (s 13(1), SOGA 1979). If the goods do not correspond to the description the consumer buyer will have two options. First, to treat the contract as repudiated and reject the goods. Secondly, to accept the goods and treat the breach of condition as a breach of warranty giving a right to damages assessed on normal contractual principles (ss 53 and 54, SOGA 1979). The non-consumer buyer will be limited to the second remedy if the breach is slight (s 15A, SOGA 1979, considered above).

10.3.3 Breach of the implied condition of quality and fitness

This is the breach which gives rise to most litigation. As seen at **3.10.3**, there is in a contract for the sale of goods an implied statutory condition that the goods are of satisfactory quality and fit for the purpose (s 14, SOGA 1979). If the goods are not of satisfactory quality and fit for the purpose the consumer buyer will have two options. First, to treat the contract as repudiated and reject the goods. Secondly, to accept the goods and treat the breach of condition as a breach of warranty giving a right to damages assessed on normal contractual principles (ss 53 and 54, SOGA 1979). The non-consumer buyer will be limited to the second remedy if the breach is slight (s 15A, SOGA 1979, considered above).

The new statutory test of satisfactory quality has now been considered by the courts. The analysis of Dame Brenda Hale in *Clegg v Olle Andersson (trading as Nordic Marine)* [2003] 1 All ER (Comm) 721 at paras 71–74 should be examined with care. The test is not whether a reasonable person would find the goods acceptable but is an objective comparison of the state of the goods with the standard which a reasonable person would find acceptable. Thus, for a high priced quality product, the customer may be entitled to expect that it is free from even minor defects, in other words perfect or very nearly so. The words used by Dame Brenda Hale would, no doubt, have been applied in the case of *Alpha Chauffeurs Ltd v Citygate Dealership & Lombard North Central plc* [2002] GCCR 301 if the judgment had been available then. In that case the court was concerned with a series of defects which manifested themselves (some of which persisted for six months) in a new Rolls-Royce motor car costing £112,000. The judge had no hesitation in saying that the car delivered did not meet the standard that a reasonable person would regard as satisfactory.

Neither of these decisions considered the new amendments to s 14 introduced by the Sale and Supply of Goods to Consumers Regulations 2002. It will be interesting to see whether the comments made by Dame Brenda Hale about high-priced quality products are applied more rigorously in consumer cases in the light of the new relevant circumstance in consumer cases arising from public statements on the specific characteristics of the goods. At a time when manufacturers spend vast amounts on advertising goods suggesting that they have particular characteristics (which, at very least, by implication rival products do not have), there seems to be no reason why the expectation raised by that advertising should not be a relevant circumstance in deciding what standard the reasonable person could expect.

The new provisions are to be found in s 14(2A) and (2B), SOGA 1979 which provide:

> *(2A) For the purposes of this Act, goods are of satisfactory quality if they meet the standard that a reasonable person would regard as satisfactory, taking account of any description of the goods, the price (if relevant) and all the other relevant circumstances.*
>
> *(2B) For the purposes of this Act, the quality of goods includes their state and condition and the following (among others) are in appropriate cases aspects of the quality of goods—*
>
> *(a) fitness for all the purposes for which goods of the kind in question are commonly supplied,*
> *(b) appearance and finish,*
> *(c) freedom from minor defects,*
> *(d) safety, and*
> *(e) durability.*

That condition is limited by the wording of the new s 14(2C) which provides:

> *(2C) The term implied by subsection (2) above does not extend to any matter making the quality of goods unsatisfactory—*
> *(a) which is specifically drawn to the buyer's attention before the contract is made,*
> *(b) where the buyer examines the goods before the contract is made, which that examination ought to reveal, or*
> *(c) in the case of a contract for sale by sample, which would have been apparent on a reasonable examination of the sample.*

The wording of s 14(2C)(a) is extremely similar to the wording of the former s 14(2)(a), SOGA 1979 and it is likely that the cases on defects specifically drawn to the buyer's attention will still be authoritative. It should be noted that there is no requirement that it be the seller who draws the defect to the attention of the buyer. Similarly, the wording of s 14(2C)(b) is so similar to the wording of the former s 14(2)(b) that the cases on examination of the goods will still be authoritative. The use of the word 'that' as qualifying the examination requires the court to look at the actual examination which the buyer gives the goods rather than considering what an examination could or should have revealed. The change in wording when the 1979 Act was enacted reverses the decision in *Thornett and Fehr v Beers & Son* [1919] 1 KB 486 and that change has been retained in these amendments.

10.3.4 Fitness for a particular purpose

The implied condition of fitness for a particular purpose is to be found in s 14(3), SOGA 1979 which provides:

> *(3) Where the seller sells goods in the course of a business and the buyer, expressly or by implication, makes known—*
> *(a) to the seller, or*
> *(b) where the purchase price or part of it is payable by instalments and the goods were previously sold by a credit-broker to the seller, to that credit-broker,*
> *any particular purpose for which the goods are being bought,*
> *there is an implied term that the goods supplied under the contract are reasonably fit for that purpose, whether or not that is a purpose for which such goods are commonly supplied, except where the circumstances show that the buyer does not rely, or that it is unreasonable for him to rely, on the skill or judgment of the seller or credit-broker.*

The sale must be in the course of a business or through an agent acting in the course of a business, or to a credit broker: *R & B Customs Brokers Co Ltd v United Dominion Trust Ltd* [1988] 1 WLR 321. The particular purpose must be made known at the time the contract is made. It is possible to imply a particular purpose from the circumstances of the transaction and the business of the parties: *Cammell Laird & Co Ltd v Manganese Bronze & Brass Co Ltd* [1934] AC 402. The importance of the true meaning of the particular purpose can be seen from the decision of the House of Lords in *Slater and others v Finning Ltd* [1996] 3 All ER 398. In that case the buyer had made known the purpose for which the goods were required in the sense that the camshafts being sold were to be installed in the engine of a fishing vessel. However, the vessel had an abnormal feature or idiosyncrasy consisting of excitation forces which caused excessive torsional resonance leading to wear and failure of the camshaft. It was held that the particular purpose had not been made known to the seller as the particular purpose within s 14(3) was not use in a fishing vessel but use in a fishing vessel with this abnormal feature or idiosyncrasy.

Reliance on the seller's skill and judgment is normally presumed. It is for the seller to show that there was no such reliance or that the reliance was unreasonable: *Teheran-Europe Co Ltd v S. T. Belton (Tractors) Ltd* [1968] 2 QB 545, *Aswan Engineering Establishment Co v Lupdine Ltd* [1987] 1 WLR 1. Reliance is not excluded merely because the buyer is aware of the defect before the contract is concluded: *R & B Customs Brokers Co Ltd v United Dominion Trust Ltd* [1988] 1 WLR 321.

10.3.5 Other breaches

The buyer's rights on a breach of any other term of the contract will depend upon whether the term was a condition or a warranty. The distinction has already been considered (**Chapter 3**). If the term is a condition, the buyer will have the right to reject the goods whereas if the term is merely a warranty, the buyer will only have a remedy in damages.

10.3.6 Rejection

Rejection requires an unequivocal act by the buyer amounting to clear notice of rejection. An unequivocal act by the buyer will prevent subsequent acceptance, affirmation or waiver of the right to reject: *Morton v Chapman* (1843) 11 M & W 534, *Tradax Export SA v European Grain & Shipping Ltd* [1983] 2 Lloyd's Rep 100, *Graanhandel T. Vink v European Grain & Shipping Ltd* [1989] 2 Lloyd's Rep 531.

The right to reject goods may be limited or lost as a result of express contractual terms agreed between the parties. Such terms may be subject to the statutory protection already considered (**Chapter 3**). Section 35A(4), SOGA 1979 expressly permits the parties to contract out of the right of partial rejection.

The buyer who is a consumer has a right to reject goods which do not comply with any condition of the contract, including the conditions implied by ss 11(3), 12, 13, 14 and 15, SOGA 1979 (see **Chapter 3**). The buyer who is a non-consumer (see **Chapter 3**) has the same rights unless, in relation to breaches of s 13, 14 or 15, the breach is so slight that it would be unreasonable of him to reject (s 15A, SOGA 1979). The burden of proof is on the seller under s 15A, SOGA 1979. Thus the remedy of a non-consumer is limited to damages only if the breach is shown by the seller to be so slight that it would be unreasonable for the buyer to reject. On a justified or lawful rejection the buyer is entitled to refuse to pay for the goods, to recover any money already paid upon a total failure of consideration and may have the right to claim further damages if he has suffered any additional loss (such as the additional cost of buying elsewhere).

A right to reject goods also exists if the delivery is of the wrong quantity. A consumer can accept all the goods, reject all of the goods, or reject the excess (s 30(2)). A non-consumer's rights are limited in that he cannot reject the goods if the delivery is too small, or reject the whole delivery if too much was delivered, if the shortfall or excess is so slight it would be unreasonable for him to do so (s 30(2A)). The burden of showing that it would be unreasonable to reject is on the seller.

If rejection takes place before expiry of the period allowed by the contract for performance by the seller, the seller can cure the defective delivery by delivering other goods complying with the contract: *Borrowman Phillips & Co v Free & Hollis* (1878) 4 QBD 500.

If property has already passed to the buyer before rejection it will revert to the seller and the goods will be held at the seller's risk, but the buyer who retains possession will be a bailee of the goods. Section 36, SOGA 1979 provides:

> *Unless otherwise agreed, where goods are delivered to the buyer, and he refuses to accept them, having the right to do so, he is not bound to return them to the seller, but it is sufficient if he intimates to the seller that he refuses to accept them.*

The right to reject is quite different to the new right to rescind in consumer contracts which is now to be found in Part 5A , SOGA 1979.

10.3.7 Part 5A, SOGA 1979

The new Part 5A, SOGA 1979, introduced by the Sale and Supply of Goods to Consumers Regulations 2002 with effect from 31 March 2003, gives consumers additional remedies (see text at beginning of this chapter).

The remedy of specific performance can be awarded by the court for breach of the obligation to repair or replace under s 48B. Specific performance has traditionally been regarded as a discretionary remedy awarded in limited category of cases and where damages are not an adequate remedy. There may be situations in which a repair can realistically be carried out by the seller only (either because the seller has access to equipment or codes necessary to carry out the repair or because an unauthorised repair would invalidate a warranty or devalue the goods). Similarly there may be situations in which it is not possible to purchase a replacement in the market place (there may be a long waiting list for the product, or it may truly be unique) and so an order for specific performance of the obligation to replace is required. These situations will be rare and damages will remain the usual remedy.

In exercising the new power to rescind the contract, the court has the power to order that the sum to be reimbursed to the buyer is reduced so as to take account of the use of the goods. This discretionary power may make the grant of an order more likely as the court will not feel that the buyer thereby unfairly makes no payment at all for the use of the goods. The creation of this discretionary power avoids the problem of a restitutionary claim where, for example, title did not pass to the buyer so that the buyer (see **10.3.1**) might be thought to have a windfall where the goods are depreciating (eg cars).

10.4 Rejection of part of the goods

Where the contract is severable a buyer may reject an individual instalment even though he has accepted other instalments (s 11(4), SOGA 1979). This right does not exist for non-consumers if the defect is so slight that it would be unreasonable for the buyer to reject (s 15A, SOGA 1979).

Where the contract is not severable, acceptance of some but not all of the goods will not prevent rejection of the remainder unless there is a contrary intention, express or implied, in the contract (s 35A, SOGA 1979). The right to reject some goods and accept others would extend to a single instalment under a severable contract.

10.4.1 Loss of right to reject goods

A buyer who has a right to reject the goods may lose that right in three separate ways: by waiver of any breach; by electing to affirm the contract and claim damages; or, by acceptance of the goods within the meaning of ss 11(4) and 35A, SOGA 1979. If the right to reject is lost the buyer will be able to claim damages only.

10.4.1.1 Waiver

Waiver is used in the ordinary contract law sense of one party excusing the other from proper performance of the contract and will not be binding unless:

(a) supported by consideration so as to amount to a binding variation of the contract (whereupon the label waiver becomes a misnomer); or

(b) the waiver falls within the doctrine of promissory estoppel which applies where there is a representation made by the buyer to the seller by words or conduct upon which the seller acts to his detriment so that it would be inequitable for the buyer to be permitted to enforce his strict legal rights: *Hughes v Metropolitan Railway Co* (1877) 2 App Cas 439, *Société Italo-Belge pour le Commerce et l'Industrie SA v Palm and Vegetable Oils (Malaysia) Snd Bhd (The Post Chaser)* [1982] 1 All ER 19.

Waiver will be rare in cases involving defective goods, but it would be possible for the buyer who gives some assurance to the seller which leads the seller not to deliver or tender further conforming goods to be estopped from rejecting the initial goods. The question of whether there has been an effective waiver is, as in other contracts, a mixed question of fact and law. The burden will be on the seller to show that it would be inequitable for the buyer to retract the waiver.

10.4.1.2 Affirmation

Affirmation is used in the ordinary contractual sense as an election to accept defective performance together with damages. Affirmation will place the buyer in the same position as though a breach of condition giving rise to the right to reject had been merely a breach of warranty. The difficult question is whether the buyer has to be aware of his right to reject before there can be an affirmation. At common law the position seems to be that knowledge of both (i) the facts giving rise to the right to elect, and (ii) of the right of election itself is required: *Peyman v Lanjani* [1985] Ch 457. The common-law doctrines of waiver and estoppel may also prevent rejection. The position in contracts for the sale of goods is altered by the provisions governing acceptance.

10.4.1.3 Acceptance of the goods

The concept of acceptance has already been considered in detail (**Chapter 8**). Section 35, SOGA 1979 sets out the rules for the buyer being deemed to have accepted the goods. Section 11(4), SOGA 1979 makes a breach of condition only a breach of warranty where the buyer has accepted the goods. Acceptance of all the goods will prevent rejection of any goods: acceptance of part of the goods will prevent rejection of that part only.

10.4.2 The effect of lawful rejection

If the buyer has a right to reject the goods and properly exercises that right the buyer can:

- claim the return of any money already paid upon a total failure of consideration;
- refuse to pay for the goods; and,
- the buyer may have a claim for further damages to reflect any loss suffered.

By s 36, SOGA 1979 the buyer is not bound to return the rejected goods to the seller unless the contract so provides: *Hammer & Barrow v Coca-Cola* [1962] NZLR 723. The goods remain or become the property of the seller and at his risk: *Kwei Tek Chao v British Traders & Shippers Ltd* [1954] 2 QB 459. The buyer as a bailee of the goods owes the seller a duty of care. The buyer may be able to claim the reasonable expense of looking after the goods as agent of necessity, or under the rule in *China Pacific SA v Food Corp of India (The Winson)* [1982] AC 939. The buyer cannot deal with the goods without the authority of the seller, nor can the buyer exercise a lien over the goods for return of any money already paid to the seller.

10.4.3 The effect of wrongful rejection

If the buyer rejects goods when he had no right to do so, or when he had lost his right to do so the purported rejection will be a repudiatory breach of contract by the buyer. The seller can elect to sue for the price: *Slea Shipping Corp v Bulk Oil International Ltd (The Alaskan Trader)* [1984] 1 All ER 129. Alternatively, if the breach is accepted by the seller, which will bring the contract to an end, the seller can sue for damages.

10.5 Remedies

The remedies which have to be considered in detail are recovery of money paid; damages; specific performance; and, miscellaneous remedies.

10.5.1 Recovery of money paid

The buyer will be able to recover any money paid upon a total failure of consideration if there has been a lawful rejection, and in the circumstances already outlined. Section 54, SOGA 1979 makes it plain that this right has been preserved. In addition, the buyer will be able to recover a part of the money paid where there is a divisible contract such as an instalment contract and where there has been an overpayment of money due under the contract (eg, where the price was fixed by weight and the delivery was light). Finally, a defaulting buyer may be able to recover a deposit or pre-payment from the seller when the contract is discharged, subject (a) to the seller's right to set off his damages claim and (b) any forfeiture clause.

10.5.2 Damages

The normal contractual rules of damages apply so that damages will be recovered under the first limb of *Hadley v Baxendale* (1854) 9 Ex 341 and, if the circumstances justify it, under the second limb. The normal rules of mitigation of damage apply, the burden being on the party alleging a failure to mitigate to prove it.

If the buyer rejects the goods the measure of damages will normally be the difference between the market price and the contract price (s 51, SOGA 1979). In addition, the buyer may claim any special damages and any interest (s 54, SOGA 1979).

If the buyer is unable to reject or has lost his right to reject the goods he may still recover damages where the goods are not in accordance with the contract. The measure of damages is governed by s 53 which provides that:

> *(1) Where there is a breach of warranty by the seller, or where the buyer elects (or is compelled) to treat any breach of a condition on the part of the seller as a breach of warranty, the buyer is not by reason only of such breach of warranty entitled to reject the goods; but he may—*
>
> *(a) set up against the seller the breach of warranty in diminution or extinction of the price, or*
>
> *(b) maintain an action against the seller for damages for the breach of warranty.*
>
> *(2) The measure of damages for breach of warranty is the estimated loss directly and naturally resulting, in the ordinary course of events, from the breach of warranty.*
>
> *(3) In the case of breach of warranty of quality such loss is prima facie the difference between the value of the goods at the time of delivery to the buyer and the value they would have had if they had fulfilled the warranty.*
>
> *(4) The fact that the buyer has set up the breach of warranty in diminution or extinction of the price does not prevent him from maintaining an action for the same breach of warranty if he has suffered further damage.*

10.5.2.1 Damages for non-delivery

Three special situations involving non-delivery need to be mentioned:

(a) if the seller knew that the goods were to be sold on by the buyer, the buyer may recover the normal loss of profits on the subsale, any damages which are paid to the sub-buyer, and occasionally the loss on repeat orders which are not then received by the buyer: *GKN Centrax Gears Ltd v Matbro Ltd* [1976] 2 Lloyd's Rep 555;

(b) if the buyer is able to buy the same goods from the seller at a reduced price, no loss will have been occasioned and no damages will be recovered (other than any consequential losses between the date of non-delivery and the actual purchase): *R. Pagan & Frateli v Corbisa Industrial Agropacuria Limitada* [1970] 1 WLR 1306;

(c) if the buyer has to buy better replacement goods at greater costs, if he has acted reasonably the additional costs will be recoverable without allowance for the better quality: *Blackburn Bobbin Co Ltd v T.W. Allen & Sons Ltd* [1918] 1 KB 540.

10.5.2.2 Damages for delayed delivery

The measure of damages for delayed delivery is not specified in SOGA 1979 but is the same as that for breach of the warranty. Two situations need to be mentioned:

(a) if there is an available market, the buyer may claim the difference between the market value at the time delivery should have taken place and the price when delivery actually happened but the effect on a resale will be irrelevant as the buyer could have obtained goods in the market to satisfy the sub-buyer: *Slater v Hoyle & Smith Ltd* [1920] 2 KB 11;

(b) loss of profits on the use of the goods may be claimed provided the use was within the reasonable contemplation of the parties: *Victoria Laundry (Windsor) Ltd v Newman Industries Ltd* [1949] 2 KB 528, but contrast *Cory v Thames Ironworks and Shipbuilding Co Ltd* (1868) LR 3 QB 181 where the peculiar use was not in the contemplation of the parties.

10.5.2.3 Delivery of defective goods

Four special situations involving defective delivery need to be mentioned:

(a) if the defect can be repaired the damages will be the costs of the repair together with any consequential claims for loss of profit on the use of the goods: *British Westinghouse Electrical Manufacturing v Underground Electric* [1912] AC 673;

(b) if the seller knew that the goods were to be sold on by the buyer, the buyer may recover the normal loss of profits on the subsale, any damages which are paid to the sub-buyer, and occasionally the loss on repeat orders which are not then received by the buyer: *GKN Centrax Gears Ltd v Matbro Ltd* [1976] 2 Lloyd's Rep 555 and *Bence Graphics International Ltd v Fasson UK Ltd* The Times, 24 October 1996;

(c) damages for consequential loss within the reasonable contemplation of the parties will include damage to property and persons, it is the type of loss which has to be in the contemplation of the parties and not the extent of the loss: *H Parsons (Livestock) Ltd v Uttley Ingham & Co Ltd* [1978] QB 791;

(d) an indemnity against claims from third parties may be recovered in addition to any loss of the buyer: *Lambert v Lewis* [1982] AC 225.

10.5.3 Specific performance

Claims for specific performance by buyers are comparatively rare. The right to specific performance is preserved by s 52, SOGA 1979 but is exercised in accordance with the usual practice of the court. Specific performance is a discretionary equitable remedy which will not be awarded where damages are an adequate remedy and is a claim to which the usual equitable defences apply (eg, laches, mistake, hardship). It seems that with contracts for the sale of goods the court requires the buyer to show that it is impossible rather than merely difficult to calculate the buyer's damages. In commercial terms the dividing line between difficulty and impossibility may be extremely difficult to draw: *Société des Industries Métallurgiques SA v The Bronx Engineering Co Ltd* [1975] 1 Lloyd's Rep 465, in which the remedy was refused. If the specific goods sold are unique or, at least, particularly unusual the test is more easily satisfied.

10.5.4 Other claims

In rare cases the buyer may seek an injunction against the seller. An injunction restraining a sale to anyone else can be coupled with an order for specific performance: *Behnke v Bede Shipping Co Ltd* [1927] 1 KB 649. Injunctions can also be an important remedy on breach of a 'solus' agreement where one party has agreed to deal only with the other: *Sky Petroleum Ltd v VIP Petroleum Ltd* [1974] 1 WLR 576 in which an injunction restraining the withholding of supplies until trial was granted. The common law doctrines of restraint of trade and any statutory restrictions in competition law may preclude the grant of an injunction, depending upon the facts of the case.

A declaration can be an important remedy for a buyer. If the buyer wishes to know whether he is discharged from further performance or whether a particular act amounts to a repudiatory breach a declaration can be sought: *Spettabile Consorzio Veneziano di Armamento e Navigazione v Northumberland Shipbuilding Co Ltd* (1919) 121 LT 628. A declaration can also be useful where it is necessary for one party to have a clear statement of rights which can be shown to third parties: *Patten v Burke Publishing Co Limited* [1991] 1 WLR 541.

The buyer may have a right to seek delivery up of the goods under the Torts (Interference with Goods) Act 1977, if he is already the owner thereof: *Howard E. Perry Co Ltd v British Railways Board* [1980] 1 WLR 1375.

The buyer may have a right of action in negligence against the manufacturers of defective goods if the damage is to person or property rather than pure economic loss. In addition the buyer may have a direct right of action against a manufacturer under the provisions of the Consumer Protection Act 1987.

10.6 Practical aspects of the claim by the buyer

The way in which a counterclaim can operate as a defence and the importance of carefully considering how to plead a cross-claim have already been considered (see **9.6**).

If the buyer has tendered the price to the seller but the seller has not accepted the money or has not released the goods the defence of tender before action will be available. The tender can only be used in liquidated claims: *John Laing Construction Ltd v Dastur* [1987] 1 WLR 686. The defence must be pleaded and the money must be paid into court. The defence of tender must be pleaded and the money tendered must be paid into court: CPR PD 16, para 16.2, r 37.3 and PD 37, para 2.1 (formerly RSC O 18, r 16; CCR O 9, r 12).

If the seller or a third party claims a lien on the goods and that lien is totally disputed or is disputed only as to the amount due, and the buyer's title to the goods is not in dispute, the buyer may apply to the court for an interim order that the goods be released on payment of the money claimed into court: CPR, r 25.1(m) (formerly RSC O 29, r 6 which was applied in the County Court by CCR O 13, r 7(1)(a)).

11 Electronic commerce

The growth of electronic commerce is expected to create a revolution in spending habits and the way in which business is conducted. The e-commerce industry expects a more rapid expansion in business than has been seen with credit and debit cards. Although the initial market expectations for e-commerce have not materialised, e-commerce is expanding rapidly. A comparison with the expansion of debit and credit cards is illuminating. These cards were first introduced in 1966. More than 90 million payment cards are currently in use in the UK (47 million debit cards and 43 million credit cards). The annual increase in credit card spending has been 15% in each of the last five years and now accounts for over £100 billion of annual consumer expenditure. Even if e-commerce expands at a similar rate (rather than the higher rate predicted) it will rapidly be a major element of consumer spending.

Many of the current court decisions about e-commerce have involved intellectual property rights in domain names, trade marks and passing off (including the new form known as cyber squatting). The courts have yet to deal with the way in which our existing law of sale and supply of goods fits in with e-commerce.

The aim of this chapter is to highlight some of the practical problems which the courts may have to grasp. Until specific laws for e-commerce are introduced, the courts will have to apply existing UK common law and statutory provisions.

The Consumer Protection (Distance Selling) Regulations 2000 apply to most forms of e-commerce (see **4.9**).

11.1 The types of contract

There seems little doubt that e-commerce contracts (like other contracts) can be either unilateral (known as option contracts in the USA) or bilateral contracts. Plainly, there must be at least two different parties to any contract. A unilateral contract is a contract in which only one party is contractually bound to take any action. In a bilateral contract both parties have binding obligations under the contract.

A unilateral contract is a contract which is normally accepted by performance of the obligation set out in the offer, without necessarily communicating acceptance to the offeror. The most famous example of a unilateral contract in English law is surely to be found in the case of *Carlill v Carbolic Smoke Ball Co Ltd* [1893] 1 QB 256. Prior to the Estate Agents Act 1979, the most common form of unilateral contract was a multiple estate agency contract for the sale of property. Each estate agent instructed was only paid commission if he or she was the effective cause of the sale of the property, but there was no contractual obligation on any of the agents to do anything to find such a sale (only a financial incentive to do so). With sole estate agencies the contract was arguably bilateral with the agent being obliged to make some efforts (eg, use reasonable endeavours) to find a purchaser. With the greater control of estate agents under the Estate Agents Act 1979 (and the regulations made thereunder) and the requirement for written contract terms, most estate agents now accept an obligation to make some efforts to sell the property so that the contract is a bilateral contract.

In e-commerce, sellers will often protect themselves from making unintended offers by making it plain that any advert is not an offer or a unilateral contract but merely an invitation to treat. The offer then comes from the buyer and, upon acceptance, a binding contract will be created. The seller will seek to equate his advertisement with a display of goods on the shelf of a shop which, in UK law is always regarded as an invitation to treat: *Pharmaceutical Society of Great Britain v Boots Cash Chemists (Southern) Ltd* [1951] 2 QB 795 and *Fisher v Bell* [1961] 1 QB 394. This approach enables the seller to select the acceptable customers and to control the volume of sales. If an offer is made on the Web which is accepted by customers merely contacting the seller, the seller will be at risk that more contracts are created than he or she can perform.

Finally, the courts may have to consider the effect of e-commerce auctions which are becoming increasingly common. Some are attempts to carry out a true auction with bids for a lot being made by e-mail rather than at the auction house or by telephone. Other sale described as auctions are more akin to a sale by tender where all bids are considered at the closing date of the tender period and the highest bid secures the lot. In a sale by auction s 57(2), SOGA 1979 provides that the sale is completed when the auctioneers hammer falls or in any other customary manner. In an e-commerce auction there is no hammer to fall and as yet, no other means of deciding the exact point of sale is sufficiently well known to be regarded as a customary manner.

11.2 Formation of the contract

The problems of forming a contract with e-commerce auctions have already been mentioned. As there are no mandatory formalities for the creation of a contract for the sale of goods or supply of services, it is not necessary to consider when an e-commerce contract would be a contract in writing nor when a signature can be said to exist in e-commerce.

Whether the offer is made by the seller or the buyer, at some point the courts will have to deal with the problem of garbled offers or acceptances. The commercial cases on garbled telexes and facsimiles suggest that the court will have to adopt a flexible approach to e-commerce. An interesting but, as yet, unresolved question is whether the court will try to apply the postal acceptance rule to e-commerce. It could be argued that the court will not apply the postal acceptance rule, adopting the same approach as to telexes: *Brinkibon v Stahag Stahl und Stahlwarenhandelsgellschaft mbH* [1983] AC 34. However, telexes and facsimiles are transmitted direct and the sender ought to be able to tell whether they have been received properly. E-mail is different as the message is sent over the internet and control of the message is lost (rather like posting a letter to someone).

A further complication with e-commerce will be deciding the timing of offers and acceptances. In the case of facsimiles and telexes the court has adopted the approach that an acceptance sent outside normal business hours will be deemed effective only on the opening of normal business hours: *Schelde Delta Shipping BV v Astarte Shipping Ltd*

(The Pamela) [1995] 2 Lloyd's Rep 249. Quite how far the court will take the concept of normal business hours using e-commerce remains to be seen.

E-commerce is likely to force the court to give further consideration to other areas of contract law. As minors use computers, the issue of the validity and enforcement of minors' contracts is likely to arise. Equally, issues about the identity of the parties to the contract may cause new problems. Where there is a mistake as to the identity of one of the parties will the court adopt the approach that a e-commerce transaction is made between the parties in the presence of each other so that the presumption is that the parties intended to contract with each other, or will the contract be regarded as in writing so that the persons bound are the persons named and no one else? Some of the problems about the identity of parties may be avoided by the use of passwords, pin numbers and other security devices.

Now that the Distance Selling Directive is in force (see **4.9**) this will apply to e-commerce where one party is a consumer and the other acts in the course of his or her business. Further regulation will exist if the current proposal for a EU Directive on e-commerce in the internal market results in a Directive being issued and that Directive is then made into UK law. Unfortunately this seems a long way off.

11.3 Terms of the contract

E-commerce is likely to cause a rush of new decisions over the incorporation of standard terms of trading and onerous contract terms. Before considering whether a term may be void or unfair within the statutory regime (see **Chapter 4**), the courts will have to consider whether the term is incorporated into the contract at all. In e-commerce there are currently four main options for incorporating standard terms:

(a) first, the advertisement for goods or services could merely refer to the existence of standard terms of trading which are either not available unless requested, or are available elsewhere on the Web;

(b) secondly, there could be a reference to the standard terms with a hyperlink to the actual terms of trading — this is a popular option as, by comparison to the well-known ticket cases, the terms may be held to be incorporated into the contract even if they have not been read;

(c) thirdly, the terms could be displayed as part of the advertisement. This is not a popular option as it detracts from the advertisement and, as with a hyperlink, the buyer may still not read the terms;

(d) fourthly, the terms can be incorporated into some type of order form or order system in which the buyer has to confirm that he or she has read and accepted the standard terms before the order can be placed or will be accepted. This is the best way for a seller to ensure that his or her standard terms are incorporated into the contract.

The various ways of incorporating standard terms have to be considered in the light of the distinction between invitations to treat and offers. If the advertisement contains detailed terms of trading that may suggest that the advertisement is, in UK law, an offer. An advertiser who wishes to avoid this risk can adopt the fourth option above so that the buyer sending the completed standard order form back (incorporating the sellers standard terms of trading) makes the offer which the seller can then accept.

11.4 Payment

Much of the press comment upon e-commerce has focused on the risks of giving credit, debit card or bank account details out over the Web. The evidence does not suggest that this practice is markedly more dangerous than allowing a shop assistant to take away a debit or credit card to process it, or using a debit or credit card for telephone booking and ordering. The risks of unauthorised access to these details is reduced if one of the encryption systems is used to transact any business. The UK Government has made proposals to licence systems for secure cryptography. The White Paper was issued on 1 July 1998. It is not yet clear when legislation will be enacted.

11.5 Jurisdiction

E-commerce will also raise interesting issues of jurisdiction. The courts will have to decide the proper law of the contract and which country has jurisdiction over disputes in relation to the contract. At present, this will be decided by the courts on the same basis as other jurisdictional issues.

12 Checklists

The purpose of these short checklists is to give a quick guide to the provisions you may have to consider when dealing with common practical sale of goods problems. They are each based on the assumption that the contract is a sale of goods contract.

12.1 The seller is relying upon general 'small print' in the contract to avoid or limit his liability

- Is the small print incorporated into the contract? See **3.3**.
- What is the correct interpretation of the small print? See **3.4**.
- Can the small print be avoided as unusual or onerous terms? See **3.5**.
- Was or is the agreement cancellable? See **4.4**.
- Does UCTA 1977 apply? See **4.3**.
- Do the Unfair Terms in Consumer Contracts Regulations apply? See **4.5**.

12.2 The seller has not delivered the goods at all

- What is the delivery obligation? See **7.3**.
- Can time now be made of the essence? See **7.2**.
- Is there a repudiation of the contract which can be accepted? See **10.1**.

12.3 The seller is demanding payment before delivery

- What were the payment terms of the contract? See **8.4**.
- If nothing was expressly or impliedly agreed? See **8.4.1**.

12.4 A third party is claiming title to the goods

- What were the stipulations as to title in the contract? See **3.10**.
- Did the buyer acquire title under an exception to the *nemo dat* rule? See **6.2**.
- Can the buyer reject the goods? See **10.3**.

12.5 The buyer finds the goods unsatisfactory

- Was the contract a sale by description or sample? See **3.10.2**, **3.10.4**.
- Are the goods of satisfactory quality? See **3.10.3**.
- Was the defect drawn to the attention of the buyer? See **3.10.3**.
- Was the defect apparent from the examination of the goods? See **8.3**.
- Are the goods fit for their purpose? See **10.3.3**.
- Were the goods for a specific purpose? See **10.3.3**.
- Can the buyer reject? See **10.3.6**.
- Can the buyer obtain damages? See **10.5**.
- Is this a consumer contract made after 31 March 2003, so the buyer can use the new statutory remedies? See **10.3**.

Part II

Consumer credit

13

Introduction

In modern Britain it is virtually certain that most people will enter into some form of credit agreement (whether in the form of a loan, use of a credit card or entry into a hire-purchase or conditional sale agreement) to finance a major transaction in the course of their lives. Much litigation arises from such credit transactions and the civil practitioner can expect to deal with these cases almost as a matter of routine.

13.1 Scope of the Manual

Restriction of space prevents an examination of the full scope of consumer credit law. This Manual deals with only some of the main features of the law and practice of unregulated and regulated consumer credit agreements. Hire-purchase agreements, conditional sale agreements, credit sales and fixed term loans are dealt with as fully as space allows. Credit card transactions are examined cursorily in **Chapter 24** but fare more happily than, for example, mortgages (and any transaction involving land) and leases (known as consumer hire agreements in the Consumer Credit Act 1974) which are not considered at all in this Manual. There is no mention (save for this) of the regulatory and licensing regime, although it is important, or of the criminal offences. Discussion of these areas can be found in the further reading materials referred to at the end of this chapter.

13.2 Primary legislation

Just as SOGA 1979 is the towering monolith of the law relating to sale of goods, so the Consumer Credit Act 1974 (CCA 1974) towers over the law relating to consumer credit. However, as we shall see, it applies only to some consumer credit transactions. Since most consumer credit finances transactions involving the sale and supply of goods and services it is necessary to bear in mind the provisions of SOGA 1979, SOGITA 1973 and SOGSA 1982 (see **Chapter 4**). Statutes relating generally to the law of contract are also of some importance, eg, UCTA 1977, the Consumer Protection Act 1987 and the Misrepresentation Act 1967. The Timeshare Act 1992 contains regulatory provisions over the extension of credit by a creditor who knows or ought to know that it is to be used to purchase a timeshare.

13.3 Secondary legislation

CCA 1974 has spawned a large and complex regime of regulations and orders. Indeed, in laying down a skeleton in the form of the Act and flesh in the form of the regulations made under it, it can be regarded as a model of much recent legislation. The most important regulations are mentioned as necessary in the text. Apart from them, bear in mind the provisions of the Consumer Protection (Cancellation of Contracts Concluded away from Business Premises) Regulations 1987 (see **Chapters 4** and **16**).

13.4 Cases

Cases involving credit transactions appear in all the major series of law reports and some specialist series. Since CCA 1974 re-enacted some provisions of the old Hire Purchase Acts, cases on those Acts can still be of some relevance — but always check whether CCA 1974 has changed the statutory picture. Bear in mind that since most litigation involving interpretation of and practice under CCA 1974 is heard in the county court and involves relatively small sums of money (so appeals to the Court of Appeal are relatively rare), there is a dearth of reported cases about the workings of CCA 1974.

13.5 Further reading

There are three main practitioner books in widespread use:

Benion, Consumer Credit Control, Sweet & Maxwell (a looseleaf work) which includes the Consumer Credit Law Reports (CCLR).

Encyclopedia of Consumer Credit, Sweet & Maxwell (a looseleaf work).

Goode, Consumer Credit Law and Practice, Butterworths (a looseleaf work) which includes Goode, Consumer Credit Reports (GCCR).

14

Applications of CCA 1974 and definitions thereunder

In every case the vital preliminary stage is to examine whether the agreement is regulated by the Consumer Credit Act 1974 (CCA 1974).

Enacted on the recommendations of the Crowther Report (Report of the Committee on Consumer Credit under the Chairmanship of Lord Crowther, Cmnd 4596 (1971)), CCA 1974 provides a compendious, although not exhaustive, code to the accommodation of credit. Many agreements are regulated by the Act and a working knowledge of it is therefore vital.

Unfortunately, before we can come to grips with CCA 1974, we need to understand the definitions it uses. Note that the statutory definitions of hire-purchase, conditional sale and credit sale agreement codify the common law position. The definitions which appear below therefore apply equally well to unregulated hire-purchase, conditional sale and credit sale agreements. That apart, do not use terms created by CCA 1974 in relation to unregulated agreements. This Manual contains a solecism in that (for ease of convenience) it refers to 'creditor' and 'debtor' in relation to unregulated agreements when the correct legal terminology is 'owner' and 'hirer' in respect of hire-purchase agreements and 'owner' and 'buyer' in respect of conditional sale and credit sale agreements.

14.1 Application of the 1974 Act

CCA 1974 applies to all agreements which meet the following criteria:

(a) The debtor must be an individual. An individual is defined by s 189 as including a partnership or unincorporated body of persons not consisting entirely of bodies corporate. Thus limited companies are not individuals but, for example, solicitors' firms and barristers' chambers are.

(b) The credit provided by the creditor must not exceed a specified limit. There have been three different limits during the lifetime of the Act. Until 19 May 1985 the limit was £5,000. Between 20 May 1985 and 30 April 1998 the limit was £15,000. Since 1 May 1998 the limit has been £25,000.

(c) The agreement must not be exempt under s 16 or the Consumer Credit (Exempt Agreements) Order 1989. For present purposes it serves to note that:

(i) No hire-purchase agreement or conditional sale agreement is exempt.

(ii) No credit sale agreement (or other fixed sum debtor–creditor supplier agreement) is exempt unless the debtor is to repay the credit in four instalments or less.

(iii) A running-account debtor–creditor–supplier agreement is exempt if the debtor is required to make a single periodic payment in settlement of the account (eg, a charge card: see **24.1.3**).

(iv) A debtor–creditor agreement is exempt if the total charge for credit is interest alone at a rate which cannot be higher than bank base rate plus 1% or 13% (so an interest-free or low interest loan is exempt).

14.1.1 Agreements which are exempt from some of the 1974 Act's provisions

We have just seen that some types of agreement are totally exempt from the provisions of CCA 1974. Now we must briefly note two types of agreement which are exempt from many of the Act's strictures.

14.1.1.1 Non-commercial agreements

Non-commercial agreements are agreements into which a creditor does not enter in the course of business.

14.1.1.2 Small agreements

These are agreements for credit not exceeding £50. This exemption does not, however, extend to hire-purchase or conditional sale agreements (not that there is ever likely to be such an agreement for credit of less than £50).

14.2 Definitions

14.2.1 'Creditor' and 'debtor'

A creditor is defined by s 189 as a person who extends credit under a consumer credit agreement. A debtor is defined by s 189 as an individual who receives credit under a consumer credit agreement.

14.2.2 Hire-purchase agreements

Under a hire-purchase agreement, possession of the goods but not title to them, passes to the debtor straight away. The debtor may, but is not obliged to, take title to the goods. Title may pass in one of the following ways:

(a) when the agreement expires by effluxion of time unless the debtor exercises a right to terminate before then (ie, the debtor has to do something to stop himself acquiring title);

(b) when the agreement confers on the debtor an option to purchase the goods by payment of a further sum (ie, the debtor has to do something in order to acquire title).

14.2.3 Conditional sale agreements

At common law, a conditional sale agreement is identical to a hire-purchase agreement except that title will automatically pass to the debtor at the end of the agreement. However, as will be seen in **Chapter 22**, if a conditional sale agreement is regulated by the CCA 1974, the debtor can avoid taking title by terminating the agreement. The debtor in a regulated conditional sale agreement is deemed not to have bound himself to buy (s 25(2), SOGA 1979).

When considering whether an agreement takes effect as a hire-purchase or conditional sale agreement the court looks at the substance of the agreement and not the form. This is illustrated by *Forthright Finance Ltd v Carlyle Finance Ltd* [1997] 4 All ER 90. In that case an agreement was described as a hire-purchase agreement. One clause provided that when the debtor had discharged all sums owing to the creditor then he would be deemed to have exercised the option to purchase. Another clause provided that the debtor could avoid taking title by giving notice to the creditor before paying all the sums due under the agreement. The Court of Appeal held that the agreement was a conditional sale agreement. One would expect the debtor to exercise the option not to take title only in the most unusual circumstances. The Court of Appeal noted but did not decide an argument that an agreement which included a positive option to take title for a nominal payment would be a conditional sale agreement rather than a hire-purchase agreement.

In *Close Asset Finance Ltd v Care Graphics Machinery Ltd* [2000] GCCR 2617 the High Court on appeal from the Master had to decide whether an agreement with a £50 option fee to purchase the goods was a hire-purchase agreement or a conditional sale agreement. The value of the goods was about £2.5 million so the fee of £50 was, arguably, nominal. The court distinguished the *Forthright Finance* case on the ground that, in that case, there was an automatic deemed exercise of the option without further payment if all instalments had been paid. This particular agreement was therefore a hire-purchase agreement and outside s 25, SOGA 1979 (on the same ground it would have been outside s 9, Factors Act 1889).

14.2.4 Credit sale agreements

As with a conditional sale agreement, title is obliged to pass from the creditor to the debtor. However, unlike a conditional sale agreement title passes when the agreement is entered into (subject to the rules in sale of goods about specific and unascertained property). In effect, whereas with hire-purchase and conditional sale agreements the creditor has the security of ownership of the goods for the credit it has given to the debtor, in a credit sale agreement it is giving unsecured credit to the debtor.

14.2.5 Credit and total charge for credit

Credit is defined by s 9 of the Act as 'a cash loan or any other form of financial accommodation'. This definition was considered by the Court of Appeal in *Dimond v Lovell* [1999] 3 WLR 561. Scott V-C said that credit involved 'the deferral of payment of a sum which, absent of agreement, would be immediately payable'. The subsequent appeal in the House of Lords did not really address this issue and it is submitted that the Court of Appeal's definition is binding.

The definition adopted by the Court of Appeal is potentially extremely wide and it is likely that it will take some time for the implications to be tested. At first blush it would appear, for example, to include solicitors who agree to wait for an unsuccessful litigant to pay a cost order before pursuing their own client for costs. The Court of Appeal's definition has been subject to academic criticism (see especially Goode) and it seems likely that the issue will be tested again in the courts.

It is important to distinguish between the amount of credit extended to the debtor and the cost to him of taking the credit:

(a) In *Watchtower Investments Ltd v Payne* [2001] EWCA Civ 1159 the Court of Appeal had to consider whether in a re-mortgage the agreement was enforceable or unenforceable, which turned on whether the payment made to discharge the mortgage arrears was part of the credit or part of the cost of the credit. The Court of Appeal decided that the purpose of the loan was a re-mortgage and so the discharge of the earlier arrears was part of the credit and not part of the cost of the credit. The case was then remitted for other issues to be determined.

(b) In *McGinn v Grangewood Securities Ltd* [2002] GCCR 251 the Court of Appeal was concerned with appeals from decisions in the county court. The Court of Appeal expressed some surprise and horror that one of the county court hearings had lasted eight days. The Court decided that where arrears on an earlier mortgage were discharged as a condition of the further advance, they were part of the cost of the credit and fell within the definition of the total charge for credit. This resulted in the agreement being unenforceable and it was not necessary for the court to decide other questions on broker's fees and legal costs, although views were expressed. This is a highly questionable decision. It is odd to distinguish between the situation where the borrower wishes to discharge earlier credit (whether in arrears or not) so the money advanced to do so is the 'purpose' of the loan and not the cost of the new loan, from the situation where in order to obtain the new loan there is a requirement to discharge arrears. The absurdity of this situation is increased when it is noted that there is no requirement to specify the purpose of the loan in the agreement, so that the creditor who does so where it is to pay off earlier credit is placing in jeopardy the enforceability of the agreement.

Thus, in the case of a hire-purchase agreement, for example, the 'credit' element of the agreement is the creditor's agreement to let the debtor pay for the goods after delivery (whereas normally payment and delivery are concurrent conditions (s 28, SOGA 1979)). In considering whether credit falls above or below the £25,000 regulatory limit, reference must be made to the capital amount borrowed by the debtor. Interest is excluded. Thus where Mr Bloggs is advanced £24,999 by a finance house in order to buy a car, the agreement will be regulated (all other criteria being satisfied) even if the agreement provides that he has to repay over £30,000 because of the interest being charged on the money lent. Similarly, whilst in any commercial hire-purchase, conditional sale or credit sale agreement the total credit bargain will exceed the sale price of the goods (since the creditor will want to make a profit on the transaction) it is the sale price of the goods (subject to deduction of any deposit) which determines whether or not the agreement is regulated by the CCA 1974.

The total charge for credit is defined by s 20 and the Consumer Credit (Total Charge for Credit) Regulations 1980. The basic idea is that it includes all charges (including interest) which the debtor is obliged to incur under the terms of the agreement and which he would not have had to incur had he entered into the same supply transaction for cash. Therefore, for example, the cost of having goods delivered does not fall within the total charge for credit but the option to purchase fee in a hire-purchase agreement does. **Form 14.1**, taken from a regulated hire-purchase agreement, shows how different charges are split between the statutory definitions of credit and total charge for credit.

In order to ensure that all creditors quote the same cost for the credit they offer, s 20 requires all advertisements and agreements to quote an annual percentage rate (APR). The APR is calculated according to complex formulae in the Consumer Credit (Total Charge for Credit) Regulations 1980. The APR reflects not just the interest charged on the credit afforded to the debtor, but the overall cost to him of the credit.

Form 14.1

Financial Details and Payments			
Particulars of Goods		**Cash Price incl. VAT**	
Qty.	Description	£	p
	Identification Nos:		
	Total Cash Price (incl. VAT)	£	
	Less: Pt.Ex. £______ Cash £______ = Deposit (a)	£	
	= Amount of Credit	£	
	Hire Purchase Charge £______		
	Documentation Fee* £______		
	Option to Purchase Fee* £______		
	= Total Charge for Credit	£	
	APR______%		
	Balance Payable (b)	£	
	Payable by:		
	A first payment (including documentation fee) of:†	£	
	______ payments each of:	£	
	A final payment (incl. option fee) of:†	£	
	Each payment payable the same day of each succeeding month, commencing ______		
	Total Amount Payable (a) + (b)	£	

*Must include VAT if together more than £10 in total. Omit if not needed.

†Delete if not needed.

14.2.6 Restricted-use credit

This concept is created by s 11 of the CCA 1974. A restricted-use credit agreement is an agreement which does not leave the debtor free to choose how he uses the credit supplied to him by the creditor. Any other credit agreement is an unrestricted-use credit agreement.

Thus all hire-purchase, conditional sale and credit sale agreements are restricted-use credit agreements because the debtor has no choice about how he uses the credit facility which the creditor has afforded him. It is always for the goods the subject matter of the agreement.

A loan, however, may be a restricted-use or unrestricted-use credit agreement depending upon the terms upon which it is granted. A loan to buy a car is restricted — use if it must be used for the purchase of the car.

14.2.7 Debtor–creditor–supplied agreements and debtor–creditor agreements

Sections 12 and 13, CCA 1974 create the concept of debtor–creditor–supplier agreements (also known as DCS agreements) and debtor–creditor agreements (also known as DC agreements). The practical importance of the distinction is that the debtor may have legal remedies against the creditor in a debtor–creditor–supplier agreement if the goods are faulty (see **Chapter 23**), but that he will have no such remedy against the creditor in a debtor–creditor agreement.

14.2.7.1 Definition of debtor–creditor agreements

This is easy! A debtor–creditor agreement is an agreement that is not a debtor–creditor–supplier agreement.

14.2.7.2 Definition of debtor–creditor–supplier agreement

A debtor–creditor–supplier agreement can be created in three ways:

(a) Section 12(a)

Where the agreement is a restricted-use credit agreement which is being used to finance a transaction between the debtor and creditor. All hire-purchase agreements, conditional sale and credit sale agreements are debtor–creditor–supplier agreements. This is because the credit is always being used to finance a transaction (ie, the sale of goods) between the debtor and creditor. This is because the creditor in such an agreement is always the legal supplier of the goods even if it does not actually deliver them to the debtor or even see them.

(b) Section 12(b)

Where the agreement is a restricted-use agreement to finance a transaction between the debtor and a third party (the supplier) and is made by the creditor under a pre-existing arrangement, or in contemplation of a future arrangement, with the supplier. All purchases by credit card (apart from store cards — see **Chapter 24**) fall within s 12(b) as there will be a pre-existing arrangement with the card company that they can be used, and so do some personal loans.

(c) Section 12(c)

Where an unrestricted-use credit agreement is made by the creditor under pre-existing arrangements with the supplier in the knowledge that the credit is to be used to finance a transaction between the debtor and the supplier. These loans are relatively rare — an example would arise if a supplier has arranged for a finance house to make personal loans to his customers and the finance house makes the loan to the debtor. In practice, most finance houses either make loans in the form of a cheque made payable to the supplier (so the transaction would be within s 12(b)) or do not make the loan pursuant to pre-existing arrangements with the supplier (eg, a bank loan for a fitted kitchen would be a debtor–creditor agreement rather than a debtor–creditor–supplier agreement).

14.2.8 'Fixed sum' and 'running account credit'

Although these are important concepts they can be dealt with quite shortly since this book does not deal with running account credit agreements. 'Fixed sum' credit is credit involving one single advance. Thus all hire-purchase, conditional sale and credit sale agreements are fixed sum credit agreements. Running-account credit, however, allows the debtor a fluctuating level of credit up to a prescribed limit, for example, bank overdrafts, credit cards or charge cards.

14.2.9 Linked transactions

A linked transaction is a transaction which is ancillary to the principal credit agreement. An example would be a maintenance contract on a photocopier which was the subject of a regulated hire-purchase agreement. The importance of defining linked transactions is that they are automatically cancelled under s 69 of the Act if the debtor cancels the principal agreement (cancellation is dealt with in **Chapter 16**).

14.2.9.1 Definition of a linked transaction

Section 19 defines linked transactions as:

- a transaction which the debtor is obliged to enter into under a term of the principal agreement; or
- a transaction financed by a debtor–creditor–supplier agreement; or
- a transaction which was entered into by the debtor at the suggestion of the creditor (or someone with a business connection with him):

  to induce the creditor to enter into the principal agreement; or

  for another purpose related to the principal agreement; or

  for a purpose related to a transaction financed by the principal agreement where the principal agreement is a restricted-use credit agreement.

We must note four exceptions to these definitions. The first appears in s 19 itself and the others in the Consumer Credit (Linked Transactions) (Exemptions) Regulations 1983 (SI 1983 No 1560). They are:

- contracts of security (eg, guarantee or indemnity);
- insurance contracts;
- contracts of guarantee of goods; and
- transactions comprising (or made under) any agreement for the operation of a deposit or current account.

There is considerable criticism of the second and third exemptions. These can leave a consumer liable for insurance premiums for goods which he has not received, or paying for a warranty on goods after he has cancelled an order for those goods. The fourth exemption is intended to cover a situation where a debtor opens a current account with a bank in order to obtain a loan: withdrawal from the loan does not make the current account inoperative.

15

Formalities of regulated agreements and enforcement orders

Sections 60 to 65, CCA 1974, and the regulations thereunder, contain detailed provisions about the form and content of regulated agreements. There are no equivalent requirements about the form and content of unregulated agreements save for the common law rules applicable to all contracts (see **Chapter 3**).

The practical importance of complying with the requirements of CCA 1974 is that an agreement which does not comply with the formalities is 'improperly executed'. An improperly executed agreement will not be enforceable by the creditor without leave of the court (s 65) and may not be enforceable at all (s 127) (the debtor, on the other hand, will always be able to enforce an agreement whether or not it complies with the statutory requirements). To assist you in deciding whether or not an agreement is properly executed and, if not, whether it is enforceable, see the flowchart reproduced as **Form 15.1**.

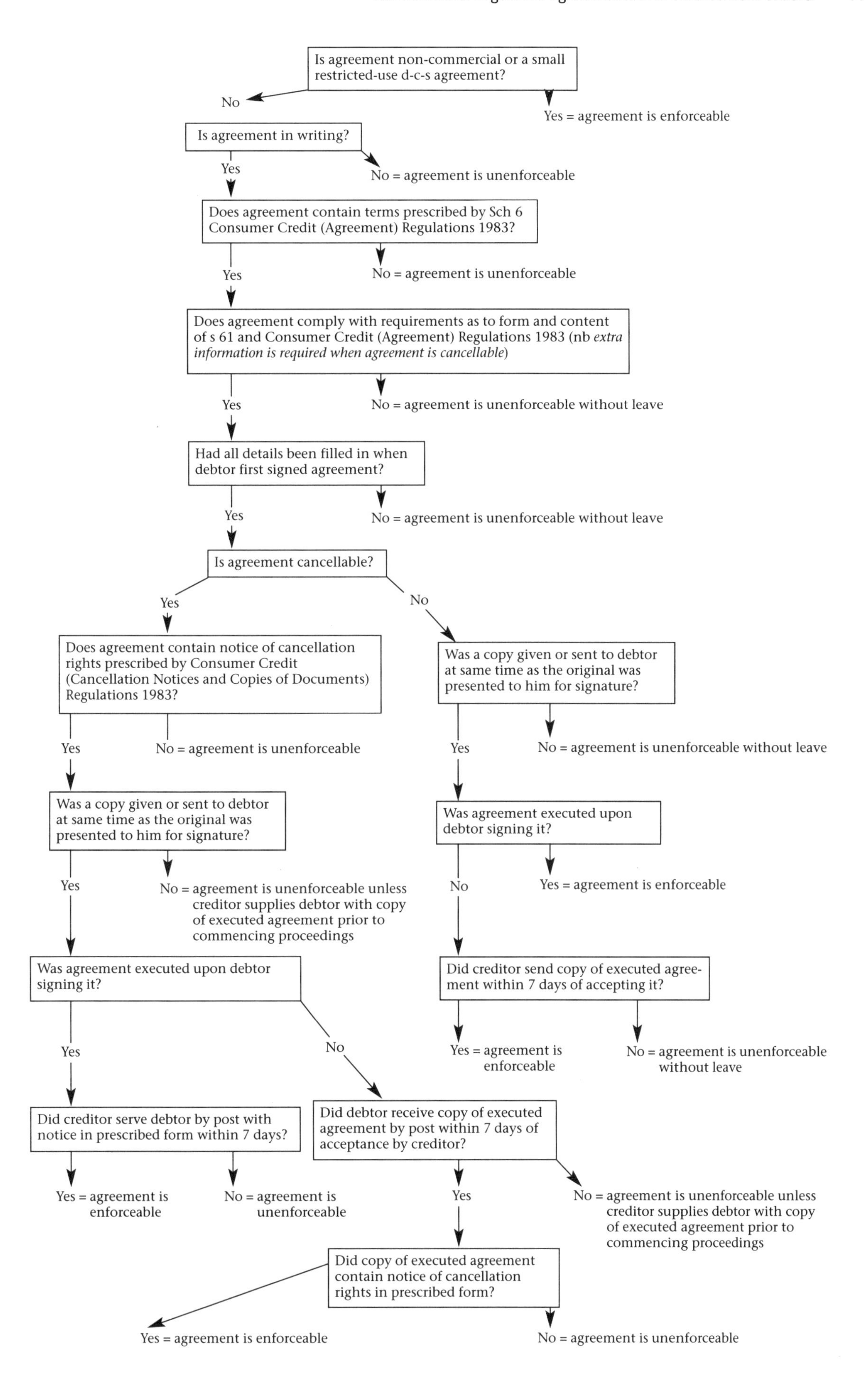

Form 15.1 Is a regulated consumer credit agreement enforceable?

Certain agreements are excepted from these requirements. These are non-commercial agreements, or any small, restricted-use debtor–creditor–supplier agreements. For present purposes it serves to note that no hire-purchase or conditional sale agreement is excepted save for a non-commercial one (ie, where the creditor is not acting in the course of business) and no credit sale agreement for over £50 is excepted save for a non-commercial one. In other words, most agreements which become the subject of litigation are covered by the formality provisions.

The aim of the provisions of CCA 1974 is to ensure that a prospective debtor is aware of the terms and costs of the agreement into which he is about to enter and of his rights and obligations under it. The provisions even extend to ensuring the legibility of documents.

15.1 Prescribed terms

Schedule 6 to the Consumer Credit (Agreements) Regulations 1983 (SI 1983 No 1553) contains prescribed terms which must be included in writing in an agreement. If they are absent, the creditor cannot enforce the agreement. There are different prescribed terms for different types of agreement. In the case of hire-purchase, conditional sale and credit sale agreements the prescribed terms are the time and amount of repayments by the debtor and any power of the creditor to vary what is payable.

15.2 Prescribed form

The agreement must be in the prescribed form. If it is not, it is an improperly executed agreement (s 65) and is enforceable only with the leave of the court (s 127).

In the case of a restricted-use debtor–creditor–supplier agreement for fixed-sum credit to finance the acquisition of identified or specified goods or services the required contents are:

- the appropriate heading (eg, Hire-Purchase Agreement regulated by the Consumer Credit Act 1974);
- the names and addresses of the parties to the agreement;
- a description of the goods to which the agreement relates and the cash price thereof;
- the amount of any advance payment or deposit;
- the amount of credit;
- the total charge for credit;
- the total amount payable;
- the APR;
- details of any charges that accrue if the debtor is in default;
- details of any security supplied by the debtor.

In addition, there is certain other compulsory information which must appear in the agreement. This includes notice of the debtor's statutory rights to terminate a hire-purchase or conditional sale agreement early (see **Chapter 22**) and the wording of information which must appear in a box provided for the debtor's signature. An example of a regulated cancellable hire-purchase agreement which complies with the statutory requirements is reproduced as **Form 15.2**.

Form 15.2

HPC (g) **Hire-Purchase Agreement** *regulated by the Consumer Credit Act 1974* **Second Copy**

With right of cancellation

Agreement No. 3789758

This Hire-Purchase Agreement sets out below and overleaf the terms on which we (the owners) agree to let and you (the customer) agree to hire the goods described below:

The Owners (Name and address) RALPH NICKLEBY FINANCE PLC
GOLDEN SQUARE LONDON

The Customer (Full names please) WACKFORD SQUEERS

Address DOTHEBOYS HALL, DOTHEBOYS, YORKSHIRE

Financial Details and Payments

Qty.	Description (Particulars of Goods)	Cash Price incl. VAT £	p
20	ENCYCLOPEDIAS	2000	00
	Identification Nos:		
	Total Cash Price (incl. VAT)	£ 2000	00
	Less: Pt.Ex. £ ____ Cash £ 200 – Deposit (a)	£ 200	00
	– Amount of Credit	£ 1800	00
	Hire Purchase Charge £ 360		
	Documentation Fee* £ ____		
	Option to Purchase Fee* £ ____		
	– Total Charge for Credit	£ 360	00
	APR 19.75 %		
	Balance Payable (b)	£ 2160	00
	Payable by: A first payment (including documentation fee) of: †	£ 90	00
	22 payments each of:	£ 90	00
	A final payment (incl. option fee) of: †	£ 90	00
	Each payment payable the same day of each succeeding month, commencing 1 JUNE 1997		
	Total Amount Payable (a) + (b)	£ 2360	00

*Must include VAT if together more than £10 in total. Omit if not needed.

† Delete if not needed.

Signature of (or on behalf of) Owners S. Room

Date of Owners' Signature (Date of Agreement) 1-5-97

TERMINATION: YOUR RIGHTS

You have a right to end this agreement. If you wish to do so, you should write to the person authorised to receive your payments. We will then be entitled to the return of the goods and to half the total amount payable under this agreement, that is £ ____ .[1] If you have already paid at least this amount plus any overdue instalments, you will not have to pay any more, provided you have taken reasonable care of the goods.

1 Insert one half of the total amount payable

REPOSSESSION: YOUR RIGHTS

If you fail to keep to your side of this agreement but you have paid at least one third of the total amount payable under this agreement, that is £ ____ ,[2] we may not take back the goods against your wishes unless we get a court order. (In Scotland, we may need to get a court order at any time.) If we do take them without your consent or a court order, you have the right to get back all the money you have paid under the agreement.

2 Insert one third of the total amount payable.

DECLARATION BY CUSTOMER

By signing this agreement you declare that:

- ★ You have carefully examined the goods and your attention has been drawn to Clause 12 overleaf.
- ★ The information given by you before entering into this agreement is correct. You realise that we will rely on that information in deciding whether to enter into this agreement.
- ★ You are aware that before granting credit we may search the files of one or more credit reference agencies which will keep a record of our enquiry. We may also disclose details about the account and your conduct of it to that agency (or agencies). Information thus held is used only to help make credit decisions or occasionally for fraud prevention or tracing debtors.

This is a Hire-Purchase Agreement regulated by the Consumer Credit Act 1974. Sign it only if you want to be legally bound by its terms.

Signature(s) of Customer(s) Wackford Squeers

Date(s) of Signature(s) 25th April, 1997

The goods will not become your property until you have made all the payments. You must not sell them before then.

This is a copy of your agreement for you to keep.

It includes a notice about your cancellation rights which you should read.

See overleaf for notice of cancellation rights

Witness: Signature J Browdie

Name (Block letters please) JOHN BROWDIE

Address 2 COBBLESTONE ROAD
GRIMSDALE YORKSHIRE

✂ CANCELLATION FORM

(Complete and return this form ONLY IF YOU WISH TO CANCEL THE AGREEMENT).

To: ____ [1]

I/We* hereby give notice that I/we* wish to cancel agreement ____ [2].

Signed ____

Date ____

Name ____

Address ____

Notes for cancellation form:

1 Owners to insert name and address.
2 Owners to insert reference number, code or other identification details.
* Delete inapplicable pronoun.

HPC (g) Second

TERMS OF THE AGREEMENT

1 Payment

Before signing this agreement you must have paid the deposit shown overleaf. By signing this agreement you agree to pay the Balance Payable by making the payments set out overleaf, by their specified dates, to us at the address stated overleaf or to any person or address notified by us in writing. Punctual payment is essential. If you pay by post you do so at your own risk.

2 Failure to pay on time

We have the right to charge interest at the annual percentage rate shown overleaf (less that part attributable to any documentation or option to purchase fee) on all overdue amounts. This interest will be calculated on a daily basis from the date the amount falls due until it is received and will run before and after any judgment.

3 Ownership of the goods

You will become the owner of the goods only after we have received payment off all amounts payable under this agreement, including under Clauses 2 and 11, and any option to purchase fee shown overleaf. Until then the goods remain our property and your rights are solely those of a hirer.

4 Selling or disposing of the goods

You must keep the goods safely at your address and you may not sell or dispose of them or transfer your rights under this agreement. You may only part with the goods to have them repaired. You may not use the goods as security for any of your obligations.

5 Repair of the goods

You must keep the goods in good condition and repair at your own expense. You are responsible for all loss of or damage to them (except fair wear and tear) even if caused by acts or events outside your control. You must not allow a repairer or any other person to obtain a lien on or a right to retain the goods.

6 Change of address

You must immediately notify us in writing of any change of your address.

7 Inspection

You must allow us or our representative to inspect and test the goods at all reasonable times.

8 Insurance of the goods

You must keep the goods insured under a fully comprehensive policy of insurance at your own expense. You must notify us of any loss of or damage to the goods and hold any monies payable under the policy in trust for us. You irrevocably authorise us to collect the monies from the insurers. If a claim is made against the insurers we may at our absolute discretion conduct any negotiations and effect any settlement of the claim with the insurers. You agree to abide by such settlement and to pay us any shortfall under the agreement. Subject to the provisions of Clause 10 any loss of or damage to the goods shall not affect the continuance of this agreement.

9 Your right to end the agreement

You have the right to end this agreement as set out in the notice 'Termination: Your Rights' overleaf. You must then at your own expense return to us the goods, together with in the case of a motor vehicle, the registration document, road fund licence and test certificate.

10 Our right to end the agreement

We may end this agreement, after giving you written notice, if:

(a) you fail to keep to any of your obligations under clauses 1, 4, 5, 7 or 8, the complete and punctual performance of which is of the essence of this agreement;

(b) a meeting is called of your creditors or any arrangement, composition or trust deed is made or proposed with or for the benefit of them;

(c) a petition is presented for the making of a bankruptcy order against you or you are deemed unable to pay your debts or you become apparently insolvent within the meaning of the Insolvency Act 1986 or the Bankruptcy (Scotland) Act 1985 respectively;

(d) you cease to carry on business or, being a partnership, it is dissolved or proceedings for its dissolution are commenced;

(e) execution or, in Scotland, any poinding or arrestment (otherwise than on the dependance of an action) is levied or attempted against any of your assets or income;

(f) the landlord of the premises where the goods are kept threatens or takes any step to distrain on or, in Scotland, exercise any right of hypothec over the goods or any of your other goods.

(g) you have given false information in connection with your entry into this agreement;

(h) the goods are destroyed or the insurers treat a claim under the above policy on a total loss basis.

If we end this agreement then, subject to your rights as set out in the Form 'Repossession: Your Rights' overleaf, we may retake the goods. You will also then have to pay to us all overdue payments and the rest of the Total Amount Payable under the agreement remaining unpaid less:

(i) a rebate for early payment required by law and

(ii) the net proceeds of sale of the goods (if any) after deduction of the cost of recovery, insurance, storage and sale.

You must also return to us the documents listed in Clause 9.

11 Expenses

You must repay on demand our expenses and legal costs for:

(a) finding your address if you change address without first informing us or finding the goods if they are not at the address given by you;

(b) taking steps, including court action, to recover the goods or to obtain payment for them.

12 Exclusion

(a) If you are dealing as consumer (as defined in the Unfair Contract Terms Act 1977) nothing in this agreement will affect your rights under the Supply of Goods (Implied Terms) Act 1973.

(b) In all other cases:

(i) you rely on your own skill and judgement as to the quality of the goods and their fitness for their intended purpose;

(ii) we will not be responsible for their quality, their fitness for any purpose or their correspondence with any description or specification.

13 General provisions

(a) The word 'goods' includes replacements, renewals and additions which we or you may make to them.

(b) No relaxation or indulgence which we may extend to you shall affect our strict rights under this agreement.

(c) Where two or more persons are named as the customer, you jointly and severally accept the obligations under this agreement. This means that each of you can be held fully responsible under this agreement.

(d) We may transfer our rights under this agreement.

14 When this agreement takes effect

This agreement will only take effect if and when it is signed by us or our authorised representative.

IMPORTANT — YOU SHOULD READ THIS CAREFULLY
YOUR RIGHTS

The Consumer Credit Act 1974 covers this agreement and lays down certain requirements for your protection which must be satisfied when the agreement is made. If they are not, we cannot enforce the agreement against you without a court order.

The Act also gives you a number of rights. You have a right to settle this agreement at any time by giving notice in writing and paying off all amounts payable under the agreement which may be reduced by a rebate.

If you would like to know more about the protection and remedies provided under the Act, you should contact either your local Trading Standards Department or your nearest Citizens' Advice Bureau.

YOUR RIGHT TO CANCEL

You have a right to cancel this agreement. You can do this by sending or taking a WRITTEN notice of cancellation to the owners whose name and address is shown overleaf. You have FIVE DAYS starting with the day after you received this copy. You can use the form provided.

If you cancel this agreement, any money you have paid, goods given in part-exchange (or their value) and property given as security must be returned to you. You will not have to make any further payment.

If you already have any goods under the agreement, you should not use them and should keep them safe. (Legal action may be taken against you if you do not take proper care of them.) You can wait for them to be collected from you and you need not hand them over unless you receive a written request. If you wish, however, you may return the goods yourself.

Note: Your notice of cancellation will not affect your contract for insurance.

The form for exercising your right to cancel is on the front of this agreement.

15.3 Signatures

The agreement must be signed by the debtor at a time when all the terms of the agreement (save implied terms) are set out in the document and in a state that is readily legible. Thus, where a standard pre-printed form is supplied with blanks to be filled in by hand (eg, for the amount of each repayment), these blanks must be filled in before the debtor signs. The debtor must sign within the statutorily prescribed signature box.

15.4 Copies

Sections 62 and 63, CCA 1974 require the creditor to supply to the debtor a copy or copies of the agreement. How many copies the debtor receives will depend on when the agreement is executed (an executed agreement is a document signed by both parties embodying the terms of a regulated agreement; an unsigned document is an unexecuted agreement: see s 189).

The debtor should always receive one copy when he signs the agreement (either by being given one in person if the document is presented to him personally for signature or by post if he is being sent a document to sign). If the agreement is concluded upon the debtor's signature being affixed to the document then only that copy is needed.

Usually the agreement is not concluded at this stage. Usually the document will then be sent on to the creditor to sign and the agreement will only be executed when it does so. If this is the case then the debtor must be given or sent a second copy within seven days of the agreement being concluded. Note that copies of some documents referred to in agreements must be served with the copies of the agreement.

15.5 Cancellable agreements

If the agreement is cancellable (as to which see **Chapter 16**) then even more stringent rules apply. First, further information must appear in the agreement if it is to be enforceable, such as the nature of any advance payment (eg, cash or part exchange). Secondly, notice of the debtor's right to cancel must be included in the form prescribed in the Consumer Credit (Cancellation Notices and Copies of Documents) Regulations 1983: s 64.

We have just seen that if the agreement is executed upon the debtor signing it then the creditor need present him with only one copy. However, if the agreement is cancellable then a notice (again in the prescribed form) must be sent by post within seven days. If the creditor is obliged to give a second copy of the agreement to the debtor (because it is concluded upon the creditor signing it) then the second copy of the agreement must be sent by post.

15.6 Enforcing an improperly executed agreement

If an agreement is improperly executed then the court has a discretionary power to allow the creditor to enforce the agreement, notwithstanding the default in compliance with the formality provisions. In practice, the court will usually grant an enforcement order because it can use its powers under ss 129, 135 and 136 (see **Chapter 21**) to cure any prejudice caused to the debtor. However, in three circumstances the court has no discretionary power to allow the creditor to enforce the agreement (s 127(3))

15.6.1 Improperly executed agreements that cannot be enforced

We have already noted one of these exceptions to the general rule: a failure to include the relevant prescribed terms in the agreement. The other two relate only to cancellable agreements. If the requirements of s 64 (ie, notice of cancellation rights) are not complied with then the agreement is improperly executed and is not enforceable. If copies have not been supplied properly under ss 62 and 63 and the creditor has not supplied the debtor with a copy of the executed agreement and any document referred to in it before the commencement of proceedings, then the agreement is improperly executed and is not enforceable.

15.6.1.1 Section 127(3): is it still good law?

In the remarkable decision of the Court of Appeal in *Wilson v First County Trust Ltd* [2001] QB 407 and *Wilson v First County Trust Ltd (No 2)* [2001] 3 WLR 42 the Court made the historic first declaration of incompatibility with the European Convention on Human Rights under the Human Rights Act 1998. This was on the basis that the effect of the subsection was to deny a creditor a legal remedy in breach of Article 6(1) of the Convention and Article 1 of the First Protocol.

On 10 July 2003 the House of Lords overturned the decision in *Wilson v First County Trust Limited (No 2)*. There is nothing incompatible in the prohibition on enforcement in s 127(3). It follows that s 127(3) is still good law.

15.6.2 Meaning of enforce

Enforcement means not only issuing proceedings but also repossessing goods associated with the agreement. Thus the creditor cannot enforce the agreement in any way without first acquiring an enforcement order from the court (s 65). Further, the creditor cannot enforce any security (whether given by the debtor or a third party) without first obtaining an enforcement order in respect of the agreement (s 113).

15.6.3 Making of an application for an enforcement order

The application can be made by either a claim of its own or in the course of a claim for payment of money or possession of goods. Thus a creditor need only issue one set of proceedings against a debtor although, of course, he is at risk on costs if he fails to get the enforcement order.

15.6.4 Exercise of court's discretion in considering an application under section 65

The court will usually grant an enforcement order. This is because s 127 provides that the court shall dismiss an application only if it considers it just to do so having regard to the prejudice caused to any person by the contravention in question, and the degree of culpability for it and the powers conferred on the court by s 127(2) and ss 135 and 136. The powers conferred on the court by s 127(2) and ss 135 and 136 should usually be sufficient to cure any prejudice caused to the debtor by the creditor's contravention of the statutory requirements.

15.6.4.1 Court's powers under s 127(2)

Under s 127(2) the court may reduce the sum payable by the debtor or surety in order to compensate him for any prejudice which he has suffered by reason of the creditor's contravention. For a graphic example of the way in which this operates against the creditor see *Rank Xerox Finance Ltd v Hepple and Fennymore* [1994] CCLR 1 in which damages of £5,000 for breach of a consumer hire agreement were reduced to £500 due to the failure of the agreement to comply with the requirements of the Consumer Credit (Agreements) Regulations 1983.

15.6.4.2 Court's powers under ss 135 and 136

The court's powers under s 135 (to suspend any order it makes) and s 136 (to re-write the terms of an agreement) are dealt with in **Chapter 21**, as are time orders which a court can consider making under s 129 when considering an application for an enforcement order.

15.6.5 Court's powers under section 142

Under s 142 the court can make a declaration that the creditor cannot take the action which it required an enforcement order to take and that no further application for an enforcement order shall be entertained. It appears that the court can make such a declaration: (a) of its own motion when dismissing an application for an enforcement order on substantive grounds (s 142(1)(a)); or (b) on an application by any interested party if the creditor has made no application for an enforcement order; or (c) when such an application has been dismissed on technical grounds (s 142(1)(b)).

16

Withdrawal and cancellation

A particular concern of CCA 1974 is to allow a debtor time to cool off before committing himself to a regulated agreement. This is done by making it easier for him to withdraw an offer to contract with the creditor than is the case at common law and by introducing a statutory right to cancel an agreement in certain circumstances. These rights are in addition to the statutory rights considered at **16.3.7**.

Before we consider these aspects of the Act, it is convenient to consider the position first under common law and second under the Act of the creditor's vicarious liability for the dealer.

16.1 Dealer as agent of creditor

16.1.1 The common law position

In a vast number of hire-purchase, conditional sale and credit sale transactions the creditor will be a faceless financial institution as far as the debtor is concerned. The debtor will rarely meet a representative of the creditor. The creditor will rarely see the goods. Although the creditor is the legal supplier of the goods the actual supplier will be the dealer. It is on the dealer's premises that the debtor will see the goods he wishes to buy; it is the dealer who will demonstrate and recommend them to the debtor; and it is the dealer who will arrange for the debtor to enter into the finance transaction. At common law the dealer is not usually the creditor's agent: *Branwhite v Worcester Works Finance Ltd* [1969] 1 AC 522. Consequently, the creditor is not liable for any mistakes or misrepresentations made by the dealer and the debtor will have no remedy against the dealer (since there is no contract between them) unless he can show that there was a collateral warranty with the dealer (see **23.1.1**), or that the dealer made a negligent misstatement (*Hedley Byrne & Co Ltd v Heller & Partners Ltd* [1964] AC 465).

16.1.2 Effect of section 56, CCA 1974

The common law position is radically altered by s 56, CCA 1974. This provides that:

> ***56. Antecedent negotiations***
>
> *(1) In this Act 'antecedent negotiations' means any negotiations with the debtor or hirer—*
>
> *(a) conducted by the creditor or owner in relation to the making of any regulated agreement, or*
>
> *(b) conducted by a credit-broker in relation to goods sold or proposed to be sold by the credit-broker to the creditor before forming the subject-matter of a debtor—creditor—supplier agreement within section 12(a), or*

(c) conducted by the supplier in relation to a transaction financed or proposed to be financed by a debtor—creditor—supplier agreement within section 12(b) or (c),

and 'negotiator' means the person by whom negotiations are so conducted with the debtor or hirer.

(2) Negotiations with the debtor in a case falling within subsection (1)(b) or (c) shall be deemed to be conducted by the negotiator in the capacity of agent of the creditor as well as in his actual capacity.

(3) An agreement is void if, and to the extent that, it purports in relation to an actual or prospective regulated agreement—

(a) to provide that a person acting as, or on behalf of, a negotiator is to be treated as the agent of the debtor or hirer, or

(b) to relieve a person from liability for acts or omissions of any person acting as, or on behalf of, a negotiator.

(4) For the purposes of this Act, antecedent negotiations shall be taken to begin when the negotiator and the debtor or hirer first enter into communication (including communication by advertisement), and to include any representations made by the negotiator to the debtor or hirer and any other dealings between them.

16.1.2.1 Importance of fixing creditor with vicarious liability for dealer

The practical importance of s 56 is that it makes the creditor liable for misrepresentations made by the dealer (see **Chapter 23**) and, as we shall now see, that it has significance when we consider the debtor's right to withdraw from or cancel a regulated agreement.

16.2 Withdrawal

We have seen that consumer credit agreements are commonly made by a prospective customer signing a document (the 'unexecuted agreement') which is then sent to the creditor for approval and that the agreement is executed when the creditor signs (see **15.4**). In such circumstances the debtor is the offeror and the creditor is the offeree. At common law the offeror can revoke his offer at any time prior to acceptance either orally or in writing. Revocation of an offer is effective when it is received by the offeree. Thus an offer by a prospective customer to enter into an unregulated hire-purchase, conditional sale or credit sale agreement can be withdrawn only before the creditor accepts it by communicating his decision.

16.2.1 Effect of CCA 1974 on common law position

Section 57, CCA 1974 makes it easier for a prospective debtor to withdraw from a prospective regulated agreement that is not a small restricted-use debtor–creditor–supplier agreement or non-commercial agreement (s 74). It does this by providing that notice may be given to anyone deemed to be the agent of the creditor under s 56 (s 57(3)(a)) or anyone who, in the course of business, acted for the debtor in pre-contract negotiations (s 57(3)(b)).

By s 57(1), the effect of withdrawal from a regulated agreement is the same as if the debtor had cancelled it under s 69 (see below).

16.3 Cancellation

The object of ss 67 to 73, CCA 1974 is to provide a debtor with the opportunity to resile from a regulated agreement when oral representations were made to him prior to the contract being made at premises other than the trade premises of the creditor, his agent or a party to a linked transaction other than the debtor or his relative. The object of the provisions was to allow a cooling-off period for a debtor who was visited at home by a door-to-door salesman and felt pressurised into signing an agreement (although there is no requirement that the debtor has been or feels pressurised). However, the provisions work in such a way that a debtor who signs a creditor's standard form of agreement in a shop is not entitled to cancel the agreement while one who takes the same form away and signs it at home and then returns it to the shop is entitled to cancel. The effect of cancellation is to rescind the agreement and any linked transaction.

We noted in **Chapter 15** the importance of a creditor complying with the statutory requirements to give the debtor notice of his right to cancel in the written agreement.

We must now examine the statutory right to cancel in more detail. The flowchart reproduced as **Form 16.1** will help you decide whether or not an agreement is cancellable.

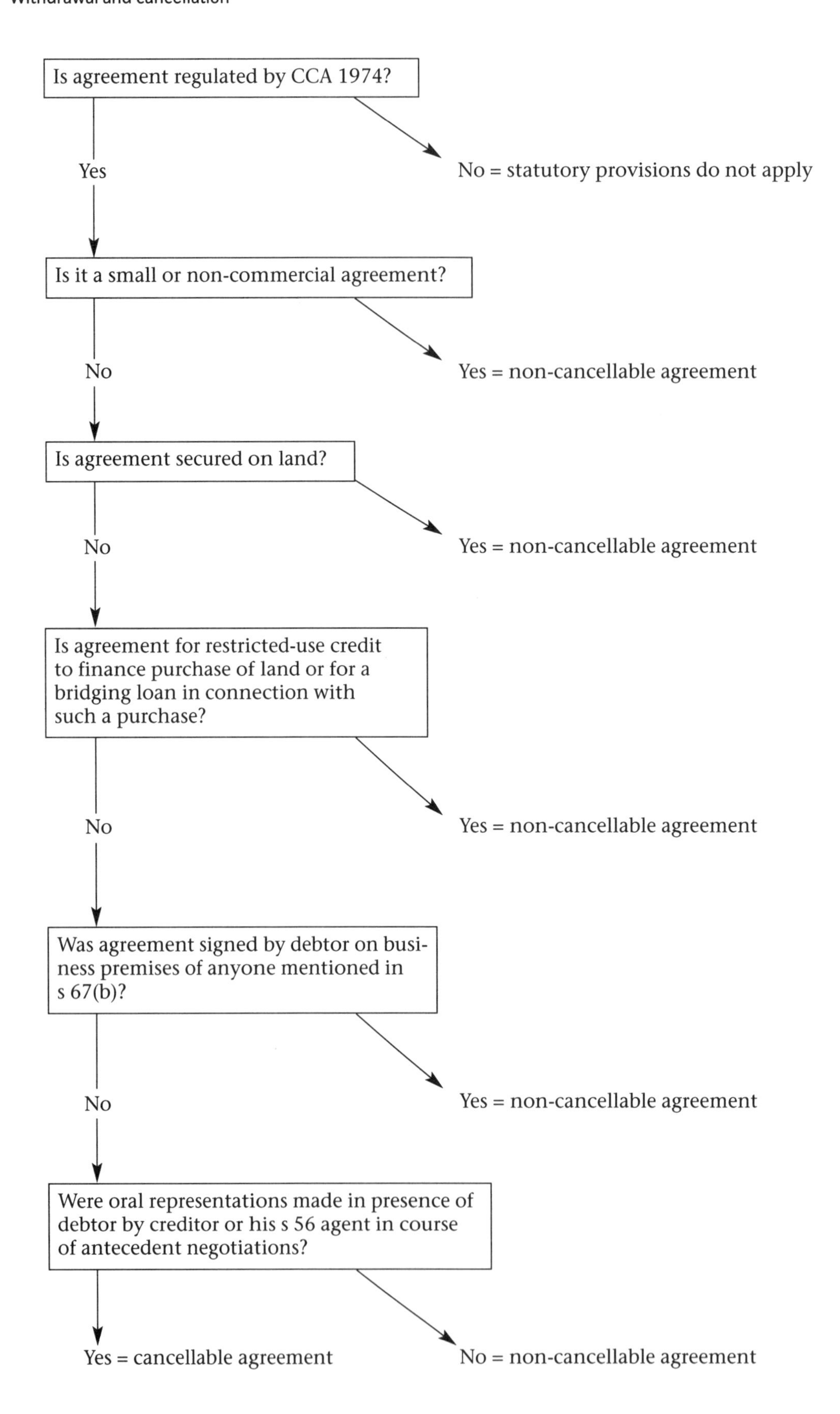

Form 16.1 Is agreement cancellable?

16.3.1 Creation of statutory right to cancel

Section 67, CCA 1974 provides that the debtor will have a statutory right to cancel a regulated debtor—creditor—supplier agreement (which is not a non-commercial or small agreement) if, before conclusion of the agreement, oral representations forming part of the antecedent negotiations were made in the presence of the debtor by the creditor or someone deemed to be an agent of the creditor under s 56.

In *Moorgate Services Ltd v Kabir* The Times, 25 April 1995, the Court of Appeal held that any statement of fact or opinion or an undertaking as to the future which was capable of inducing the proposed borrower to enter the agreement was a representation within the meaning of s 67. It was unnecessary for the debtor to show that he had been so induced.

16.3.1.1 Restriction on statutory right to cancel

Section 67, CCA 1974 provides that the debtor does not have the statutory right to cancel the agreement if either:

(a) the agreement is secured on land or is a restricted-use credit agreement to finance the purchase of land or is an agreement for a bridging loan in connection with the purchase of land; or

(b) the unexecuted agreement is signed by the debtor at premises where the creditor, someone deemed to be his agent under s 56 or any party to a linked transaction (other than the debtor or his relative) carries on business.

16.3.2 Time for exercising the statutory right to cancel

The debtor only has a limited time in which to exercise his statutory right to cancel the agreement (s 68(a)). He must do so within five clear days (ie, not counting the date of receipt) of receiving a copy of the executed agreement or his notice of cancellation rights (see **15.5**). If he posts his notice of cancellation then cancellation is effective when it is posted (s 69(7)).

If the creditor does not comply with ss 63(2) or 64(1)(b) by posting a copy of the executed agreement or notice of cancellation rights to the debtor, or if the debtor does not receive it, then the time limit on the debtor's right to cancel does not begin to run. Consequently, the agreement remains cancellable by the debtor unless he waives his right to cancel (eg, by exercising his right to terminate) or judgment is entered against him: *V.L. Skuce & Co v Cooper* [1975] 1 WLR 593. It will be difficult for the creditor to obtain a judgment against the debtor which cannot be set aside since non-compliance with ss 63(2) or 64(1)(b) renders the agreement unenforceable.

16.3.3 Exercising the right to cancel

The debtor must give written notice to the creditor, an agent of the creditor under s 56 or anyone who acted for the debtor in the course of business in the antecedent negotiations (s 69(6)). Although the creditor must include a 'clip-out and send' cancellation notice in the documentation (see **Form 15.2**), there is no prescribed form for a notice of cancellation and anything which indicates the intention of the debtor to withdraw from the agreement will suffice (s 69(1)).

16.3.4 Effect of cancellation

Cancellation of a regulated agreement also automatically cancels a linked transaction (see **16.3**). The effect of cancellation is that the agreement and any linked transaction shall be treated as if they had never been entered into (s 69(4)). Consequently the creditor must repay all and any sums paid by the debtor and the debtor must return the goods.

When considering how this works in practice we must distinguish between two different types of agreement: first, restricted-use credit debtor–creditor–supplier agreements (ie, agreements falling within s 12(a) and (b)); and secondly unrestricted-use credit debtor–creditor–supplier agreements (ie, agreements falling within s 12(c)) and debtor–creditor agreements (see **14.2.7**).

16.3.5 Section 12(a) and (b) agreements

16.3.5.1 Refund of payments made by debtor

We shall begin by examining the creditor's obligation to refund all sums paid by the debtor. This is covered by s 70. Money is repayable by the person to whom the debtor paid it. So where the debtor has paid a cash deposit it is the dealer who is under the obligation to repay. The exception to this general rule is that a creditor is jointly liable with the supplier in a s 12(b) agreement and has a right of indemnity against the supplier.

Of course the debtor may not have paid any money to the dealer — he may have traded in his own goods in part-exchange and those goods will have been included in the deposit (see **2.6**). The position in these circumstances is governed by s 73. The dealer can return the goods within ten days of the agreement being cancelled. If he does not do so, the debtor can: (a) demand their part-exchange value (s 73(2)); (b) demand the part-exchange value from the creditor (*Branwhite v Worcester Works Finance Ltd* [1969] 1 AC 552); or (c) sue the dealer for conversion.

16.3.5.2 Exceptions to the debtor's right to a refund

Because of the effect of s 69(2), the debtor will not be entitled to a full refund where the cancelled agreement financed:

(a) the doing of work, or supply of goods, to meet an emergency; or

(b) the supply of goods which, prior to cancellation, had by the act of the debtor or a relative become incorporated into any land or thing not comprised in the agreement or any linked transaction.

In these cases all the debtor's financial obligations under the agreement end, except an obligation to pay for the work done or goods supplied.

16.3.5.3 Debtor's obligation to return goods in his possession

We turn now to consider the debtor's obligation to return the goods. This is governed by s 72. Goods can be returned to any person to whom notice of cancellation could have been given (s 72(6) — see **16.3.3**). The debtor is under a duty to retain possession of the goods and take reasonable care of them for 21 days after cancellation. If the other party (defined in s 72(2) as the person from whom the debtor obtains possession: in this context it means the creditor from whom he receives legal possession) has not made a written request for restoration of the goods by that time then the debtor is merely under the common law duty of a bailee. If the creditor has made such a written request and the debtor unreasonably fails to comply then the 21 day period is extended until he does comply.

The debtor can end his duty to care for the goods at any time by delivering them to any of the persons to whom he can return them or sending the goods to any such person.

If, within the 21 days, the debtor receives a written request from the other party then he is under a duty to do so. However, he does not have to take any steps to deliver or return the goods — it is sufficient for him to allow the other party to recover them from the debtor's premises.

16.3.5.4 Exceptions to debtor's duty to restore goods

(a) The debtor is allowed to exercise a lien over goods in his possession for ten days following cancellation for the return of part-exchange goods (s 73(5)). He can exercise a lien without time limit for the value of part-exchange goods and for the return of any sums paid (ss. 73(5) and 72(4)).

(b) The debtor is under no duty to restore perishable goods (whether perished or not) (s 72(9)(a)).

(c) The debtor is under no duty to restore goods which were consumed before cancellation (s 72(9)(b)).

(d) The debtor is under no duty to restore goods supplied to meet any emergency (s 72(9)(c)).

(e) The debtor is under no duty to restore goods which had become incorporated in any land or thing not comprised in the cancelled agreement or any linked transaction (s 72(9)(d)).

Note that in the final two exceptions the debtor is under a duty to pay for the goods (see **16.3.5.2** above) and there is therefore no injustice in allowing him to keep them. In the case of the previous two exceptions, however, the debtor is entitled to the benefit of having goods without having to pay for them.

16.3.6 Section 12(c) and section 13 agreements

The debtor's obligation to restore goods (to the supplier since the creditor will not have title to them) is exactly the same as above. But the debtor remains liable to repay the credit which he has received and interest (s 71) provided that, where credit is repayable by instalments and the debtor has not repaid the total credit which he received by the time that the first instalment falls due, the creditor must first serve a notice on the debtor under the Consumer Credit (Repayment of Credit on Cancellation) Regulations 1983 (SI 1983 No 1559) setting out the amount to be paid under the debtor's revised liability.

Note that interest is not payable on any amount repaid by the debtor within one month of cancelling the agreement or by the date that the first instalment falls due.

16.3.7 Other statutory rights to cancel

The Consumer Protection (Cancellation of Contracts Concluded away from Business Premises) Regulations 1987 (discussed in **Chapter 4**) and the Timeshare Act 1992 apply to unregulated and regulated but non-cancellable consumer credit agreements. Regulated cancellable consumer credit agreements do not fall within the scope of the Regulations or the 1992 Act. The Regulations and the 1992 Act contain similar provisions to ss 67 to 73, CCA 1974.

17

Termination of hire-purchase and conditional sale agreements by creditor: the common law position and contractual devices to circumvent it

Much consumer credit litigation is concerned with the consequences of the creditor's termination of a hire-purchase or conditional sale agreement. This chapter examines the common law position. CCA 1974 modifies the common law position in some ways as we shall see in **Chapter 18**. But it is easier to understand the statutory provisions once you understand the common law position. The classification of contract terms was considered at **3.1**.

The creditor's right to terminate a hire-purchase or conditional sale agreement can arise:

(a) automatically, or at the creditor's option, on the occurrence of a specified event;

(b) upon the debtor committing a repudiatory breach of the agreement or a breach of condition;

(c) upon the debtor committing a breach which does not amount to a repudiation of the agreement and is not a breach of a condition but which confers a contractual right to terminate the agreement on the creditor.

Before we go any further it is as well to point out that, of course, a creditor need not terminate a contract because the debtor is in breach. Probably the most common breach committed by debtors is to fall into arrears with their payments. The creditor can always simply sue for arrears on a regulated or unregulated agreement. It need not serve a s 76 or default notice if the agreement is regulated (see **Chapter 18**). The creditor is entitled to claim interest pursuant to contract or statute (s 35A, Supreme Court Act 1981 or s 69, County Courts Act 1984) but cannot claim contractual interest on late payments due under regulated consumer credit agreements which is higher than that payable under the contract as a whole (s 93).

17.1 Examples of events leading to termination

17.1.1 Termination on occurrence of a specified event

Agreements often specify that they will be terminated either automatically or at the option of the creditor in the event of, for example, the debtor becoming bankrupt or his landlord distraining against him (see **20.2**). Clause 10(b) to (f) of the agreement reproduced as **Form 15.2** are typical examples of provisions which allow a creditor to terminate without the debtor having committed any breaches of the agreement.

17.1.2 Repudiatory breach

A common example of a debtor committing a repudiatory breach is when he disposes of the goods to which the agreement relates. The Court of Appeal has held that the owner of a car is entitled to immediate possession of it if the person hiring the car does anything inconsistent with the hire-purchase agreement: *Union Transport Finance Ltd v British Car Auctions Ltd* [1978] 2 All ER 385, per Roskill LJ at p 390:

> ... if the bailee acts in a way which ... destroys the basis of the contract of bailment, the bailor becomes entitled at once to bring that contract to an end, and thus at once acquires the right to immediate possession of the article bailed.

17.1.3 Breach of condition

If the contract expressly provides for time of payment of instalments to be of the essence then that term is a condition and late payment entitles the creditor to treat the agreement as having been repudiated by the debtor: *Lombard North Central plc v Butterworth* [1987] QB 527 (see **3.2**). Perhaps unsurprisingly, most agreements in fact provide for most of the debtor's obligations to be of the essence (see clause 10(a) of **Form 15.2**).

17.1.4 Non-repudiatory breach

There may be circumstances in which the debtor is in breach of a term of the agreement but that term is not a condition and the debtor's breach does not allow the creditor to treat the agreement as repudiated. In such a case the creditor cannot terminate the agreement unless there is an express clause in the agreement allowing it to do so. An example may be where the term requiring the debtor to make payments is not a condition (because it does not make time of the essence) but the agreement nevertheless confers a right of termination on the creditor.

17.2 When termination occurs

The agreement will determine whether termination has to be on notice or whether it is automatic on the occurrence of a certain event. In *Eshun v Moorgate Mercantile Credit Co* [1971] 1 WLR 722, Lord Denning MR suggested that a notice should be served before the creditor could terminate the agreement but since the legislature passed a codifying Act three years later which did not enact this dictum it is submitted that the dictum is of no weight.

17.3 The consequences of termination

Upon termination the creditor becomes entitled to repossession of the goods and may be entitled to damages.

17.4 Repossession of goods

The right to possession of the goods will re-vest in the creditor when it terminates a hire-purchase or conditional sale agreement (it will be recalled that the creditor has retained title to the goods in these agreements). The creditor does not obtain a right to possession of goods under a credit sale agreement because, of course, title passes to the debtor at the outset of such an agreement.

The creditor is therefore entitled to take possession of the goods upon termination of the agreement. In practice this may create problems, for if the goods are on the debtor's premises then the creditor cannot seize them without the debtor's permission or it will be committing a trespass. Therefore, most agreements expressly provide that the creditor can enter upon the debtor's premises to repossess the goods in the event of termination.

If there is no such contractual provision and the debtor does not consent to the creditor taking possession of the goods then the creditor will have to bring a claim for wrongful interference and seek either (a) delivery up of the goods or (b) the value of the goods as damages together in each case with consequential damages.

17.4.1 Measure of damages

Upon common law termination the creditor is entitled to claim all arrears due to the date of termination (if any) and the cost of repairing the goods if the debtor is in breach of his duty to take reasonable care of them. Whether or not the creditor is entitled to any further damages upon termination will depend upon the reason for termination and the terms of the agreement.

17.4.1.1 Measure of damages for repudiatory breach or breach of condition

Upon termination for either of these reasons, the creditor is entitled to damages for loss of profit on the transaction: *Yeoman Credit Ltd v Waragowski* [1961] 1 WLR 1124. The formula for calculating damages for loss of profit is to take the total price from which must be deducted:

(a) all sums which should have been paid by the debtor at the date when the claim is made, whether paid or not (the creditor must include a separate claim for arrears if any of these payments have not been made);

(b) any option to purchase fee (in the case of hire-purchase agreements); and

(c) the value of the goods recovered by the creditor (if they have not been recovered then the creditor must claim separately for damages for their value at the date of termination).

Suppose that Usurius Finance plc enters into a hire-purchase agreement in respect of a car with Mr Baker. The total price payable under the agreement is £6,000 which Mr Baker agrees to repay over a period of five years by monthly payments of £100. Suppose that Mr Baker makes the first three payments but then falls into arrears. Three months later Usurius terminates the agreement, repossesses the car and sells it for £1,000 and three months after obtains judgment in default against Mr Baker. At this point the sum will be as follows:

Total hire-purchase price = £6,000

Deduct from it:

	£
The sums already paid 300	
Arrears due before termination	300
Option to purchase fee	30
Value of goods recovered	1,000
	1,630

£6,000 – £1,630 = £4,370

If the formula stopped there, then in cases where the agreement was terminated at an early enough point in its term, the creditor would be in a better position by reason of the termination than it would have been if the debtor had performed the agreement.

Therefore, the creditor must give a discount for accelerated receipt of the total price: see *Overstone Ltd v Shipway* [1962] 1 WLR 117. In that case, the Court of Appeal eschewed any mathematical formula for calculating the rebate — the court must simply assess such sum as it thinks appropriate. The requirement to give a discount for accelerated receipt of money is also found in many actions for wrongful dismissal, for personal injuries (for future losses) and in ancillary relief (where periodical payments are capitalised). The discounts range from 1% in *Lavarack v Woods of Colchester Ltd* [1967] 1 QB 278 to 7% agreed between counsel in *Shove v Downs Surgical plc* [1984] ICR 532. In a more recent decision in personal injury actions, the House of Lords adopted an assumption that money paid early would give a return of 3%: *Wells v Wells* [1998] 3 WLR 329.

17.4.1.2 Damages flowing from termination for non-repudiatory breach

What is significantly different about the measure of damages on termination by the creditor in this case is that he cannot sue for any payments which the debtor would have made in the future: see *Financings Ltd v Baldock* [1963] 2 QB 104. This is because the creditor's loss of future profit derives not from the debtor's breach but from its own decision to terminate the agreement.

Not unnaturally finance companies have attempted to circumvent the decision in *Financings Ltd v Baldock*. The most effective way for them to do so is to dress up as many of the debtor's obligations as possible as conditions so that a breach by the debtor does entitle them to treat the contract as repudiated and thus entitle them to claim damages which include the outstanding balance due under the agreement.

Another device which finance companies have attempted to use is a contractual minimum payment clause. A minimum payment clause will provide for a debtor to pay a fixed sum to the creditor upon termination. However, such clauses are subject to the doctrine of penalties (see **3.8**). The courts have not been slow to hold that such clauses are often penalty clauses. Thus, an agreement which included a minimum payment clause which provided that the creditor was entitled to two-thirds of the total hire-purchase price and the return of the goods upon termination was held to be a penalty clause because, depending on the value of the goods, the creditor could recover more than 100% of the total hire-purchase price: *Bridge v Campbell Discount Co Ltd* [1962] AC 600. Similarly a minimum payment clause which attempted to make the debtor liable for *Waragowski* damages on termination was held to be a penalty because it applied to breaches for which at common law the *Financings Ltd v Baldock* measure of damages applied: *Capital Finance Co Ltd v Donati* (1977) 121 SJ 270.

17.4.1.3 Damages for termination following a non-breach event

The doctrine of penalties has one significant limitation: it does not apply to a liquidated damages clause which comes into effect not when the debtor is in breach but on the occurrence of a specified event: see *Associated Distributors v Hall* [1938] 2 KB 83 and *Export Credits Guarantee Department v Universal Oil Products Co* [1983] 1 WLR 399.

17.4.1.4 Overview on damages

Since the decision of the Court of Appeal in *Lombard North Central plc v Butterworth* [1987] QB 527, it is likely that most agreements will provide for the debtor's obligations to be conditions.

Although the claim for loss of profit could be mounted as a claim for unliquidated damages, most agreements provide for the outstanding balance to be paid as liquidated damages according to the *Waragowski* formula. The advantage of this from a creditor's point of view is that it can sue for a debt and thus avoid the necessity of an assessment of damages hearing if it obtains judgment in default. For an example of a liquidated damages clause, which gives effect to the Waragowski measure of damages upon termination for repudiatory breach or termination on the occurrence of certain events, see clause 10 of the hire-purchase agreement set out as **Form 15.2**.

17.5 Debtor's right to relief

The High Court and county court have jurisdiction to grant relief: see **3.8**.

18

Termination of regulated hire-purchase and conditional sale agreements by creditor

Straightaway we must note certain limitations in CCA 1974. The Act does not codify the common law position as to breaches. It contains no provision analogous to those in landlord and tenant legislation which restricts a landlord's right to possession of premises by limiting the grounds on which the landlord may regain possession. Whether or not a debtor is in breach of an agreement will depend upon the express and implied terms of that agreement. What the Act does provide is limited protection for the debtor. It does this in three ways:

(a) It provides that the creditor cannot terminate an agreement without giving prior notice to the debtor. This creates a breathing space in which the debtor has time to put right any breaches, apply to the county court for more time to do so if necessary or terminate the agreement himself.

(b) It substantially restricts the creditor's right to repossess goods.

(c) It arguably caps the debtor's exposure to damages.

We must now examine in detail how the Act achieves this protection.

18.1 No termination without notice

We have seen that unregulated agreements may provide for the creditor to terminate an agreement without notice or on the occurrence of a specified event. Where the agreement is regulated by CCA 1974, however, the creditor cannot simply terminate the agreement. He must first serve one of three types of notice under ss 76, 87 and 98, CCA 1974. We shall now examine each type of notice in more detail.

18.1.1 Default notices

By s 87 of the Act the creditor must serve a 'default notice' before it:

- terminates the agreement;
- demands earlier payment of any sum (ie, enforces an accelerated payment clause: see **19.1**);
- recovers possession of any goods;

- treats any right conferred on the debtor by the agreement as terminated, restricted or deferred; or
- enforces any security

because of any breach by the debtor.

The default notice must be in the prescribed form (set out in the Consumer Credit (Enforcement, Default and Termination Notices) Regulations 1983 (SI 1983 No 1561)) and, by s 88, CCA 1974, must include:

(a) the nature of the breach;

(b) the action required to remedy it or, if it is not remediable, the amount to be paid as compensation;

(c) the exact date by which the breach must be remedied or the compensation paid (which must be at least seven days from the date of service of the notice on the debtor);

(d) the consequences if the debtor does not comply with the notice.

An example of a default notice is included as **Form 18.1**.

18.1.1.1 Debtor's choice of action when served with a default notice

A debtor can do one of four things when served with a default notice:

(a) Comply with it. If the debtor complies with the notice within the prescribed time then the breach must be treated as if it had never occurred (s 89). Thus the debtor is always given one last chance to remedy a breach and if he does then the creditor cannot thereafter terminate the agreement because of it.

(b) Apply for a time order under s 129, CCA 1974 if he is able to remedy the breach but needs more time than the creditor has allowed in the notice to do so. (Time orders are considered at **21.1**.)

(c) Apply for relief on the basis that the agreement is extortionate (see **21.5**).

(d) Terminate the agreement himself under s 99 (see **22.2**). He will still lose the goods but may reduce his liability for damages.

If the debtor does not comply with the notice within the prescribed time (or within such extension of time as he may be given by the court) nor terminate the agreement then the creditor can pursue its remedies. Thus if the breach is repudiatory within the terms of the agreement then the creditor can accept the debtor's repudiation and terminate the contract.

18.1.1.2 Consequences of failing to serve a valid default notice

If the creditor fails to serve a default notice prior to taking any of the steps set out in s 87, or if the default notice that is served is defective because it does not comply with the requirements of s 88 and the regulations thereunder, then the creditor cannot validly take any of the steps set out in s 87. The failure of the creditor to comply with the strict requirements of s 87 thus affords a complete defence to the debtor in any legal proceedings that follow. In addition, of course, if the agreement has not been properly terminated then neither has the debtor's right to possession of the goods so the creditor cannot lawfully repossess them. The debtor will therefore have a claim for wrongful interference with the goods if the creditor repossesses without first having served an effective default notice, in addition to any rights of the debtor under CCA 1974 (as to which see **18.2.2** below).

Form 18.1

NDHP(a)

IMPORTANT — YOU SHOULD READ THIS CAREFULLY

Default Notice

Served under Section 87(1) of the Consumer Credit Act 1974

Dated 16 JULY 1997

To: WACKFORD SQUEERS
(Debtor's Name and Address)
DOTHEBOYS HALL, DOTHEBOYS, YORKSHIRE

From RALPH NICKLEBY FINANCE PLC
(Name and Address)
GOLDEN SQUARE LONDON Tel. No. 0171 353 8554

*Delete inapplicable words.

We hereby give you notice of default under your *Hire-Purchase/Conditional Sale Agreement with us, namely Agreement No. 3789758 dated 1 MAY 1997 ('the Agreement')

1. **Terms of the Agreement that you have broken**
You have broken the following provisions of the Agreement:
Clause(s) 1

2. **Nature of your breach and remedy**
You have failed to make the following payment(s) by the due date(s)†:

†If breach is not failure to pay delete and substitute applicable details.

£90 DUE ON 1 JUNE 1997
£90 DUE ON 1 JULY 1997

Total amount due: £ 180.00

To remedy the breach you must pay us the total amount due at our address stated above by 26 JULY 1997

IF THE ACTION REQUIRED BY THIS NOTICE IS TAKEN **BEFORE THE DATE SHOWN** NO FURTHER ENFORCEMENT ACTION WILL BE TAKEN IN RESPECT OF THE BREACH.

IF YOU DO **NOT** TAKE THE ACTION REQUIRED BY THIS NOTICE **BEFORE THE DATE SHOWN** THEN THE FURTHER ACTION SET OUT BELOW MAY BE TAKEN AGAINST YOU (*OR A SURETY).

3. **Action we intend to take**
If you fail to make the payment referred to in paragraph 2 by the date stated in that paragraph we will:

*Delete inapplicable items.

- * terminate the Agreement, without further notice, on 30 JULY 1997
- * recover possession of goods under the Agreement, if necessary by court action
- * enforce any guarantee or indemnity in respect of the Agreement
- * demand earlier payment of £ 1,676.40 (comprising £ 1,980 less a rebate of £ 303.60) by 30 JULY 1997 against which we will credit you with any net proceeds of the sale of goods to which you may be entitled under the Agreement.

BUT IF YOU HAVE PAID AT LEAST ONE-THIRD OF THE TOTAL AMOUNT PAYABLE UNDER THE AGREEMENT SET OUT BELOW (OR ANY INSTALLATION CHARGE PLUS ONE-THIRD OF THE REST OF THE AMOUNT PAYABLE), WE MAY NOT TAKE BACK THE GOODS AGAINST YOUR WISHES UNLESS WE GET A COURT ORDER. (IN SCOTLAND WE MAY NEED TO GET AN ORDER AT ANY TIME.) IF WE DO TAKE THEM WITHOUT YOUR CONSENT OR A COURT ORDER, YOU HAVE THE RIGHT TO GET BACK ALL THE MONEY YOU HAVE PAID UNDER THE AGREEMENT SET OUT BELOW.

Total amount payable under the Agreement (less any installation charge)	£ 2,360
Installation charge (if any)	£
Total amount paid by you to the date of this notice	£ 200

IF YOU HAVE DIFFICULTY IN PAYING ANY SUM OWING UNDER THE AGREEMENT OR TAKING ANY OTHER ACTION REQUIRED BY THIS NOTICE, YOU CAN APPLY TO THE COURT WHICH MAY MAKE AN ORDER ALLOWING YOU OR ANY SURETY MORE TIME.

IF YOU ARE NOT SURE WHAT TO DO, YOU SHOULD GET HELP AS SOON AS POSSIBLE. FOR EXAMPLE YOU SHOULD CONTACT A SOLICITOR, YOUR LOCAL TRADING STANDARDS DEPARTMENT OR YOUR NEAREST CITIZENS' ADVICE BUREAU.

If you have not contacted us in response to previous reminders you should do so now since this may enable problems to be resolved.

18.1.2 Section 76 notices

By s 76, a notice must be served where the creditor intends to enforce a term of a regulated agreement by:

- demanding earlier payment of any sum;
- recovering possession of any goods or land; or
- treating any right conferred on the debtor or hirer by the agreement as terminated, restricted or deferred

because of the occurrence of a specified event.

Notices served under s 76 are sometimes called 'non-default notices' to distinguish them from default notices and sometimes 'enforcement notices', but we shall call them s 76 notices.

A s 76 notice must be in the prescribed form (s 76 and Consumer Credit (Enforcement Default and Termination) Notices 1983). The notice simply gives the debtor at least seven days' notice of the creditor's intention to enforce one of the terms of the agreement. Since the notice is being served in circumstances where the agreement entitles the creditor to terminate the agreement or rely on an accelerated payments clause without the debtor being in breach, the debtor can do nothing to remedy his situation and consequently, unlike a default notice, a s 76 notice does not tell the debtor how he can avoid the agreement being terminated or an accelerated payments clause from becoming operative. The breathing space created by service of the notice does, however, allow the debtor time to make an application for a time order (see **21.1**). An example of a s 76 notice is set out as **Form 18.2**.

18.1.3 Termination notices

Under s 98, CCA 1974 a creditor cannot terminate a regulated agreement when the debtor is not in default without first serving a 'termination notice' in the prescribed form (Consumer Credit (Enforcement Default and Termination) Notices 1983). If the agreement provides that it will terminate automatically upon the occurrence of some specified event then it is unnecessary to serve a notice under s 98. The section applies where an agreement provides that it may terminate at the option of the creditor (otherwise than on a breach by the debtor).

The termination notice must give the debtor at least seven days' notice of the termination. Since it is unlikely that a creditor will wish to terminate an agreement without also relying on at least one of its remedies (which it cannot do without also serving a s 76 notice), it can serve a 'rolled-up' s 76 and s 98 notice.

18.1.3.1 Effect of non-compliance with s 76 and/or s 98

Failure to serve valid notices under s 76 and s 98 as appropriate will mean that the creditor is not entitled to pursue the remedy or terminate the agreement. The debtor is in the same position as if an ineffective default notice had been served (see **18.1.1.2** above).

18.1.4 Overview of notices

We can see that a s 76 or default notice must always be served before a creditor can rely on any of his remedies when a termination clause in any regulated hire-purchase or conditional sale agreement becomes operative or when the creditor elects to terminate an agreement pursuant to his common law right on repudiation or breach of condition by the debtor. From the point of view of the litigator we can put it more simply by observing that a default notice or s 76 notice must be served before the creditor takes any legal action other than a debt claim for arrears or an action for rescission of the agreement.

Form 18.2

NE Suitable for all types of Regulated Agreements

IMPORTANT — YOU SHOULD READ THIS CAREFULLY

ENFORCEMENT NOTICE

Served under Section 76(1) of the Consumer Credit Act 1974

DATED 16 JULY 1997

To: WACKFORD SQUEERS
(Name and Address)
DOTHEBOYS HALL, DOTHEBOYS, YORKSHIRE

From: RALPH NICKLEBY FINANCE PLC
(Name and Address)
GOLDEN SQUARE LONDON

We hereby give you notice of our intention to enforce the following term of our agreement with you.

Agreement

Type HIRE PURCHASE No. 3789758 Dated 1 MAY 1997

Term of Agreement to be enforced CLAUSE 10 (f): YOUR LANDLORD
(or reference to and short description of term)
DISTRAINING ON YOUR GOODS

Intended Action (one or more of the following, delete the remainder)

We intend to (a) demand earlier payment of £1,676.40
(b) recover possession of the goods.
(c) treat as terminated/restricted/deferred* your right to POSSESSION OF THE GOODS LET UNDER THE AGREEMENT
*Delete as appropriate

by COURT PROCEEDINGS
(manner and circumstances in which action intended to be taken)

Date of intended action 26 JULY 1997

Amount payable by you (see (a) above) Total Amount:	£ 1,980 : 00
Less: Rebate Allowable (if payment made by the above date)	£ 303 : 60
Amount payable by you	£ 1,676 : 40

IF YOU HAVE DIFFICULTY IN PAYING ANY SUM OWING UNDER THE AGREEMENT YOU CAN APPLY TO THE COURT WHICH MAY MAKE AN ORDER ALLOWING YOU OR ANY SURETY MORE TIME.

IF YOU ARE NOT SURE WHAT TO DO, YOU SHOULD GET HELP AS SOON AS POSSIBLE. FOR EXAMPLE YOU SHOULD CONTACT A SOLICITOR, YOUR LOCAL TRADING STANDARDS DEPARTMENT OR YOUR NEAREST CITIZENS' ADVICE BUREAU.

18.2 Termination after service of a valid default or section 76/98 notice

We must first consider the impact of CCA 1974 on the common law position as to damages and then its significant alterations to the creditor's right to repossession of the goods.

18.2.1 The measure of damages

Perhaps curiously, CCA 1974 does not appear to provide for the measure of damages which flow from a creditor's termination of a regulated agreement (in this respect CCA 1974 provides less protection for the debtor than the Hire Purchase Act 1965 which expressly capped the debtor's liability upon termination by any party for any reason). Thus it would appear that the creditor is entitled to claim *Waragowski* damages (*Yeoman Credit Ltd v Waragowski* [1961] 1 WLR 1124) as unliquidated damages (if termination is due to a repudiatory breach or breach of condition) or Financings Ltd v Baldock damages (if termination is for any other reason) or (more likely) to rely on any liquidated damages clause in the agreement.

However, some academic authors argue that CCA 1974 does impliedly cap a debtor's liability for damages. This is because s 99 allows a debtor to terminate an agreement and s 100 provides a statutory formula for his liability for compensation if he does so (this is examined in detail in **Chapter 22**). Goode (at para IC/45.56) suggests that when the creditor terminates the agreement the debtor's liability cannot be any higher than it would have been had the debtor terminated the agreement. Goode suggests that a liquidated damages clause which attempted to impose a higher liability would be struck down as a penalty and that in assessing unliquidated damages the court would take the debtor's right to terminate and consequent exposure to loss into account when fixing the measure of the creditor's loss. Rosenthal suggests that the s 100 cap would be imposed as a result of s 173(1) which provides that a clause in any regulated agreement is 'void if, and to the extent that, it is inconsistent with a provision for the protection of the debtor ...' (so that a liquidated damages clause which provided for a debtor to pay more than he would have done under s 100 would be void). It seems very strange that the point does not appear to have been the subject of judicial consideration. In practice most creditors appear to claim damages pursuant to a liquidated damages clause which gives contractual effect to the Waragowski measure of damages and this will probably continue unless and until there is judicial approval for the arguments of Goode and/or Rosenthal.

18.2.2 Repossessing goods

We saw in the previous chapter that a creditor has an absolute right to possession of the goods upon termination of an unregulated agreement but that he needs a contractual or consensual right to enter upon the debtor's premises to enforce it. CCA 1974 alters this position in two ways. First, it may prevent a creditor from repossessing 'protected' goods without a court order. Secondly, it prohibits a creditor from entering upon any debtor's premises without a court order, whether or not the agreement confers a right of entry upon the creditor and whether or not the goods are protected.

18.2.2.1 Protected goods

We shall begin by examining the definition of protected goods. Section 90, CCA 1974 provides that goods are protected when under a regulated hire-purchase or conditional sale agreement:

- the debtor is in breach;
- he has paid more than one-third of the total balance due under the agreement (see s 90(2) for the position when this includes installation charges); and
- title to the goods has remained with the creditor.

Next we must notice three significant caveats — s 90 does not apply:

- where the debtor has terminated the agreement;
- where the creditor has terminated the agreement but the debtor is not in breach;
- if the debtor gives his consent at the time of repossession, that repossession will be valid: s 173(3).

Consent within s 173(3) must be unqualified and informed: *Chartered Trust v Pitcher* [1987] RTR 72. In *Mercantile Credit Co Ltd v Cross* [1965] QB 205 the Court of Appeal held that there was valid consent as the hire-purchase agreement contained the necessary statutory information about the right of the debtor to seek a court order for the restructuring of the agreement (per Willmer J at p 215):

> If a hirer chooses not to read what the notice required to be inserted in his hire-purchase agreement, he himself is, to my mind, the only sufferer.

In the *Chartered Trust* case no statutory information had been included in the agreement and the Court of Appeal held that the defendant was ignorant of his rights under the Hire Purchase Act 1965. It is submitted, therefore, that provided the agreement signed by the debtor does include the notice of his rights on repossession which are prescribed by the Consumer Credit (Agreements) Regulations 1983 and that a default notice does include a notice of the position on protected goods (if required), the debtor will be held to have been informed of his statutory rights.

18.2.2.2 Obtaining a court order for repossession of protected goods

In order to obtain a court order for repossession of goods (technically, a 'return order'), the creditor must commence an action in the county court claiming possession of the goods (CPR PD 7B, para 3.1). The creditor must have made a written request for delivery up of the goods prior to commencing proceedings either by including such a requirement in the default notice or by making a written request for delivery (s 134(1), CCA 1974). For the court's powers to make a return order see **21.2**.

18.2.2.3 Consequences of repossessing protected goods without a court order

Perhaps oddly, all too many creditors repossess goods without first obtaining a court order. The consequences for doing so are draconian (see s 91). The agreement will be treated as terminated (if it has not already been terminated by the creditor), the debtor shall be released from all liability under the agreement and can recover from the creditor all sums that he has paid under the agreement. Where an agreement is terminated under s 91 any security is avoided and the surety can recover any payments he has made to the creditor (s 113). Termination under s 91 also discharges the debtor or a relative from liability under a linked transaction (s 96).

A debtor can enforce his right to the return of all the sums paid by action. Note that any interested party (presumably the creditor, debtor, surety or party to a linked transaction) can seek a declaration under s 142 of the Act that an agreement has been terminated under s 91.

18.2.2.4 Prohibition against repossessing goods from any premises

Even if goods are not protected they are still safe from the creditor if stored on the debtor's (or on a third party's) premises (s 92, CCA 1974). A contractual provision entitling the creditor to enter the debtor's or any other premises is void (s 173(1)). The debtor can consent to the repossession of goods at the time of repossession despite his protection under this section (see **18.2.2.1** above for a discussion about the meaning of consent in this context).

18.2.2.5 Obtaining a court order for repossession

A court order for repossession of goods protected by s 92 is obtained by a claim brought pursuant to CPR PD 7B, para 3.1(4). The court is not obliged to make an order but may make a time order instead (see **21.1**).

18.2.2.6 Consequences of repossessing goods from any premises without first obtaining a court order

A creditor who enters onto a debtor's premises and repossesses goods without a court order is liable for damages for breach of statutory duty. The debtor may also apply for an injunction to force the creditor to return the goods (s 170(3)).

19

Early settlement of hire-purchase, conditional sale, credit sale and loan agreements

We have seen that the original plan under these types of agreement is that the debtor should make instalment payments over a fixed period of time until his indebtedness to the creditor is discharged. However, circumstances may change.

The creditor may wish to make the debtor pay up the outstanding amount in one lump sum (in the case of credit sale and loan agreements this is virtually all the creditor can do if the debtor falls into arrears since it has no contractual right to repossess the goods). Although accelerated payments clauses usually come into effect only if the debtor is in breach, enforcement of such a clause does not mean that the contract is terminated; rather it is a speeding-up of its operation. Title will still pass to the debtor under a conditional sale agreement.

The debtor may wish to pay up the outstanding balance in one lump sum rather than continue with an ongoing financial liability. He has no common law right to do so but has a statutory right in the case of regulated consumer credit agreements under s 94, CCA 1974.

19.1 Accelerated payments clauses

Rather than terminate an agreement, the creditor might want to rely on an accelerated payments clause. This is a clause entitling the creditor to require the debtor to make an early repayment of all sums due under the agreement. Such agreements are common in conditional sale and credit sale agreements. There is no authority about whether it is appropriate to include such clauses in hire-purchase agreements (when the clause would have the effect of exercising the debtor's option to purchase the goods one way or the other) although in *Wadham Stringer Finance Ltd v Meaney* [1981] 1 WLR 39 Woolf J seemed to assume that it was.

An accelerated payments clause might be attractive to a creditor in two circumstances. First, where the debtor is in a non-repudiatory breach of the agreement (for as we have seen, if the creditor terminates it may be difficult for it to recover any of the outstanding balance from the debtor) and secondly, where it is going to be difficult for it to repossess the goods or where the goods are unlikely to be worth much (so that it does not make economic sense for the creditor to terminate the agreement and repossess the goods).

As a matter of common law such a clause is subject to the doctrine of penalties — the clause must provide for a rebate or discount for accelerated receipt of all the monies due under the agreement or it will be void as a penalty — *Wadham Stringer Finance Ltd v Meaney*. As with *Waragowski* damages, a creditor would be in a considerably better position if he operated an accelerated payments clause and did not have to give a rebate for early receipt of the balance due under the agreement.

In practice most finance houses use the so-called Rule of 78 to calculate the rebate (see Goode, para IC/36.49 for a mathematical explanation) due under an agreement which provides that the debtor should make payments of equal instalments at equal intervals. The formula was approved in *Wadham Stringer Finance Ltd v Meaney*. It is:

$$\frac{a\,(a + 1) \times \text{total charge for credit on which rebate allowed}}{b\,(b + 1)} = \text{rebate}$$

where

a = the number of payment periods still to run at the date of settlement; and

b = the number of payment periods in the contract.

Let's see how this works in practice. Suppose that under an unregulated conditional sale agreement a boat is being sold to Mr Baker by Usurius Finance plc. The cash price of the boat is £18,000 and Mr Baker must make 48 monthly payments of £1,000. The total charge for credit is the amount which Mr Baker must pay under the agreement less the price of the boat (£48,000 [48 x £1,000] – £18,000), so the figure in this example is £30,000. Let's suppose that Mr Baker settles the agreement after six months, so a = 42 and b = 48. The sum is now:

$$\frac{42 \times 43 \times \pounds 30{,}000}{48 \times 49} = \pounds 23{,}035.71$$

So Mr Baker's liability has been reduced from £42,000 (42 payments of £1,000) to just under £19,000 (£18,964.29).

19.1.1 The position under CCA 1974

We must now consider how CCA 1974 modifies the common law position.

19.1.1.1 Necessity of serving s 76 or default notice before accelerated payments clause can take effect

First, the creditor cannot enforce an accelerated payments clause without first serving a s 76 or default notice (since either must be served before the creditor is to be entitled to demand earlier payment of any sum).

For the statutory requirements relating to the form and contents of ss 76 and 87 notices, the debtor's choices of action when served with one and the effect of the creditor not complying with the relevant section see **Chapter 18**.

Note that if the debtor fails to comply with a default notice by paying the accelerated sum due, the creditor need not serve a fresh default notice before suing him (s 88(3)).

19.1.1.2 Statutory calculation of rebate

CCA 1974 ensures that the debtor is granted an appropriate rebate. This is done by requiring the creditor to give the debtor the higher of two rebates:

- the rebate expressly provided in the agreement; and
- a rebate under s 95, CCA 1974 calculated in accordance with the Consumer Credit (Rebate on Early Settlement) Regulations 1983 (SI 1983 No 1562).

The Regulations provide different rebates for different types of agreement: one of them gives statutory effect to the Rule of 78 for agreements where the debtor must make equal periodic instalment repayments.

19.1.1.3 When does a rebate arise?

The debtor is only entitled to a rebate at the point when he pays the sum due under the accelerated payments clause in full: *Forward Trust Ltd v Whymark* [1990] 2 QB 670. For observations on statements of case in a debt action for an unpaid amount due under an accelerated payments clause, see **25.2.3.1**.

19.2 Debtor's statutory right to early settlement

Under s 94, CCA 1974, the debtor has a right to settle the agreement upon payment of the outstanding balance (with a rebate for early settlement calculated in accordance with s 95). In effect the position is the same as under an accelerated payments clause: the creditor is paid off early and, in conditional sale agreements, title is transmitted to the debtor earlier than would have been the case if the agreement had run its course.

19.2.1 Exercise of right to early settlement

Section 97, CCA 1974 provides that if a debtor requests a settlement statement (notifying him of the amount required to settle the outstanding balance) then the creditor must supply him with one within 12 working days. The figure given is binding on the creditor (unless the court grants relief under s 172) and the creditor may be estopped from revising and correcting a mistake if the debtor has relied on it: *Lombard North Central v Stobart* [1990] CCLR 53.

20

Interference with the creditor's title by a third party

We have seen that a crucial feature of hire-purchase and conditional sale agreements is that title remains vested in the creditor until the debtor has made all the payments due under the agreement. It is not uncommon, however, for a third party to acquire, or threaten to acquire, possession of and/or title to the creditor's goods. This chapter examines the creditor's rights and remedies in such a situation.

20.1 Wrongful disposal of the goods by the debtor

If the debtor purports to sell goods before he has acquired title to them, title will not pass to the purchaser unless he is able to rely on one of the nemo dat exceptions (see **6.2**).

20.1.1 Measure of damages for conversion of goods subject to a hire-purchase or conditional sale agreement

Where title has not passed to the purchaser, the creditor can sue him for delivery up of the goods and/or damages. Whilst the usual measure of damages for conversion is the market value of the goods at the date of conversion, where the creditor has received some payments under the hire-purchase or conditional sale agreement, the measure of damages is the lesser of the outstanding balance due under the agreement or the value of the goods: see *Wickham Holdings Ltd v Brooke House Motors Ltd* [1967] 1 WLR 295 and *Chubb Cash v John Crilley & Sons* [1983] 1 WLR 599.

Under s 3(6), Torts (Interference with Goods) Act 1977, the court can order the converter to pay the difference between the value of the goods and the outstanding balance due under a hire-purchase or conditional sale agreement instead of ordering him to deliver up the goods.

20.1.2 Creditor's remedies against debtor

Where title has passed to the purchaser or the creditor prefers to sue the debtor for conversion, it can either sue for damages for conversion (subject to the rule on damages above) or rely on the contract which, as we have seen (**17.1.2**), will almost certainly have been repudiated by the debtor parting with possession of the goods.

20.2 Distress levied against goods

The debtor's landlord is entitled to levy distress against his goods for unpaid rent. If goods which are the subject of a hire-purchase agreement or conditional sale agreement are on the debtor's premises when distress is levied then they may also be seized by the landlord. Can the creditor regain possession of them and prevent them being sold?

The Law of Distress Amendment Act 1908 allows the owner of goods in the possession of a party against whom a landlord has levied distress to protect himself by serving a notice of ownership on the landlord. Thereafter the landlord may not proceed with the distress. However, the Act appears significantly to restrict the right of a creditor to avail itself of this protection. Section 4A of the 1908 Act provides that there is no protection where the goods are the subject of a hire-purchase or conditional sale agreement (whether regulated or unregulated) unless the agreement had been terminated at the time when distress was levied. Since a creditor cannot terminate a regulated agreement without first serving a default or s 76 notice (see **Chapter 18**) a creditor will also fall within this exception if, at the time that distress was levied, a default or s 76 notice was in existence.

For this reason most agreements provide for automatic termination in the event of a landlord levying distress. However, even that may not save the creditor. For if the goods are in the possession of the tenant with the consent of the owner and in the reputed ownership of the tenant then the creditor cannot serve a notice of ownership (s 4A of the 1908 Act). In order to withdraw consent the creditor must serve some sort of notice on the debtor: a clause in the agreement withdrawing consent in the event of automatic termination will not suffice: *Times Furnishings Co Ltd v Hutchings* [1938] 1 KB 775.

20.3 Execution in aid of judgment

The goods might be seized by a sheriff executing a writ of fi. fa. or a bailiff issuing a warrant of execution to enforce a judgment debt against the debtor. The creditor can seek the return of the goods prior to sale by issuing interpleader proceedings. If it does not do so, and the goods are sold, then the buyer will obtain good title. The creditor, however, may be entitled to the proceeds of sale (see s 98, County Courts Act 1984).

20.4 Death of debtor

Section 86, CCA 1974 provides that if a debtor dies while a regulated agreement is still operative, the creditor cannot take any of the steps set out in s 87(1) (see **18.1**) if the agreement is 'fully secured'. The result is that the debtor's personal representatives step into the debtor's shoes. If the agreement is not fully secured then the creditor can take any of the steps in s 87 but must first apply to the court (ss. 86 and 128) and prove to the court that it has been unable to satisfy itself that the debtor's present and future obligations under the agreement are likely to be discharged.

20.4.1 Making the section 86(2) application

An application is made in the same way as an application for an enforcement order (see **Chapter 15**) save that the debtor's personal representatives (or if there are none, such persons as the court shall direct) shall be joined as parties to the application (see CPR, PD 7B, paras 9.3 to 9.6).

20.4.2 Meaning of 'fully secured'

There is an odd lacuna in CCA 1974: it does not define the term 'fully secured'. There are differing academic views about what it means but no case law. The differing academic views can be shortly summarised:

(a) Security is defined in s 189 as meaning a mortgage, pledge, bond, debenture, indemnity, guarantee, bill note or other right provided by the debtor or at his request. Thus if the debtor has given some form of guarantee which is sufficient to cover the entire debt then the agreement is fully secured (Goode, II/5.369).

(b) The goods bailed to the debtor are the security and if the agreement expressly provides that the creditor has a right to possession on termination then the agreement is fully secured.

The absence of case law on the point suggests that in practice creditors and personal representatives are able to reach agreement about what should happen following a debtor's death — note that the debtor's personal representatives can consent to the agreement being enforced without a court order (s 173(3)).

21

Statutory protection of the debtor

CCA 1974 confers statutory protection on a debtor against whom a creditor is enforcing, or threatening to enforce, an agreement. This is achieved through:

- the regime of time orders, return orders and transfer orders set out in ss 129 to 136, CCA 1974; and
- relief on the basis that the agreement is an extortionate credit bargain (ss. 137 to 140, CCA 1974).

We must notice an important distinction between these methods of statutory protection. The former (time orders etc) can be made only in relation to agreements regulated by CCA 1974. However, a debtor may seek relief on the basis that the agreement is an extortionate credit bargain whether that agreement is regulated or not provided that the debtor is an individual within the meaning of the Act (see **14.1**).

Always bear in mind that the debtor may be better off exercising his statutory right to terminate the agreement than allowing the creditor to do so (see **Chapter 22**).

21.1 Time orders

Section 129(1)(b) provides that a debtor may seek the protection of a time order:

- when served with a default notice; or
- when served with a s 76 notice or s 98 notice.

Thus the court has jurisdiction to make a time order before a creditor has issued proceedings against a debtor.

In addition, the court may of its own motion make a time order (or the debtor can ask it to do so):

(a) when considering an application by the creditor for an enforcement order (s 129(1)(a)); and

(b) in an action brought by the creditor to enforce a regulated agreement or security, or to recover possession of any goods to which a regulated agreement relates (s 129(1)(c)).

The court can grant one or both of the following types of time order (s 129(2)):

(a) Payment by the debtor of any sum owed under a regulated agreement in such instalments as the court, having regard to the debtor's means, considers reasonable.

(b) The remedy by the debtor of any breach (other than non-payment of money) within such period as the court may specify.

21.1.1 Some notes about section 129(2)(a) time orders

In practice, most applications for time orders relate to the debtor wanting more time to make payments to a creditor.

We must first examine what sums the debtor can seek time to pay. Remember the court's jurisdiction to make a time order extends only to 'any sum owed'.

Thus, whatever the sort of agreement, the debtor can seek time to pay arrears which have fallen due by the time the court considers the application for a time order. However, this may be of cold comfort to the debtor. After all, if he could not afford to pay previous instalments when they fell due then he may well be unable to afford to pay future instalments when they fall due. Can a time order extend to future instalments?

Under s 130(2) the court may, when making a time order under s 129(2)(a) in relation to a hire-purchase or conditional sale agreement only, also deal with future instalments. No such provision exists in relation to credit sale or loan agreements.

However, a debtor under a credit sale or loan agreement may be able to obtain the relief of a time order in relation to the outstanding balance due under the agreement if, when the application for a time order comes before the court, an accelerated payments clause has come into effect: see *First National Bank plc v Syed* [1991] 2 All ER 250 and *Southern and District Finance plc v Barnes* (1996) 27 HLR 691, and the commentary in Goode, IC/46.172–73. It is submitted that this is plainly correct where the creditor is seeking to enforce an accelerated payments clause (for in such a case the debtor owes the creditor that money), it is a moot point whether it is correct when the agreement allows the creditor to enforce an accelerated payments clause but it is not in fact seeking to do so.

A time order rescheduling payment of a debt is not limited merely to the time in which such sums should be paid. Section 136 grants the court wide powers to 'include such provision as it considers just for amending any agreement or security in consequence of a term of the order'. Thus, for example, the court can reduce (or even eliminate) the contractual rate of interest charged on late payments (in *Equity Homes Ltd v Lewis*, one of the conjoined appeals heard with *Southern and District Finance plc v Barnes*, the Court of Appeal upheld an order made by the judge reducing the rate of interest from an APR of 44.1% to nil for otherwise the amount of interest which would have built up over the extended period of repayment would have made the grant of the time order in the first place pointless).

21.1.2 Some notes about section 129(2)(b) time orders

The second type of time order obviously cannot be granted when a creditor has served a s 76 or s 98 notice since service of such a notice is predicated on the debtor not having committed a breach of the agreement. Nevertheless, in practice the protection afforded by s 129(2)(a) may be of assistance if the creditor is seeking, for example, to enforce an accelerated payments clause.

Applications for the second type of time order are rare since breaches other than non-payment of money are likely in practice to be irremediable. Nevertheless, there may be situations where a debtor can remedy a breach but needs longer than the time allowed by the creditor in a default notice to do so, for example, where he has parted with possession of the goods in breach of the agreement but hopes to be able to regain them.

Section 130(5) provides that when a time order is made under s 129(2)(b) the creditor cannot, during the period of time granted by the order, take any steps set out in s 87(1) or treat as operative any clause in the agreement which becomes operative only on the occurrence of an event to which the time order relates. If the breach is remedied during the period of time granted by the court then the breach is to be treated as not having occurred.

21.1.3 Effect of a time order

When a time order is made in relation to a regulated hire-purchase or conditional sale agreement then the debtor is to be treated as the bailee of the goods under the terms of the original agreement as modified by the time order even if the agreement has been terminated (s 130(4)).

21.1.4 Court procedure

The only court of first instance which can grant time orders is the county court. The High Court does not have jurisdiction to grant time orders (s 129 provides that 'the court' may make time orders and 'the court' is defined by s 189 as meaning the county court.) Moreover, only the county court has jurisdiction to determine proceedings relating to the enforcement of a regulated agreement (s 141) and only the county court has jurisdiction to hear an application for an enforcement order (s 65).

21.1.4.1 Application by debtor on receipt of a default or s 76 or s 98 notice

PD 7B, para 7.3 sets out the matters to be included in the particulars of claim of a debtor seeking a time order. The claim must be issued in the court for the district where the creditor resides or carries on business (PD 7B, para 4.3).

21.1.4.2 Application made in the course of proceedings

This could be made at an interim stage or at the hearing of the action itself, although the court has jurisdiction to make the order of its own motion.

21.1.4.3 Evidence of means

It is clearly desirable for the debtor to provide evidence of his means in the form of a witness statement. Presumably the debtor must give disclosure of any documents relevant to his means if he intends to ask the court to make a time order at some stage in the proceedings.

21.1.4.4 Time orders by consent

Whilst a court is normally obliged to consider the debtor's means before making a time order, where the parties agree terms for a time order under s 129(2)(a), the court may make the order in the agreed terms without hearing evidence of means (s 130(1)).

21.1.4.5 Guidelines for exercise of the court's discretion

In *Southern and District Finance plc v Barnes* (1996) 27 HLR 691, the Court of Appeal considered the approach a court should take in considering an application for time order:

(a) The court must consider whether it is just to make the order. That requires consideration of all the circumstances of the case and of the position of the creditor and of the debtor.

(b) When a time order is made it should normally be made for a stipulated period on account of temporary financial difficulty. If, despite the giving of time, the debtor is unlikely to be able to resume repayment of the total indebtedness by at least the amount of the contractual instalments, no time order should be made. It is more equitable to enforce the agreement.

(c) When a time order is made relating to the non-payment of money, the court must consider what instalments would be reasonable both as to amount and timing, having regard to the debtor's means.

(d) The court may include in the order any amendment to the agreement which it considers just and is a consequence of the order under s 136 (see **21.1.1** above).

(e) Making a time order when the outstanding balance is due under the agreement (eg, under an accelerated payments clause) will inevitably have consequences for the term of the loan or the rate of interest or both.

The conjoined appeals in *Southern and District Finance plc v Barnes* all related to possession proceedings brought by creditors to enforce mortgages granted by the debtors as securities against loans advanced by the creditors. The Court of Appeal went on to hold that where a time order was made in those cases, possession orders should be suspended so long as the terms of the time order were complied with. It is submitted that by analogy the court should also suspend any return order it makes in respect of goods (see **21.2** below).

21.2 Return orders

We have already seen that it is necessary for the court to make a return order before a creditor can repossess protected goods which are the subject of a regulated hire-purchase or conditional sale agreement. The provision for return orders is set out in s 133. In practice it is rare for a court not to make a return order. It is more common for return orders to be suspended, usually in conjunction with a time order. The court has powers to suspend orders under s 135(1)(b) either until such time as the court subsequently directs or until the occurrence of a specified act or omission.

For example, a court might make a time order under s 129(2)(a) and a return order under s 133 but suspend the operation of the latter under s 135(1)(b). If the suspension order provides that the suspension shall lapse if the debtor fails to make a payment due under the terms of the time order then the creditor will be able to repossess the goods; if the suspension order is made under s 135(1)(b)(i) then the creditor will need to make a further application to the court.

21.3 Transfer orders

In practice transfer orders are extremely rare. They apply in cases of a regulated hire-purchase or conditional sale agreement concerning separate goods. The court can make an order returning some of the goods to the creditor and transferring some to the debtor (see s 133(3) and (7) for the condition precedent to a transfer order). In practice, separate goods are rarely the subject of a regulated hire-purchase agreement or conditional sale agreement (an example might be a three-piece suite) and it is rare for anyone to seek a transfer order.

21.4 Overarching right of debtor to claim title

Note that under s 133(4), if a debtor pays the balance of the total price before a creditor has repossessed the goods then he may claim the goods notwithstanding any return or transfer orders. In practice this is likely to be of benefit only to a Pools or National Lottery winner!

21.5 Extortionate credit bargains

Section 138(1) provides that a credit bargain is extortionate if the credit agreement (together with, if applicable, other transactions whose charges are to be taken into account in calculating the total charge for credit) requires the debtor or his relative to make payments which are grossly exorbitant or which grossly contravene ordinary principles of fair dealing. Although the point must be raised by the debtor or surety, it is for the creditor to prove that the bargain is not extortionate (s 171(7)). There are proposals to change the current 'grossly exorbitant' test to an 'excessive payments' test; to enable the court to look at matters arising after the agreement was made (perhaps including falls in interest rates); and the court may be allowed to consider whether the transaction involved 'deceitful or oppressive or otherwise unfair or improper' conduct (the test used in fitness for a consumer credit licence). Whether these changes will be implemented and when, remains to be seen.

21.5.1 Making the application

A debtor or surety must make an application to the court to re-open the agreement on the basis that it was extortionate; the court cannot do so of its own motion. The application can be made either by the debtor or surety before proceedings have been commenced (s 139(1)(a)). (The County Court has jurisdiction to hear the application whatever the size of the agreement (High Court and County Courts Jurisdiction Order 1991, article 2(1)(h).) The application can be made even if all payments due under the agreement have been made provided that it would not have the effect of altering any judgment (s 139(4)).

Alternatively, an application can be raised in the course of proceedings to enforce the agreement, any security or linked transaction related to it (s 139(1)(b)) or where proceedings have commenced and the amount paid or payable under the credit agreement is relevant (s 139(1)(c)).

A claim under s 138(1)(a) is a Consumer Credit Act claim (PD 7B, para 3.1(5)). Notice of an intention to make an application under s 139(1)(b) or (c) must be made within 14 days of service of the claim form on the applicant and is to be treated as a defence (CPR, PD 7B, para 10).

21.5.2 Factors taken into account in determining the application

Section 138 requires the court to have regard to the following factors when considering whether a credit bargain is extortionate:

(a) interest rates prevailing at the time it was made;

(b) the debtor's age, experience, business capacity and state of health and the degree of financial pressure on the debtor when he entered into the credit bargain;

(c) the degree of risk accepted by the creditor having regard to the value of any security provided, its relationship to the debtor and whether or not a colourable cash price was quoted for any goods or services included in the credit bargain;

(d) how far the linked transaction (if any) was reasonably required for the protection of the debtor or creditor and how far it was in the interest of the debtor.

When considering these factors the court has to focus on the agreement when it was made: *Paragon Finance plc v Staunton* [2001] 2 All ER (Comm) 1025 (a case involving variable rate mortgages, where there was also an issue over the fixing of the rates from time to time). That decision was followed in *Broadwick Financial Services v Spencer* [2002] GCCR 51.

21.5.3 Court's powers

If a court finds that a credit bargain was extortionate, it may take any of the steps set out in s 139(2), namely:

(a) direct accounts to be taken;

(b) set aside the whole or any part of any obligation imposed on the debtor or surety by the credit bargain or any related agreement;

(c) require the creditor to repay the whole or any part of any sum paid under the credit bargain or any related agreement by the debtor or a surety;

(d) direct the return to the surety of any property provided for the purposes of the security; or

(e) alter the terms of the credit agreement or any security instrument.

Note further that the court can require a creditor to repay sums received by a third party to the agreement even if this places a burden on the creditor and confers an unfair advantage on another person who is a party to a linked transaction (s 139(3)).

21.5.4 Section 137 relief in practice

In practice, applications for a credit bargain to be re-opened on the basis that it is extortionate are rare. This is probably because the regulatory regime weeds out 'bad' creditors. Nevertheless the question does arise from time to time (see *A. Ketley Ltd v Scott* [1981] ICR 241 for an example of a credit bargain which was found not to be exorbitant and *Castle Phillips & Co Ltd v Wilkinson* [1992] CCLR 83 for an example of one that was).

21.5.5 Limitation period

The limitation period for an application under s 137 is 12 years: see ss 8 and 9, Limitation Act 1980 and *Rahman v Sterling Credit Ltd* [2001] 1 WLR 496.

21.6 Declaration under section 142

Note that a debtor can pre-empt a creditor's application for an enforcement order by applying for a declaration that he is not entitled to one (see **15.6.5**).

22 Debtor's right to terminate

In this chapter we shall examine the debtor's contractual right to terminate and the statutory modification imposed on this aspect of consumer credit law by CCA 1974. We shall examine the debtor's common law right to terminate the agreement where the creditor is in breach of a condition in **Chapter 23**.

22.1 The common law position

It is by no means uncommon for hire-purchase and conditional sale agreements to include a provision allowing the debtor to terminate the agreement. If the position was left there then the debtor would simply be liable for his obligations prior to termination (eg, to pay all instalments up to the date of termination and keep the goods in good repair) and to return the goods to the creditor. Unfortunately for debtors, most creditors are hard-nosed financial institutions unwilling to let them off so lightly. Most agreements will provide for the debtor to pay some additional sum to the creditor if he exercises his contractual right to terminate. Since the debtor is not in breach of the agreement by terminating it such a clause is not open to attack under the doctrine of penalties (although it might be open to attack under s 137 — see **21.5.4**). The paradoxical position is reached that it is better for a debtor to make the creditor terminate the agreement (provided that it is not for a repudiatory breach or breach of condition by the debtor) since his exposure to damages will be lower.

22.1.1 Protection of debtor

The courts have been concerned to protect a debtor who exercises a contractual right to terminate and unwittingly exposes himself to a greater claim for compensation from the creditor than he would have done if he had waited for the creditor to terminate. Thus in *United Dominions Trust (Commercial) Ltd v Ennis* [1968] 1 QB 54, Lord Denning MR said that a debtor 'is not to be taken as exercising such an option unless he does so consciously, knowing of the consequences and avowedly in exercise of his option.' We must note that this protection can now be neatly avoided by a creditor drafting the agreement to make as many of the debtor's obligations as possible conditions (see **17.1.3**).

22.2 The position under sections 99 and 100, CCA 1974

Section 99 confers a statutory right upon a debtor to terminate a regulated hire-purchase or conditional sale agreement. Section 100 caps the amount the debtor has to pay. If the agreement provides for the debtor to pay more upon his exercise of a contractual or the statutory right to terminate then that clause is void (s 173).

The statute does not modify the common law position that the debtor remains liable for any arrears that accrue prior to the date of termination. Section 100(4) provides that the court must order the debtor to compensate the creditor for any failure to take reasonable care of the goods prior to termination. Section 100(5) allows the court a discretionary power (not to be used unless it considers just to do so) to order the debtor to pay the creditor the value of the goods rather than return them.

Note that the prohibition on the creditor repossessing protected goods (see **Chapter 18**) does not apply when the debtor has terminated the agreement under s 99.

22.2.1 Exercise of the statutory right to terminate

The right is exercised by giving written notice to any person entitled or authorised to receive sums payable under the agreement. The right must be exercised before the final payment becomes due. Thus, if the creditor has exercised an accelerated payments clause, the final payment has become due and the debtor has lost his statutory right to terminate (*Wadham Stringer Finance Ltd v Meaney* [1981] 1 WLR 39). Note, however, that an accelerated payments clause cannot be exercised before expiry of a s 76 or default notice so the debtor can exercise his statutory right to terminate in the period between service of such a notice and its expiry.

22.2.2 The statutory cap on the debtor's liability

Section 100 provides that the amount to be paid by the debtor shall be the difference between one half of the total price of the goods and the sum of payments paid and due prior to termination.

In some cases, the total price will include an installation charge as well as the price of goods (eg, sale of a fitted kitchen to a debtor by hire-purchase agreement). In such cases the figure from which the payments paid and due prior to termination must be deducted is the sum of the aggregate of the installation charge and one half of the remainder of the total price (s 100(2)).

22.2.2.1 Circumstances where the debtor pays less than the s 100 liability

There may, however, be circumstances where the debtor has to pay less than the s 100 measure of damages or indeed nothing at all to the creditor. These are:

(a) If the agreement contains a clause under which the debtor would have to pay less than he would under s 100. The debtor is liable only for the smaller amount.

(b) If the agreement contains no provision for the debtor to pay anything at all upon termination (so we are left in the bizarre position where an agreement must either contain a clause setting out the effect of s 100 (which applies anyway) or which exposes the debtor to a greater liability (which is unenforceable under s 173)).

(c) If the amount of payments paid and due by the date of termination exceeds one half of the total price of the goods (so termination of the agreement towards the end of the contract term will result in the debtor not having to pay anything further to the creditor).

(d) Where in any action the court is satisfied that the creditor's loss by reason of the debtor's termination would be less than is due under s 100(1) in which case the court may award the lower sum (s 100(3)). The Act does not suggest how the creditor's loss might be measured. Since an express contractual right to pay a lower sum will be enforced under s 100(1) and the common law measure of damages for early termination is always lower than the statutory formula created by s 100(1), the section is either practically meaningless or a reduction of s 100(1) to statutory impotence. Goode expresses the view that loss is to be measured by the *Yeoman Credit Ltd v Waragowski* [1961] 1 WLR 1124 measure of damages (see IIB/5.190) but how would this work in practice?

23

Debtor's remedies for breaches and misrepresentations by creditor and dealer

For obvious reasons, the breaches usually committed by creditors and dealers/suppliers relate to defective goods. Unfortunately, but unavoidably, therefore, this chapter inevitably involves a great deal of cross-referencing with the earlier section of this work on sale of goods.

We should note from the outset that in debtor–creditor agreements the creditor attracts no liability for any breach of the contract which is financed by the credit he supplies. If there are any defects in the goods or services supplied under that contract then the debtor's remedies are against the supplier under SOGA 1979 and SOGSA 1982. That having been noted, we can now ignore debtor–creditor agreements for the remainder of this chapter and examine the debtor's remedies for breach of contract and misrepresentation in debtor–creditor–supplier agreements.

23.1 Section 12(a) agreements

We are here concerned with hire-purchase, conditional sale and credit sale agreements. Note that the position on defective goods and defective title applies to both unregulated and regulated agreements.

23.1.1 Implied terms as to quality of goods

Sections 13 to 15, SOGA 1979 apply to all credit sale and conditional sale agreements. Sections 9 to 11, SOGITA 1973 (which substantially mirror ss 13 to 15, SOGA 1979) apply to all hire-purchase agreements. The debtor's contractual remedy for breach of these implied terms lies against the creditor (who is the legal supplier), not the dealer. The dealer may be liable in negligence, under the Consumer Protection Act 1987 or under a collateral warranty to the debtor. (The latter is illustrated in *Andrews v Hopkinson* [1957] 1 QB 229, in which a dealer told a customer that he would have no trouble with a car. The customer entered into a hire-purchase agreement with a finance company for the car. Unfortunately he did have trouble with it. He crashed it because its steering mechanism was defective. It was held that the dealer was liable for breach of a collateral warranty.)

23.1.1.1 Fitness for purpose: purpose known to whom?

We saw in **Chapter 10** that a seller is only in breach of s 14(3), SOGA 1979 if he knew of the purpose for which the goods were being bought. A creditor will be liable under s 14(3), SOGA 1979 or s 10, SOGITA 1973 where the debtor is an individual (see **14.1**) who made the purpose for which he required the goods known to the creditor or anyone deemed to be his agent under s 56. Where the debtor is a corporate entity it must have made the purpose for which it required the goods known to the creditor in order to rely on s 14(3).

23.1.2 Rejection and damages for breach of warranty

It is now convenient to distinguish between two types of consumer credit transactions:

- non-consumer conditional sale agreements and credit sale agreements;
- hire-purchase agreements and consumer conditional sale agreements.

23.1.2.1 Distinction between consumer and non-consumer conditional sale agreements

We saw in **Chapter 10** that if goods are supplied in breach of ss 13 to 15, SOGA 1979, the buyer can either accept them, treat the breach of condition as a breach of warranty and claim damages or reject them and reclaim all sums paid on the basis that there has been a total failure of consideration.

We saw that the buyer can lose his right to reject at common law where he affirms the contract or by s 11(4), SOGA 1979 is deemed to have accepted the goods. However, s 14, SOGITA 1973 provides that where the debtor in a conditional sale agreement deals as a consumer within Part I of UCTA 1977, s 11(4) shall not apply. Consequently, a debtor in a conditional sale agreement who is a consumer within Part I of UCTA 1977 can only lose his right to reject under the common law doctrine of affirmation.

23.1.2.2 Position of debtor supplied with defective goods under credit sale and non-consumer conditional sale agreements

A debtor can lose his right to reject goods supplied under these types of agreement under ss 15A, 30(2A) (where applicable), 35 and 35A. (See **Chapter 10**.) Where a debtor rejects the goods he is entitled to recovery of all and any sums paid. If he affirms or accepts the goods or elects to treat the breach of condition as a breach of warranty then his measure of damages is that set out in s 53(3), SOGA 1979 (see **Chapter 10**).

23.1.2.3 Position of debtor supplied with defective goods under hire-purchase and consumer conditional sale agreements

We have seen that s 11(4), SOGA 1979 does not apply to consumer conditional sale agreements. Nor does it apply to hire-purchase agreements. Consequently, the debtor loses his right to reject only under the common law doctrine of affirmation.

A caveat must be entered: if the debtor in a hire-purchase agreement deals as a non-consumer within Part I of UCTA 1977 and the breach is so slight that it would be unreasonable for him to reject them, then the breach shall not be treated as a breach of condition but may be treated as a breach of warranty (s 11A, SOGITA 1973).

23.1.2.4 Measure of damages where debtor rejects defective goods supplied under hire-purchase and consumer conditional sale agreements

If the debtor rejects the goods straight away then he is entitled to recover all sums paid. However, situations may arise where the debtor has had use of the goods prior to rejection. In such cases, on rejection, a sum representing the benefit the debtor has received from using the goods will be deducted from the debtor's damages: *Farnworth Finance Facilities v Attryde* [1970] 1 WLR 1053.

23.1.2.5 Measure of damages for breach of warranty

In cases where the debtor elects to treat the agreement as still on foot, the debtor will be entitled to damages under s 53, SOGA 1979 (in the case of a conditional sale agreement). See *Charterhouse Credit v Tolly* [1963] 2 QB 683 for the position where the debtor raises his claim for damages by counterclaim.

23.1.3 Defect in creditor's title in goods sold under hire-purchase, conditional sale and credit sale agreements

Section 12, SOGA 1979 (see **Chapter 10**) applies to all conditional sale and credit sale agreements. Section 8, SOGITA 1973 implies a similar term into all hire-purchase agreements. It follows that if the creditor has no title at the time when property is to pass then the debtor can reject the goods and recover all sums paid on the basis that there has been a total failure of consideration: *Warman v Southern Counties Car Finance Corporation Ltd* [1949] 2 KB 576, *Barber v NWS Bank plc* [1996] 1 WLR 641.

In hire-purchase and conditional sale agreements property is not due to pass until the end of the contractual term when the debtor will exercise his option to purchase (under a hire-purchase agreement) or receive title automatically (under a conditional sale agreement). Thus if the creditor does not have title at the outset of the agreement (when the goods are delivered to the debtor — see *Mercantile Union Guarantee Corporation Ltd v Wheatley* [1938] 1 KB 490) but acquires them during the contractual term, he will be able to feed good title to the debtor: *Butterworth v Kingsway Motors Ltd* [1954] 1 WLR 1286.

In *Barber v NWS Bank plc* [1996] 1 WLR 641, a clause in a conditional sale agreement provided that property in the goods should remain vested in the creditor until the debtor had paid all sums due thereunder. It was conceded by counsel for the creditor that this was a term and the Court of Appeal held that it was a conditon, breach of which put the debtor in the same position as if there had been a breach of s 12, SOGA 1979.

23.1.4 Liability of creditor for misrepresentations made by dealer

We saw in **Chapter 16** that at common law the dealer does not ordinarily act as the creditor's agent. Consequently, the creditor is not liable for any misrepresentation made by the dealer which induces the customer to enter into an unregulated hire-purchase, conditional sale or credit sale agreement. We saw that in the case of regulated agreements the dealer may well be deemed to be the creditor's agent under s 56, CCA 1974. When the dealer is a deemed agent under s 56, the debtor can pursue his common law remedies for misrepresentation against the creditor. Note that under s 102 of the 1974 Act the debtor may rescind by serving a notice of his intention to do so on the creditor or the persons mentioned in s 102.

23.1.5 Exclusion clauses

The common law and Unfair Contract Terms Act 1977 rules apply to all hire-purchase, conditional sale and credit sale agreements, whether regulated or unregulated. See **3.5** and **Chapter 4**.

23.2 Section 12(b) and (c) agreements

We must now consider the debtor's remedies when he purchases goods or services under a contract with a supplier which is financed by a creditor.

23.2.1 Liability for breach of contract

If the goods or services are defective then the debtor can pursue his remedies against the supplier. The terms implied by SOGA 1979 apply.

However, the creditor will attract concurrent liability for any breach of contract committed by the supplier under s 75, CCA 1974 where:

- the credit agreement is a s 12(b) or (c) agreement;
- the credit agreement is not a non-commercial agreement;
- the cash price of the goods under the supply contract exceeds £100 but does not exceed £30,000.

The creditor is entitled to seek an indemnity from the supplier under s 75(2).

There is some doubt about whether the credit agreement is affected by the breach of the supply agreement. Clearly the debtor has a right of set-off against any money he owes under the credit agreement. In two Scottish cases it has been held that if the debtor can rescind the supply agreement then he can also rescind the credit agreement under s 75 — *United Dominions Trust v Taylor* [1980] CCLR 29; *Forward Trust Ltd v Hornby* [1996] CCLR 18 — but the issue remains contentious.

23.2.2 Liability for misrepresentations

Section 75 imposes joint liability on the creditor for any misrepresentation made by the supplier. But if the debtor rescinds the supply agreement the credit agreement will still stand unless the debtor can argue that the supplier was a deemed agent of the creditor under s 56 and that he was induced to enter into the credit agreement by the supplier's misrepresentations; so that he may similarly rescind the credit agreement.

23.2.3 Exclusion clauses

Exclusion clauses in the contract of supply between the supplier and debtor will also affect the creditor's liability under s 75. Note, however, that the parties cannot contract out of s 75 (s 173(1)).

24

Paying with plastic

In this chapter we shall briefly examine some of the legal points which arise in transactions paid for with 'plastic' ie, cards. We shall not examine the legal liability for misuse of cards although it is a thorny and real problem.

24.1 The types of card

We must first consider the various types of card that the ordinary individual might use and the legal transactions that arise from their use (largely set out by Millett J in *Re Charge Card Services Ltd* [1987] 1 Ch 150). We shall break them down into five.

24.1.1 Debit cards

First, there are debit cards (eg, Delta and Switch cards). A debit card is issued by a bank to the card-holder pursuant to an agreement that the bank is authorised to debit the card-holder's account with the amount of any card transaction. A supplier who accepts debit cards has a Merchant Agreement with his bank pursuant to which he is paid by his bank for goods and services provided to debit card users. Where the card-holder's and supplier's bank is not the same there will be a further contract between the banks by which the supplier's bank is reimbursed by the card-holder's bank.

24.1.2 Credit cards

Second, there are credit cards such as Visa and Mastercard. Most credit card holders can use their card to finance sale or supply transactions (eg, the purchaser buys goods with a credit card) and to obtain a cash advance. The legal effect of a purchase transaction is the same as with a debit card but we can briefly note three differences.

(a) The card may be issued by a credit card company rather than a bank.

(b) Some stores offer their own credit cards for use only in that store. Hence there is only one contract — that between the store and the card-holder.

(c) Where the card-holder obtains a cash advance from someone other than the card-issuer (for example, a cash withdrawal on a Visa card via a Barclays ATM,) there will be at least two contracts — the first between the card-holder and the card-issuer and the second between the card-issuer and the cash-issuer. The question is whether there is a unilateral contract between the cash-issuer and the card-holder as is the case between banks and payees of cheques supported by cheque card (see below).

24.1.3 Charge cards

Third, there are charge cards (eg, Diners' Club and American Express cards). Charge card holders must repay the balance owing in full within a prescribed time. The legal effects of charge card use are otherwise exactly the same as with credit cards.

24.1.4 Cheque cards

Fourth, there are cheque cards. These involve two contracts. The first, between the card-issuer bank and the card-holder, allows the bank to debit the card-holder's account with the amount of any cheque supported by the card, obliges the card-holder not to create an unauthorised overdraft and obliges the bank to honour any cheque supported by the card. The second, between the bank and the payee, obliges the bank to honour any cheque up to the limit stated on the card whether or not it creates an unauthorised overdraft on the card-holder's account.

24.1.5 ATM cards

Fifth, there are ATM cards which allow an account-holder to withdraw cash (up to a prescribed limit) from his account. Inter-bank agreements make provision for ATM card-holders to use their cards in machines of different banks to that which issued the card.

24.2 Impact of CCA 1974

We shall consider the effect of CCA 1974 in two ways. First, as to whether the provisions of s 51 apply and secondly, as to whether the provisions of s 75 apply. Before we turn to these questions we must set the scene by examining s 14 of the 1974 Act.

24.2.1 Credit-tokens and credit-token agreements

Section 14 creates a category of consumer credit agreements known as credit-token agreements. So far as material, s 14(1) provides:

> *(1) A credit-token is a card ... given to an individual by a person carrying on a consumer credit business, who undertakes—*
> *(a) that on production of it ... he will supply cash, goods and services ... on credit, or*
> *(b) that where, on production of it to a third-party, the third-party supplies cash, goods and services ... he will pay the third-party for them ... in return for payment to him by the individual.*

Section 14(2) provides:

> *A credit-token agreement is a regulated agreement for the provision of credit in connection with the use of a credit-token.*

24.2.1.1 Application of s 14 to different types of cards

There is no doubt that credit cards are caught by the 1974 Act if the credit limit on the card is less than £25,000 and the card-holder is an individual within the meaning of s 189 of the Act. Equally, there is no doubt that charge cards are exempt from the Act (Consumer Credit (Exempt Agreements) Order 1989 (SI 1989 No 869)). It is generally assumed that cheque cards are not credit-tokens (Sch 2, Example 21, CCA 1974). There is a live academic debate about debit cards and ATM cards: the preponderant view appears to be that the cards are credit-tokens (when issued for use with an account that has an authorised overdraft limit of less than £25,000) but that the agreements by which they are supplied are not credit-token agreements. Since this book offers a practical approach the debate can be noted and then ignored for the most significant features about the Act specifically exclude such cards. In the remainder of this chapter, therefore, we shall concentrate simply on the effect of the Act on an individual credit card-holder with a credit limit less than £25,000.

24.2.2 Effect of CCA 1974 on credit-token agreements

An agreement for provision of a credit card is subject to the formalities provisions of CCA 1974. A creditor may not issue unsolicited cards (s 51). (If debit cards and ATM cards are credit-tokens then they are subject to this section. Banks appear to proceed on the basis that debit and ATM cards are not covered by the Act but in practice do not issue unsolicited debit cards and ATM cards — more's the pity!)

24.2.3 Effect of CCA 1974 on credit cards

Note that in the case of credit cards other than store cards (because store cards are debtor-creditor agreements), the card-issuer is liable under s 75 (see **Chapter 23**) and vicariously liable for the supplier (when the supplier is deemed to act as the card-issuer's agent — see **Chapter 15**). Sections 56 and 75 expressly do not apply to debit cards and ATM cards (s 187(3A)). Note that there is another live academic debate about whether a second card-holder (ie, someone authorised to use a card on the card-holder's account) is a debtor within the meaning of s 75.

25

Some practical points about litigation: court procedure

25.1 Forum: High Court or county court?

Under s 141 of the Consumer Credit Act 1974 the county court has exclusive jurisdiction to hear any action brought by the creditor to enforce a regulated agreement (and any security or linked transaction related to it). The county court has exclusive jurisdiction to hear applications by the debtor for a time order, transfer order, suspended return order, declaration that the creditor cannot apply for an enforcement order or relief on the basis that the agreement is an extortionate credit bargain under s 139(1)(a) (see **21.5**).

The High Court and county court have concurrent jurisdiction to hear actions brought by the creditor to enforce an unregulated agreement and any other action brought by the debtor. In a claim issued in the High Court relating to a Consumer Credit Act 1974 agreement, the Particulars of Claim must include a statement that the action is not one to which s 141 applies (PD 16, para 9.6).

25.1.1 Effect of wrongly starting an action in the High Court

Where a case to which s 141 applies is commenced in the High Court, what action should the court take?

Section 141(2) provides that the action shall not be treated as having been improperly brought but shall be transferred to the county court. In *Sovereign Leasing plc v Ali* [1992] CCLR 1 it was held that the effect of s 141(2) was to rob the court of any discretion: the action had to be transferred to the county court. However, that case was decided before s 40 of the County Courts Act 1984 was amended to provide that the High Court had jurisdiction to strike out any proceedings brought by a party who knew or ought to have known that the action should have been commenced in the county court. In at least one case (*Barclays Bank plc v Brooks* [1997] CCLR 60), a High Court judge has struck out an action relating to a regulated consumer credit agreement which was commenced in the High Court. Note, however, that in *Restick v Crickmore* [1994] 1 WLR 420, the Court of Appeal issued guidelines for the exercise of the court's discretion under s 40 which effectively provide that an action should ordinarily be transferred to the county court rather than struck out. These points, and others, were considered but not decided by the Court of Appeal in the celebrated case of *Barclays Bank plc v Piper* The Times, 31 May 1995 (not reported on this point).

A claimant who issued a claim in the High Court which ought to have been commenced in the county court may be ordered to pay the costs of the transfer and have any award of costs reduced by up to 25% (s 51(8) and (9), Supreme Court Act 1981).

25.2 County court claims

The rest of this chapter is devoted to noting points which are special to county court claims arising out of unregulated and regulated consumer credit agreements: save where otherwise stated the normal rules of civil procedure apply.

Note that the court's powers to grant time orders, return orders and transfer orders and its powers on an application under s 137 were fully considered in **Chapter 21**.

CPR, PD 7B (see **Appendix**) is a Practice Direction devoted to Consumer Credit Act claims.

25.2.1 Venue

PD 7B, para 4.1 provides that an action for recovery of possession of goods to which a regulated hire-purchase or conditional sale agreement relates shall be commenced in the county court for the district in which the debtor resides or carries on business or resided or carried on business at the date when he last made a payment under the agreement.

PD 7B, para 4.2 provides that any other claim for the recovery of goods shall be issued in the court for the district in which the defendant resides or carries on business or where the goods are situated.

PD 7B, para 4.3 provides that a debtor shall issue a claim for a time order only in the court for the district where the claimant resides or carries on business.

25.2.2 Parties

Section 141(5) requires all parties to a regulated agreement, and any surety, to be joined as parties to any action relating to the Agreement. This requirement is relaxed by PD 7B, para 9.1 (which provides for a court to dispense with the requirement that a debtor or surety should be joined on the claimant's without notice application though it appears that the claimant must still issue proceedings against such a person since he can only apply for a dispensing order before they are served) and para 9.2 which provides that the creditor's assignor (if any) need not be joined save as the court otherwise directs. Since it is by no means uncommon for creditors to assign agreements we ought to spend a moment to consider the position that this creates in a little more detail.

25.2.2.1 Assignment

It is rare for debtors to assign agreements and common for agreements to exclude their right to do so. So we shall concern ourselves with the position when one creditor assigns the agreement to another.

An assignment may be statutory or equitable. Section 136, Law of Property Act 1925 provides that a written assignment of which the debtor is given written notice is effective to pass all of the assignor's legal rights and remedies to the assignee. Thereafter the assignor has no legal rights in respect of the contract which has been assigned. If, however, the assignment fails to meet the requirements of s 136 (for example because the debtor is not given written notice of it as in *Warner Bros. Records Inc. v Rollgreen Ltd* [1976] QB 430, a case involving Rod Stewart) then the assignment is equitable and the assignor may still have legal rights against the assignee. In order to protect the assignee, and to ensure that all disputes are before the court, the court will usually insist on the assignor or assignee's joinder and will stay the action until that is done: see *Three Rivers District Council v Governor and Company of the Bank of England* [1996] QB 292.

25.2.3 Statements of case

Particulars of Claim in a claim for recovery of goods let under a hire-purchase or sold under a conditional sale agreement to anyone other than a limited company (regulated by the Act) must include the matters set out in PD 7B, para 7.2. Although most published precedents adopt the strategy of including a schedule giving the required information, it is also possible to use the rule as a structure for the statements of case (see **Form 25.1** for an example).

Form 25.1 Particulars of Claim complying with PD 7B, para 7.2

IN THE ELSINORE COUNTY COURT CLAIM No: EL612121

BETWEEN

GERTRUDE GHOST PLC Claimant

and

BERNARD MARCELLUS *Defendant*

PARTICULARS OF CLAIM

1. By a written hire-purchase agreement dated 13th September 2002 made between the Claimant and the Defendant ('the Agreement'), regulated by the Consumer Credit Act 1974 and signed by the Defendant at his home, the Claimant let to the Defendant a Toyota Nintendo car ('the Goods').
2. The cash price of the Goods was £7,000; the deposit was £1,200; the total charge for credit was £2,200; and the hire-purchase balance of £7,999 was payable by 24 equal consecutive monthly instalments of £333.33 starting on 12th October 2002.
3. By clause 1 of the Agreement it was an express condition that punctual payment of instalments was essential. Clause 10(a) of the Agreement provided that the Claimant could terminate it upon written notice if the Defendant was in breach of clause 1. By clause 11 of the Agreement it was agreed that in the event of the Claimant exercising its right of termination under clause 10, the Defendant should forthwith pay all outstanding arrears, and a sum equal to the outstanding balance of the agreement due at the date of termination less the net proceeds of the sale of the Goods by the Claimant and a rebate of charges to be calculated in accordance with the Rule of 78.
4. The total price payable under the Agreement was £8,000. The Defendant has paid the sum of £999.99 and the amount of the unpaid balance of the hire-purchase price is £7,000.01.
5. On 12th January 2003 the Defendant failed to pay the instalment then due and on 15th January 2003 the Claimant served a default notice under section 87 of the Act on the Defendant by first class post, requiring him to pay the amount of £333.33 to the Claimant within 7 days of the service of the notice.
6. The Defendant failed to pay the sum or any sum to the Claimant within 7 days of service of the notice and the Claimant thereupon became entitled under clause 11 of the Agreement to recover possession and demand delivery of the Goods and to recover the amount due under clause 11.

PARTICULARS

Total purchase price	£8,000.00
Sums paid or in arrear at date of termination	£1,333.32
Total due:	£6,666.68

(the Claimant will give credit if necessary for the value of the Goods if recovered.)

7. Further, the Claimant is entitled to and claims interest pursuant to section 69 of the County Courts Act 1984 on any award herein at such rate and for such period as this Honourable Court shall think fit.
8. This claim is a Consumer Credit Act claim within the meaning of CPR, PD 7B.

AND the Claimant claims:

(1) An Order for delivery of the Goods or alternatively their value;

(2) £333.33 arrears of instalments;

(3) Pursuant to clause 11, £6,666.68;

(4) Interest as stated in paragraph 7 above.

FRANCIS C. O'PHELIA

Dated this th day of 2003

Statement of truth

Rosencrantz & Guildenstern
8 Halibut House,
Foetid Lane,
London EC4

TO THE DISTRICT JUDGE OF THE COURT
AND TO THE DEFENDANT

25.2.3.1 Pleading the rebate due

We saw in **Chapters 17** and **19** that a debtor can become liable to pay the outstanding balance due under an agreement in three situations:

- when the creditor invokes an accelerated payments clause;
- when the debtor becomes liable to pay unliquidated Waragowski damages;
- when the debtor becomes liable to pay liquidated damages which include a rebate for early settlement.

In *Forward Trust Ltd v Whymark* [1990] 2 QB 670, the Court of Appeal held that when pleading a debt action for recovery of sums due under an accelerated payments clause there was no need to plead the rebate. This is because the amount of a rebate to which the debtor is entitled will depend upon when he pays the debt. The court will enter judgment for the full unrebated amount due but the judgment order will inform the judgment debtor of his right to a rebate at the point of settlement. Note, however, that the agreement in the *Forward Trust* case was regulated by CCA 1974 and so interest did not run on the judgment debt (see below). It is questionable whether it is correct not to plead the rebated sum when the agreement is unregulated and interest will run on the judgment debt.

When pleading a claim for unliquidated *Yeoman Credit Ltd v Waragowski* [1961] 1 WLR 1124 damages it would appear that the claimant cannot plead a rebate since the amount to be rebated is within the court's discretion. The Particulars of Claim should include an averment that the claimant will give a discount for accelerated receipt of the outstanding balance.

When pleading a claim for liquidated damages, the liquidated damages clause should include a formula for the amount of the rebate. If it does not, it is probably vague and uncertain (see **Chapter 3**) and if it only allows a fixed sum then it is liable to attack as a penalty clause. The consensus of opinion is that, as with debt actions for unpaid accelerated payments sums, the claimant need only plead the unrebated balance due and wait until settlement of the debt to calculate the amount of rebate to which the defendant is entitled.

25.2.4 Procedure

PD 7B creates a special Consumer Credit Act procedure for most types of cases concerning regulated agreements (see PD 7B, para 3). Under the procedure a hearing date is fixed when the claim form is issued. The defendant need not file a defence although if he does not do so in 14 days and subsequently defends the claim the court may take this into account when considering costs.

25.2.5 Preservation of goods

A creditor may be unhappy about its inability to recover goods which are in the possession of the debtor. It may, however, obtain an injunction requiring the debtor to preserve the goods in good condition until the hearing of the action. This can be done either under CPR, r 25.1 or under s 131, CCA 1974.

25.2.6 Judgment interest

In the county courts, judgment interest is not payable on a judgment given in proceedings to recover money due under an agreement regulated by CCA 1974 (County Court (Interest on Judgment Debts) Order 1991, Article 2(3)(a)). There is nothing to prevent contractual interest running after judgment. Contractual clauses allowing such interest became commonplace after the decision of the House of Lords in *Economic Life Assurance v Usborne* [1902] AC 147. More recently in *Director General of Fair Trading v First National Bank plc* [2002] 1 All ER 97 the House of Lords considered such a clause in a regulated agreement. The decision was that there is nothing in the CCA 1974 which prevents such contractual interest being charged in a regulated agreement, nor does the Act require notice to be given of the rights contained in s 129 or 136, CCA 1974. Similarly, charging interest in that way is not an unfair contract term.

25.2.7 Execution

A judgment or order of a county court for the payment of a sum of money in proceedings arising out of an agreement regulated by CCA 1974 cannot be transferred to the High Court for execution (High Court and County Courts Jurisdiction Order 1991, Article 8).

APPENDIX
CIVIL PROCEDURE RULES

PD 7B Practice Direction — Consumer Credit Act claim

This practice direction supplements CPR rule 7.9

1.1 In this practice direction 'the Act' means the Consumer Credit Act 1974, a section referred to by number means the section with that number in the Act, and expressions which are defined in the Act have the same meaning in this practice direction as they have in the Act.
1.2 'Consumer Credit Act procedure' means the procedure set out in this practice direction.

When to use the Consumer Credit Act Procedure

2.1 A claimant must use the Consumer Credit Act procedure where he makes a claim under a provision of the Act to which paragraph 3 of this practice direction applies.
2.2 Where a claimant is using the Consumer Credit Act procedure the CPR are modified to the extent that they are inconsistent with the procedure set out in this practice direction.
2.3 The court may at any stage order the claim to continue as if the claimant had not used the Consumer Credit Act procedure, and if it does so the court may give any directions it considers appropriate.
2.4 This practice direction also sets out matters which must be included in the particulars of claim in certain types of claim, and restrictions on where certain types of claim may be started.

The Provisions of the Act

3.1 Subject to paragraph 3.2 and 3.3 this practice direction applies to claims made under the following provisions of the Act:

(1) section 141 (claim by the creditor to enforce regulated agreement relating to goods etc),

(2) section 129 (claim by debtor or hirer for a time order),

(3) section 90 (creditor's claim for an order for recovery of protected goods),

(4) section 92(1) (creditor's or owner's claim to enter premises to take possession of goods),

(5) section 139(a) (debtor's claim for a credit agreement to be reopened as extortionate), and

(6) creditor's or owner's claim for a court order to enforce a regulated agreement relating to goods or money where the court order is required by:

(a) section 65(1) (improperly-executed agreement),

(b) section 86(2) of the Act (death of debtor or hirer where agreement is partly secured or unsecured),

(c) section 111(2) (default notice etc not served on surety),

(d) section 124(1) or (2) (taking of a negotiable instrument in breach of terms of section 123), or

(e) section 105(7)(a) or (b) (security not expressed in writing, or improperly executed).

3.2 This practice direction does not apply to any claim made under the provisions listed in paragraph 3.1 above if that claim relates to the recovery of land.

(Provisions governing the procedure for such claims can be found in CPR Schedule 2, CCR Order 49, r 4 and related rules about the matters to be included in the particulars of claim can be found in CPR Schedule 2, CCR Order 6.)

3.3 This practice direction also does not apply to a claim made by the creditor under section 141 of the Act to enforce a regulated agreement where the agreement relates only to money. Such a claim must be started by the issue of a Part 7 claim form.

Restrictions on where to start some Consumer Credit Act Claims

4.1 Where the claim includes a claim to recover goods to which a regulated hire purchase agreement or conditional sale agreements relates, it may only be started in the county court for the district in which the debtor, or one of the debtors:

(1) resides or carries on business, or

(2) resided or carried on business at the date when the defendant last made a payment under the agreement.

4.2 In any other claim to recover goods, the claim may only be started to the court for the district:

(1) in which the defendant, or one of the defendants, resides or carries on business, or

(2) in which the goods are situated.

4.3 A claim of a debtor or hirer for an order under section 129(1)(b) of the Act (a time order) may only be started in the court where the claimant resides or carries on business.

(Costs rule 45.1(2)(b) allows the claimant to recover fixed costs in certain circumstances where such a claim is made.)

(Paragraph 7 sets out the matters the claimant must include in his particulars of claim where he is using the Consumer Credit Act procedure.)

The Consumer Credit Act Procedure

5.1 In the types of claim to which paragraph 3 applies the court will fix a hearing date on the issue of the claim form.

5.2 The particulars of claim must be served with the claim form.

5.3 Where a claimant is using the Consumer Credit Act procedure, the defendant to the claim is not required to:

(1) serve an acknowledgment of service, or

(2) file a defence, although he may choose to do so.

5.4 Where a defendant intends to defend a claim, his defence should be filed within 14 days of service of the particulars of claim. If the defendant fails to file a defence within this period, but later relies on it, the court may take such a failure into account as a factor when deciding what order to make about costs.

5.5 Part 12 (default judgment) does not apply where the claimant is using the Consumer Credit Act procedure.

5.6 Each party must be given at least 28 days' notice of the hearing date.

5.7 Where the claimant serves the claim form, he must serve notice of the hearing date at the same time, unless the hearing date is specified in the claim form.

Powers of the Court at the Hearing

6.1 On the hearing date the court may dispose of the claim.

6.2 If the court does not dispose of the claim on the hearing date:

(1) if the defendant has filed a defence, the court will:

(a) allocate the claim to a track and give directions about the management of the case, or

(b) give directions to enable it to allocate the claim to a track,

(2) If the defendant has not filed a defence, the court may make any order or give any direction it considers appropriate.

6.3 Rule 26.5(3) to (5) and rules 26.6 to 26.10 apply to the allocation of a claim under paragraph 6.2.

Matters which must be Included in the Particulars of Claim

7.1 Where the Consumer Credit Act procedure is used, the claimant must state in his particulars of claim that the claim is a Consumer Credit Act claim.

7.2 A claimant making a claim for the delivery of goods to enforce a hire purchase agreement or conditional sale agreement which is:

(1) a regulated agreement for the recovery of goods, and

(2) let to a person other than a company or other corporation,

must also state (in this order) in his particulars of claim:

(a) the date of the agreement,

(b) the parties to the agreement,

(c) the number or other identification of the agreement (with enough information to allow the debtor to identify the agreement),

(d) where the claimant was not one of the original parties to the agreement, the means by which the rights and duties of the creditor passed to him,

(e) the place where the agreement was signed by the defendant (if known),

(f) the goods claimed,

(g) the total price of the goods,

(h) the paid up sum,

(i) the unpaid balance of the total price,

(j) whether a default notice or a notice under section 76(1) or section 88(1) of the Act has been served on the defendant, and, if it has, the date and the method of service,

(k) the date on which the right to demand delivery of the goods accrued,

(l) the amount (if any) claimed as an alternative to the delivery of goods, and

(m) the amount (if any) claimed in addition to—

(i) the delivery of the goods, or

(ii) any claim under sub-paragraph (l) above with the grounds of each such claim.

7.3 A claimant who is a debtor or hirer making a claim for an order under section 129(1)(b) of the Act (a time order) must state (in the following order) in his particulars of claim:

(1) the date of the agreement,

(2) the parties to the agreement,

(3) the number or other means of identifying the agreement,

(4) details of any sureties,

(5) if the defendant is not one of the original parties to the agreement then the name of the original party to the agreement,

(6) the names and addresses of the persons intended to be served with the claim form,

(7) the place where the claimant signed the agreement,

(8) details of the notice served by the creditor or owner giving rise to the claim for the time order,

(9) the total unpaid balance the claimant admits is due under the agreement, and—

(a) the amount of any arrears (if known), and

(b) the amount and frequency of the payments specified in the agreement,

(10) the claimant's proposals for payments of any arrears and of future instalments together with details of his means;

(11) where the claim relates to a breach of the agreement other than for the payment of money the claimant's proposals for remedying it.

7.4 (1) This paragraph applies where a claimant is required to obtain a court order to enforce a regulated agreement by:

(a) section 65(1) (improperly-executed agreement),

(b) section 105(7)(a) or (b) (security not expressed in writing, or improperly-executed),

(c) section 111(2) (default notice etc not served on surety),

(d) section 124(1) or (2) (taking of a negotiable instrument in breach of terms of section 123), or

(e) section 86(2) of the Act (death of debtor or hirer where agreement is partly secured or unsecured).

(2) The claimant must state in his particulars of claim what the circumstances are that require him to obtain a court order for enforcement.

Admission of Certain Claims for Recovery of Goods Under Regulated Agreements

8.1 In a claim to recover goods to which section 90(1)[1] *applies:*

(1) the defendant may admit the claim, and

(2) offer terms on which a return order should be suspended under section 135(1)(b).

8.2 He may do so by filing a request in practice form N9C.

8.3 He should do so within the period for making an admission specified in rule 14.2(b). If the defendant fails to file his request within this period, and later makes such a request, the court may take the failure into account as a factor when deciding what order to make about costs.

8.4 On receipt of the admission, the court will serve a copy on the claimant.

8.5 The claimant may obtain judgment by filing a request in practice form N228.

8.6 On receipt of the request for judgment, the court will enter judgment in the terms of the defendant's admission and offer and for costs.

8.7 If:

(1) the claimant does not accept the defendant's admission and offer, and

(2) the defendant does not appear on the hearing date fixed when the claim form was issued,

the court may treat the defendant's admission and offer as evidence of the facts stated in it for the purposes of sections 129(2)(a)[2] *and 135(2).*[3]

---

1 *Section 90(1) provides that:*

'At any time when—

(a) the debtor is in breach of a regulated hire-purchase or a regulated conditional sale agreement relating to goods, and

(b) the debtor has paid to the creditor one-third or more of the total price of the goods, and

(c) the property in the goods remains in the creditor, the creditor is not entitled to recover possession of the goods from the debtor except on an order of the court.'

2 *Section 129(2) provides that—*

'A time order shall provide for one or both of the following, as the court considers just—

(a) the payment by the debtor or hirer or any surety of any sum owed under a regulated agreement or a security by such instalments, payable at such times, as the court, having regard to the means of the debtor or hirer and any surety, considers reasonable;

(b) the remedying by the debtor or hirer of any breach of a regulated agreement (other than non-payment of money) within such period as the court may specify.'

3 *Section 135(2) provides that—*

'The court shall not suspend the operation of a term [in an order relating to a regulated agreement] requiring the delivery up of goods by any person unless satisfied that the goods are in his possession or control.'

Additional Requirements about Parties to the Proceedings

9.1 The court may dispense with the requirement in section 141(5) (all parties to a regulated agreement and any surety to be parties to any proceedings) in any claim relating to the regulated agreement, if:

(1) the claim form has not been served on the debtor or the surety, and

(2) the claimant either before or at the hearing makes an application (which may be made without notice) for the court to make such an order.

9.2 In a claim relating to a regulated agreement where—

(1) the claimant was not one of the original parties to the agreement, and

(2) the former creditor's rights and duties under the agreement have passed to him by—

(a) operation of law, or

(b) assignment,

the requirement of section 141(5) (all parties to a regulated agreement and any surety to be parties to any proceedings) does not apply to the former creditor, unless the court otherwise orders.

9.3 Where a claimant who is a creditor or owner makes a claim for a court order under section 86(2) (death of debtor or hirer where agreement is partly secured or unsecured) the personal representatives of the deceased debtor or hirer must be parties to the proceedings in which the order is sought, unless no grant of representation has been made to the estate.

9.4 Where no grant of representation has been made to the estate of the deceased debtor or hirer, the claimant must make an application in accordance with Part 23 for directions about which persons (if any) are to be made parties to the claim as being affected or likely to be affected by the enforcement of the agreement.

9.5 The claimant's application under paragraph 9.4:

(a) may be made without notice, and

(b) should be made before the claim form is issued.

Notice to be Given to Re-open a Consumer Credit Agreement

10.1 Where a debtor or any surety intends to apply for a consumer credit agreement to be reopened after a claim on or relating to the agreement has already begun, and:

(1) section 139(1)(b);[4] *or*

(2) section 138(1)(c),

applies, the debtor or surety must serve written notice of his intention on the court and every other party to the proceedings within 14 days of the service of the claim form on him.

10.2 If the debtor or surety (as the case may be) serves a notice under paragraph 10.1 he will be treated as having filed a defence for the purposes of the Consumer Credit Act procedure.

---

[4] *Section 139(1) provides that:*

(1) A credit agreement may, if the court thinks just, be reopened on the ground that the credit bargain is extortionate:

(a) on an application for the purpose made by the debtor or any surety to the High Court, county court or sheriff court; or

(b) at the instance of the debtor or a surety in any proceedings to which the debtor and creditor are parties, being proceedings to enforce the credit agreement, any security relating to it or any linked transaction; or

(c) at the instance of the debtor or a surety in other proceedings in any court about the amount paid or payable under the credit agreement is relevant.

INDEX

E

F

G

H

Q

R

S

T

U